Adam's Dream

James Land Jones

Adam's Dream

Mythic Consciousness in Keats and Yeats

The University of Georgia Press

Athens

Library of Congress Catalog Card Number: 73–88362
International Standard Book Number: 0–8203–0340–2

The University of Georgia Press, Athens 30602

Set in 10 on 12 pt. Waverley type
Printed in the United States of America

To

My Mother

The Memory of My Father

and to

Ben

"The crown . . . is made of love and friendship."

The Imagination may be compared to Adam's dream—he awoke and found it truth.

John Keats

We shall enjoy ourselves here after by having what we called happiness on Earth repeated in a finer tone and so repeated. . . . Adam's dream will do here and seems to be a conviction that Imagination and its empyreal reflection is the same as human life and its spiritual repetition.

John Keats

The ideal of a god, I believe, is to become a man while knowing that he can recover his power; and the dream of man to become a god without losing his personality.

André Malraux, *Man's Fate*

We assent to the conclusions of reflection but believe what myth presents; belief is love, and the concrete alone is love; nor is it true that myth has no purpose but to bring round some discovery of a principle or fact. The saint may touch through myth the utmost reach of human faculty and pass not to reflection but to unity with the source of his being.

W. B. Yeats

Contents

Acknowledgments

An author invests so much of his being in the writing of a book that he is eager, upon completion of his text, to thank those persons who have given of their patience and energy to its realization. They have become, unwittingly, part of the fabric of the book, its undersong, so that the work is a palimpsest of the author's intellectual and emotional life during its completion. Although the finished book moves from its author to the realm of public ideas, there to be judged, the author still retains the spirit that informed his act of creation, a spirit generated by his first audience. Hence he gives to them thanks for what they gave to him, an opportunity not merely to write a book but to know himself.

For encouragement in the earliest stages of this work, I owe most to the genial wisdom and patience of my teacher, Richard Harter Fogle. Professor Fogle has been to his students, as Yeats's fisherman was to him, an image. The strengths of the present study are tribute to that image; the weaknesses remain with the author.

E. P. Bollier read an early draft with the tact and acumen that early drafts so badly need and so often fail to receive, offering his friendship and continued interest. Charles I. Patterson, Jr., criticized the text with uncommonly generous attention, making suggestions that spared me many small infelicities and embarrassments. When I was confronted with a major revision, his reassurance was invaluable. Edward Engelberg had the charity to say of an early draft that it was astray on the path of the chameleon, its lineaments yet indistinctly drawn. His good sense prompted a rewriting that he read as rigorously as the earlier draft.

To John Welsh, Virginia Ramsey, and Joseph I. Killorin, my colleagues at Armstrong State College, I am indebted for help in countless ways, chiefly their many unremembered acts of kindness and of love. Mrs. A. J. Waring, Jr., in her rare friendship, gave me moments of understanding she her-

Acknowledgments

self was hardly aware of—and much too humble to acknowledge. Numerous conversations with my friend and former student Lucas Carpenter renewed my sometimes flagging spirits; his knowledge of and interest in my subject were made doubly valuable by his care. To Jack E. Miller, Jr., I am grateful for many needed moments of joy and a knowledge of philosophy that cleared my head on more than one occasion. George Core, at the University of Georgia Press, was constant with his loyalty, consideration, and intelligent judgment.

I wish to thank as well Walter Coppedge, who, while President of the College of Charleston, released me from some teaching duties to complete the first draft. Hugh Pendexter at Armstrong steadfastly gave his support and made available departmental funds to help with typing. Mae Rushing, of the Armstrong Library, was cheerful and efficient in procuring materials; by sparing me labor and travel, she hastened my work considerably. For typing various drafts with attention, tolerance, and good will, I wish to thank Sharon Gutwein, Mary Ryles, and most especially Mary Winters; her sense of perfection gave me not only cause for joy but reason for shame.

With these colleagues and friends, and with the persons named on the dedication page, I have known, while writing this book, "the chief intensity."

Moon River
   Savannah, Georgia
     March 21, 1973

A Note on the Text: A quick and unobtrusive system of reference to primary sources is desirable in a comparative study, otherwise documentation is apt to burden the developing argument or hinder perception of relationships among quotations. In this study, therefore, a simple set of abbreviations,

Acknowledgments

placed in parentheses within my text, identifies quotations from Keats and Yeats. For the reader's convenience, the list of these abbreviations has been placed on page xiv.

Readers are reminded of Keats's careless spelling and punctuation in his letters; this reminder obviates the otherwise frequent and ugly editorial insertion of "sic." The names of journals are abbreviated in footnotes and bibliography in accordance with the abbreviations use in the PMLA *Bibliography, 1973.*

Abbreviations

For works by Keats

L1, L2   *The Letters of John Keats,* ed. Hyder Edward Rollins. 2 vols. Cambridge, Mass.: Harvard University Press, 1958.

K   *The Poetical Works of John Keats,* ed. H. W. Garrod, 2nd ed. London: Oxford University Press, 1958.

For works by Yeats

A   *The Autobiography of William Butler Yeats.* New York: Macmillan Co., 1953.

E   *Essays and Introductions.* New York: Macmillan Co., 1951.

EX   *Explorations.* New York: Macmillan Co., 1962.

DW   *Letters on Poetry from W. B. Yeats to Dorothy Wellesley.* London: Oxford University Press, 1964.

LY   *The Letters of W. B. Yeats,* ed. Allen Wade. London: Rupert Hart-Davis. 1954.

M   *Mythologies.* New York: Collier Books, 1969.

V   *A Vision.* New York: Macmillan Co., 1961.

Y   *Collected Poems of W. B. Yeats.* New York: Macmillan Co., 1956.

Introduction
The Motive for Myth

In his influential essay on *Ulysses*, published in 1923, T. S. Eliot praised Joyce for using the method of myth and so developing for the twentieth century a method which other writers must pursue. Eliot's definition of the method was sketchy—"manipulating a continuous parallel between contemporaneity and antiquity"—but it was sufficiently clear to draw attention to the structural device used not only by Joyce but, in *The Waste Land,* by Eliot himself. And he added, with a chronological accuracy that has often escaped literary critics: "It is a method already adumbrated by Mr. Yeats."

Eliot's essay may be said to mark the beginning in modern literary criticism of an awareness of myth in literature—and of literature's relationship to myth—that has now not only moved to the center of criticism but in some quarters has all but engulfed it. At the same time this intensive study, however revealing its reading of individual literary works, has been vitiated by imprecise definition of its key term. By some "myth" is taken in the everyday sense as a story about gods and heroes in a golden age—the mythology of classical dictionaries. This sense of the term underlies Douglas Bush's *Mythology and the Romantic Tradition in English Poetry* (1937), a book one may read for its critical insights into poems but a book offering little insight into myth's relationship to literature, beyond the allegorical use of mythology. By others "myth" is dissolved into literature itself, becoming distinguishable from it in one of two ways: by becoming, as it were, all but a genre of literature, as in Richard Chase's *Quest for Myth* (1949); or by becoming the archetypal form comprised of all works of literature, or to which they point, as in the work of Northrop Frye.

Still others have followed the ritual theory of myth promoted in the early years of this century by the Cambridge school—Jane Harrison, Gilbert Murray, Francis Cornford, A. B. Cook—which followed insights in Frazer's *Golden Bough*. These critics, such as Stanley Edgar Hyman, and, most notably, Francis Fergusson, have had at least the advantage of a working definition of their term. But often, as in the case of Hyman, they have come perilously close to dissolving literature into myth-as-ritual. Furthermore there are a good number of scholars, such as Joseph Fontenrose, who presently discredit with good argument the ritual origin of myth—and therefore the ritual structure that has been found basic to literature.

Terminological imprecision obtains in the analysis of myth in Keats and Yeats as well as in literary criticism at large. There are studies by Margaret Sherwood and Walter Evert on Keats and by Peter Ure, Morton Irving Seiden, and Daniel Hoffman on Yeats that contain in their titles the word "myth." Valuable as these works are, one looks in them in vain for any definition of myth that is clearer than those set forth above. These writers are more anthropologically sophisticated than Bush chose to be, and so are nearer to the ritual critics than to dictionaries of mythology. But the term "myth" nevertheless is used equivocally and goes begging.

The problem is formidable. Where do myth, religion, and literature part company to become separate activities and products of the mind—and what is the common ground from which they spring or which they share? The problem involves not only anthropology but philosophy as well, epistemology in particular. And there is precious little consensus. No wonder the literary critic often writes as if Humpty Dumpty's advice to Alice is sufficient: a word can mean anything we want it to mean.

Outside of the Looking-Glass world, however, it does seem that the term ought to be used in some clearly delimited sense. This is even more urgent when, because particular poets require the term, it cannot be avoided. Keats and Yeats are clearly such poets. Moreover they belong to a class of writers with which the term is, by definition, associated. I refer to Romanticism and René Wellek's definition of it.

The Motive for Myth

Wellek first defined Romanticism in 1949, in an essay countering A. O. Lovejoy's nominalism. In 1963, reviewing the major studies in Romanticism since the publication of his first essay, he found sufficient evidence to repeat his central thesis. During this period Morse Peckham published two provocative and controversial definitions. Between them, Wellek and Peckham may be said to have initiated the present directions taken in the theory of Romanticism.[1] Each posits a set of characteristics which, if Romantic, appears remarkably modern, too, comfortably allowing Yeats to be seen as the last great figure in the Romantic movement, and suggesting that modernism, rather than the break with Romanticism that it thought itself to be, is really a further extension and modification of the Romantic movement.[2]

In Wellek's definition Romanticism is an employment of imagination, symbol, myth, and organic nature "as part of the great endeavor to overcome the split between subject and object, the self and the world, the conscious and the unconscious."[3] The Romantic movement is thus seen to be, at its center, a response to the post-Enlightenment crisis in cognition, that bifurcation of nature as Whitehead called it, which grew wider as the age of reason moved from Descartes to Kant. Philosophically speaking, epistemology is, in Romanticism and Romantic poetry, prior to ethics, politics, meta-

1. Wellek's essays can be found most easily in *Concepts of Criticism* (New Haven, 1963) and Peckham's in *The Triumph of Romanticism* (Columbia, S.C., 1970).
2. This point has been made often in studies of modern literature since Peckham's first essay: John Bayley, *The Romantic Survival* (London, 1957); Frank Kermode, *Romantic Image* (New York, 1957); Robert Langbaum, *The Poetry of Experience* (New York, 1957); G. S. Fraser, *Vision and Rhetoric* (New York, 1960); Stephen Spender, *The Struggle of the Modern* (London, 1963); Monroe K. Spears, *Dionysus and the City: Modernism in Twentieth-Century Poetry* (New York, 1970); Robert Langbaum, *The Modern Spirit: Essays on the Continuity of Nineteenth and Twentieth Century Literature* (New York, 1970); Harold Bloom, *The Ringers in the Tower* (Chicago, 1971). Its general acceptance seems heeded by *The Modern Tradition: Backgrounds of Modern Literature*, ed. Richard Ellmann and Charles Feidelson, Jr. (New York, 1965), an anthology that begins with works from the Romantic movement.
3. "Romanticism Re-examined," in *Concepts of Criticism*, p. 220.

physics, or anything else. This insight is at the heart of Wellek's definition. Imagination, symbol, and myth are strategies employed in a cognitive predicament, often in poems that are themselves investigations of the cognitive process. As Stephen Spender has said, speaking of a link between Romantic and modern poetry, "The mode of perceiving itself becomes an object of perception and is included as part of the thing perceived."[4] His words "object" and "thing" are imprecise and ill-chosen, but what he is saying is correct: much of the significant poetry since 1800 does have as its content the activity of the mind in the process of cognition. If Wellek's fourth term, organic nature, was generally abandoned after Browning's *Paracelsus* (Hopkins, remaining unpublished, had no influence), the cognitive problem faced by the Romantics, and the employment of the other three elements, did not stop in 1835 or even in 1917.

Exploration of the elements isolated by Wellek is anything but new. Books on Romantic imagination and symbolism abound, and certainly myth has not been overlooked, as the authors mentioned above will attest. But the study of myth, when it has not considered myth as ritual, has had its emphasis almost exclusively on myth as narrative, or on source and analogue of mythic narratives and characters. What has been overlooked is myth as an activity of the mind with intrinsic factors which, prior to their configuration in narrative or story, find expression in the poem. As Philip Wheelwright has said, "Genuine myth is a matter of perspective first, invention second."[5] One can—like Tennyson in *The Idylls of the King* or Gide in *Theseus*—employ the mythic product, a narrative or story, without the finished work evidencing the mythic assumption, the mode of cognition. Conversely a work can exhibit the mythic perspective without the invented narrative. Before this can be shown, however, a definition of that perspective is needed.

To date there have been few accounts of myth as a mode of thinking. Because the philosophical problems involved are

4. Spender, *The Struggle of the Modern*, pp. 133–34.
5. *The Burning Fountain* (Bloomington, Ind., 1954), p. 159.

obviously formidable, most investigators prefer to limit themselves to analysis of the mythic product, the narrative. This is particularly true of anthropologists, most of whom are determined to remain empirical. In the work of three men can be found what I think is the most viable analysis: Ernst Cassirer, Mircea Eliade, and Claude Lévi-Strauss. The conjunction may seem strange: Cassirer the neo-Kantian philosopher, Eliade the student of comparative religion, and Lévi-Strauss the anthropologist with claims to empirical objectivity. But if their positions hardly share the same assumptions, their work provides remarkably parallel insights.

Curiously enough, literary critics studying or employing myth almost never refer to Cassirer's work.[6] One reason may be his antimythical bias. Though he defends the modes of thought operative in myth, religion, and art as forms of knowledge having equal value with the scientific mode of thought, he never fully escapes from the strong inclination to assume scientific thinking an improvement upon mythic forms which, in human history, it comes to replace. In this respect Cassirer's epistemology, however neo-Kantian, is not that of the Romantic poets. Some critics find him inadequate because they believe he denies that myth is narrative at all. He does use the term in a special, restricted sense: myth is a "form" or "mode" or "structure" of thought, and this is the concern of his investigation. But he does not openly deny that this form of thought may have its most fully-developed expression in narrative, that the product of the form of thought may also be called myth. He would be forced to say, I think, that as soon as this form of thought takes extended rather than fragmentary expression its product would have to be narrative or poetic hymn—or both.

A problem more relevant to the employment of Cassirer's analysis in literary study is this: by his analysis, mythic thought occurs largely before any significant disjunction of

6. The only works known to me which use Cassirer are Wheelwright's study and Hazard Adams's *William Blake: A Reading of the Short Poems* (Seattle, 1963). One essay on Yeats's mythical thought utilizing a set of insights similar to Cassirer's is Harold H. Watts, "Yeats and Lapsed Mythology," *Ren* 3 (1951), 107–12.

the self and the world. This disjunction arises with the birth of self-consciousness, and at that point myth begins to shade into religion, which, in using images and signs, "recognizes them as such—a means of expression which, though they reveal a determinate meaning, must necessarily remain inadequate to it."[7] In myth the unity of self and world is "substantial"; in religion it is "a synthetic unity: a unity of different entities. For it, therefore, differentiation remains a necessary factor, a condition for the achievement of the unity itself."[8] Hence a poet writing in 1820 or 1920 cannot be said to exhibit mythic apprehension in the strictest sense. But the *intention* of Romantic poetry, as Wellek defines it, is the reestablishment of some identification of subject and object that is not unlike the predisjunctive identification in mythic thought. Northrop Frye, in fact, sees the very thrust of Romantic myth to be the re-creation of this identity experienced in mythic consciousness.[9] Such identification cannot be, in Cassirer's term, substantial. It will be the paradoxical identity Cassirer describes for religion and Malraux defines as the human condition, in the quotation used as an epigraph for this work. But this residual disjunction does not, I think, invalidate the use of Cassirer's analysis to indicate the goal of the self-conscious mind when it desires to think mythically. Cassirer can show us what the mind desires, before it finds narratives in which to embody its desires. Finally, to consider the mythic perspective or mode of apprehension is to relate myth more firmly to the cognitive endeavor in Romantic poetry.

Cassirer's six characteristics of mythic apprehension may be set forth briefly here: (1) a feeling of sympathetic re-

7. Cassirer, *Mythical Thought*, vol. 2 in *Philosophy of Symbolic Forms* (New Haven, 1955), p. 239.
8. Ibid., 2: 251. Cassirer would distinguish poetry from myth by the same means he divides religion and myth: ". . . the images in which [myth] lives are not *known* as images. They are not regarded [as they are in poetry] as symbols but as realities," *The Myth of the State* (New Haven, 1971), p. 47.
9. "The alienated man cut off from nature by his consciousness is the Romantic equivalent of post-Edenic Adam. . . . The Romantic redemption myth then becomes a recovery of the original identity," *A Study of English Romanticism* (New York, 1968), p. 18.

The Motive for Myth

sponse to the world, dominating logical responses and perception of empirical cause-and-effect relationships; (2) a sense of the unbroken continuity and interconnectedness of everything in the world; (3) metamorphosis; (4) an experience of time into which linear progression does not enter, and the separate segments of time—past, present, and future—fuse into each other simultaneously; (5) a sense of space that causes it to be divided not primarily into quadrants and cardinal points but into two areas of different feeling and value, the sacred and the profane; (6) a refusal to admit the fact of death.

Much of Cassirer's analysis is seconded by Eliade, who in some instances develops it and in others makes additions to it. In Cassirer's analysis the unbroken continuity of all life and metamorphosis—for all intents and purposes the same characteristic—are the components of mythic apprehension; mythic time and the refusal to accept death are merely particularized instances of this structure of apprehension. In Eliade consciousness of time is the central factor; or, rather, the mythic denial of time. To him, "The chief difference between the man of the archaic . . . and the man of the modern societies . . . lies in the fact that the former feels himself indissolubly connected with the Cosmos and the cosmic rhythms, whereas the latter insists that he is connected only with History."[10] He defines archaic societies as those which, "although they are conscious of a certain form of 'history,' make every effort to disregard it."[11] Prehistoric man is certainly "aware" of chronological time, of the past, present, and future. But to him this chronological time always bends back on itself, as in seasonal renewal, and so it becomes mythic and unhistoric. The man of mythic apprehension does not assume, as we do, that time is linear. Consequently our sense of history, which we take for granted, is as alien to him as his sense of mythic time is alien to us. Since he lives in a temporal world, he can *conceive* of chronological time, but he

10. Mircea Eliade, *Cosmos and History: The Myth of the Eternal Return* (New York, 1959), p. vii.
11. Ibid., p. xi.

does not *experience* it. We, on the other hand, can conceive of
mythic time but, by and large, do not frequently experience
it. The experience of time is what is in question here; we are
returned to Cassirer's first point, a feeling response. And Cassirer insists from his neo-Kantian framework that men experience time differently with differing structures of consciousness.

Why these structures differ and how man moves from
mythic to historic time, or from myth to religion (and
thence to science), becomes a central question. Cassirer posits
increased self-consciousness as the causal agent, and I follow
him in this. At the same time it seems to me that evolution of
man's self-consciousness (which is history) must disturb the
a priori nature of the structures. Cassirer does not resolve
this problem to my satisfaction.[12] But one can hardly fault
him. For the question abandons us immediately in epistemological seas that no one has successfully charted yet.

Eliade tries to avoid these troubled waters by focusing on
metaphysics. He undertakes to study "certain aspects of archaic ontology—more precisely, the conceptions of being and
reality that can be read from the behavior of the man of premodern societies," finding that "the symbol, the myth, the
rite express . . . a complex of coherent affirmations about the
ultimate reality of things, a system that can be regarded as
constituting a metaphysics."[13] He tries again to avoid the
problem by calling himself an historian of religions. Yet he
never discusses with any thoroughness either the developing
stages of religious consciousness or of any religion. Consequently his position implies what Cassirer's affirms—a priori
structures. That he discusses mythic thinking without any
clearly formulated assumptions about the mind is, it seems
to me, the gravest weakness in his work. Stressing ontology,
he returns again and again to the idea that myth and religion

12. The best critique of Cassirer's position, in so far as his thought is
relevant to my study, is the essay by David Bidney, "On the Philosophical Anthropology of Ernst Cassirer and its Relation to the History of
Anthropological Thought," in *The Philosophy of Ernst Cassirer*, ed. Paul
Arthur Schilpp (New York, 1958), pp. 465–544.
13. Eliade, *Cosmos and History*, p. 3.

are concerned with the sacred because the sacred is concerned with being.[14] Cassirer would probably agree (my argument will show that I do), but he insists on and is interested in the differing structures of consciousness through which being is revealed.

Lévi-Strauss would chart epistemological seas by attending to the empirical data of myths and rituals themselves. There, by comparative analysis, he finds consistent structural components and from them draws an *ur*-structure, as it were, for all myth. He believes this extrapolation warranted by the evidence, though some of his critics, like Edmund Leach, think he overgeneralizes from his data: what is undoubtedly true of the Indian myths of Brazil may not necessarily be true of all myths. But Lévi-Strauss plunges ahead. He moves from the data of myths to the mind of the believer in myth, arguing for a mental structure he believes is universal. In a general sense, his conclusion is similar to Cassirer's assumption.

The question raised by Lévi-Strauss's work is formulated quite cogently by Piaget:

Have these composite wholes always been composed. . . . Did not someone compose them? . . . Do structures call for *formation*, or is only some sort of eternal *preformation* compatible with them? . . . the former would make [them] revert to that atomistic association to which empiricism has accustomed us; the latter constantly threaten[s] to make [them] lapse into a theory of Husserlian essences, Platonic forms, or Kantian *a priori* forms of synthesis.[15]

14. Eliade does not clearly distinguish between myth and religion, treating them for the most part synonymously. For example, much of his description of myth in *Cosmos and History* is repeated in *The Sacred and the Profane* (New York, 1961), where the term myth has been replaced by religion. The dividing line is perhaps impossible to establish. Cassirer is probably accurate in saying that it involves an increase in self-consciousness. He has an excellent discussion of the stages of religious thought in *Language and Myth* (New York, 1946), pp. 17–23 ff.

15. Jean Piaget, *Structuralism* (New York, 1970), p. 9. Piaget's analysis of his subject, it must be added, shows structuralism itself to be related to assumptions common to the Romantic period and to mythic apprehension: "In short, the notion of structure is comprised of three key ideas: the idea of wholeness, the idea of transformation, and the idea of self-regulation," p. 5.

Introduction

To me the attempt to settle the *formation-preformation* dilemma is evidence of what I think is the central thrust of the human mind: to find unity among disparate or contrary factors—an attempt symbolized by the quotation from Malraux found in the opening epigraphs. This quest for a unity that does justice to multiplicity, for permanence that does not deny change, is the very intention of human consciousness, to borrow Husserl's term—or, at least, it is the very intention of mythic consciousness. Lévi-Strauss's theory of myth points in this direction: mythic narratives are structured so that opposing elements find reconciliation by the interposition of a mediating action or image. I cannot escape believing the efficient cause for this formal result to be some a priori structural factor in the human mind itself. This is the assumption behind the present study, and because of it Eliade and Lévi-Strauss are often employed in a context of Cassirer's assumptions rather than their own.

Two possible criticisms follow from my use of myth. First, it would seem that my interest lies ultimately not in the poetry of Keats and Yeats but in their minds—what has been called the intentional fallacy. This criticism is met by saying clearly that the subject of my study is the poetic universe of Keats and Yeats. Their poetry, with their prose that throws light on it, is what interests me. I find in the evidence a particular kind of consciousness. That hypothesis, given body by Cassirer and Eliade, lends direction to my attention; if it limits what I see, it also brings into focus material otherwise obscured. But it is the material, the poetry, that is the subject of my investigation. In brief I am not interested in using the poems to prove some theory about consciousness or the particular minds of Keats and Yeats. I am interested in using a theory about consciousness to interpret their work. Mythic consciousness as such becomes my subject only in the Conclusion where, summarizing its nature in Keats and Yeats, I attempt to outline its relationship to post-1800 poetry in general.

The second possible criticism would rest in my use of Eliade and Lévi-Strauss: reading them as if they share Cas-

The Motive for Myth

sirer's assumptions. To this criticism there are two replies. The first has already been made in passing: whatever their differences in philosophical assumption, Cassirer, Eliade, and Lévi-Strauss draw from their data a number of remarkably parallel insights. The second reply is really an extension of the answer to the first criticism: how "true" Cassirer's thesis may be, weighed against other interpretations of myth, is finally irrelevant, for this book is only indirectly about myth; its chief subject is poetry.

I use Cassirer and Eliade for two reasons. It is commonly assumed today that myth and poetry do, in some fashion, share some similar functions or structural elements, however little agreement there may be about the nature of their interrelationship. Cassirer's assumptions and Eliade's insights allow us to see interrelations between myth and poetry at the same time these two endeavors remain separate. Second, the poetry of Romanticism, given Wellek's definition, is considered today to be the most mythic body of poetry in our literature. Hence a focus on mythic thinking reveals similarities in Keats and Yeats that further substantiate the recent sense of interconnection between nineteenth- and twentieth-century poetry.

My central purpose is to show that the poetry of Keats and Yeats is informed by a set of assumptions, a mode of apprehension, which marks it as a certain kind of poetry: Romantic poetry, as Wellek generally defines it, characterized in particular by the elements of mythic thinking analyzed by Cassirer and Eliade. In chapter 1, with a discussion of self-consciousness—the separation of the self from the world—I relate the concept of the self developed by Keats and Yeats to the chief intention of mythic consciousness: the experience of Being through which the self establishes unity with the world. The chapter closes with a discussion of the faculty—Keats called it "a greeting of the Spirit"—by which the self relates to the Other. This faculty, an aspect of the Romantic concept of imagination, is central to mythic apprehension.

Chapter 2 presents the most fundamental assumption of

mythic apprehension: the felt solidarity of all life. This may be called, in Eliade's terms, the ontological content of mythic thought. Keats and Yeats experience within objects an "energy," "essence," or "beauty" (the concepts are all but synonymous) that manifests the primal reality in mythic apprehension: divine power, the numinous, or Being.

The other characteristics of mythic consciousness are agents contributing to the apprehension of this reality. Chapter 3 investigates them in separate sections: a sense of metamorphosis, that everything may turn into everything else; a sense of reciprocity in the cosmos, found among the seasons, the four elements, and life and death; two particular senses of time, the first a fusion of the past or future with the present (Cassirer), the second an eternal return to the beginning of things, to rebirth (Eliade); the denial of death. The first three I subsume in the general term "process," the "vast idea" that gives the chapter its name. Under consideration in this chapter are these aspects of mythic apprehension when they occur separately.

Very often in the work of Keats and Yeats the factors of mythic apprehension come into play together and an epiphany results which, borrowing Yeats's term, I call the Great Moment. It is the subject of chapter 4. Prerequisite to it is a paradoxical mood of intensity and stillness; its result is the paradoxical reconciliation of opposites that Yeats called "tragic joy" and Keats called "melancholy." In this experience the self joins with or is made ready to join the Other, discovering that *being* in which the ego and the Other are grounded; the solidarity of life is affirmed. In this chapter, I explicate several poems by Yeats that exhibit almost all the characteristics of mythic apprehension hitherto investigated singly: *Vacillation, Chosen,* and *Leda and the Swan.*

Chapter 5 is devoted exclusively to Keats. This narrowed focus serves two purposes. First, I believe that the struggle to accept the mythic sense of time innate with him is the key to Keats's development after the early months of 1818, and to see this development clearly it is necessary to look at his work alone. Hence section 1 looks at a number of his poems with this theme in mind, in particular the *Ode to a Nightingale* and the verse *Epistle to Reynolds*. My second purpose is to end with a detailed reading of poems in which mythic apprehension finally embodies itself in mythic narrative. The second section is thus devoted to the two *Hyperions*. In these poems Keats not only exhibits the full range of his mythic consciousness but also creates a mythic narrative. This narrative has as its theme the very problem from which this book began: the fall into self-consciousness. In this narrative Keats, like Yeats in the poems discussed in chapter 4, transforms self-consciousness into a higher, more inclusive consciousness. Even as fragments the two *Hyperions* are remarkable feats, one of the pinnacles of the Romantic imagination. They are, as well, summary and paradigm for that imagination's relationship to mythic thought.

Chapter One
Soul Making

When twentieth-century criticism undertook the reading of Shakespeare, one of its principal tasks was prying Hamlet loose from Coleridge. In the eyes of modern critics Coleridge was at fault for reading into Hamlet the problems of his own personal nature. Hamlet the procrastinator, A. C. Bradley argued, is very much Coleridge sicklied o'er with the pale cast of thought. The point was well taken and necessary if the fullness of Shakespeare's play was to become available again. But what Bradley did not know, evidently, is what modern scholarship has shown: Coleridge to a large extent borrowed his Hamlet from Schlegel. This being so,, we must modify Bradley and say that Coleridge read into the Prince of Denmark not merely his personal situation but, more importantly, the situation of his age, the metaphysical and epistemological crisis inherited from Descartes and the British Empiricists.

It may be this fact, this relationship of Coleridge's Hamlet to the Romantic situation, that accounts for the common reader's clinging to him, even when he is told that that Hamlet may be more nearly Coleridge's invention than Shakespeare's creation. For the Romantic situation is still very much of our time, and the common reader sees his own predicament in the Hamlet defined by Coleridge. He lives in a culture that echoes with "identity crisis," what Arnold called "this strange disease of modern life," and the literary protagonists of that culture are such gentlemen as Conrad's Heyst and Faulkner's Quentin Compson. Coleridge's self-conscious Hamlet may be the child of a Romantic mind, but he is also one of modern man's chief images of himself.

An important body of recent criticism would support this common reader's intuition. For the work of such men as Langbaum, Frye, Hartman, and Bloom makes self-conscious-

Soul Making

ness the key term in Romanticism and Romanticism the beginning of the modern movement.[1] As seen by these critics, Romanticism is a response to a crisis in consciousness—or, more precisely, *of* consciousness, for it is consciousness itself that is problematic, the content of the problem and hence the subject of the crisis.

In this problem of consciousness Romanticism and myth directly meet: Romanticism employs mythic consciousness to heal the wounds of self-consciousness; modes of consciousness—and the definitions of self that they entail—become the theme of much Romantic poetry, emerging in the two *Hyperions* (to be examined in chapter 5) as the subject of a narrative myth. But to know the remedy, one must know the wound; self-consciousness must be defined before mythic consciousness is explored. Hence the subject of the section that follows is what Keats, using the older word for consciousness, called "curious Conscience," that faculty from which, in the sonnet *To Sleep*, he begs to be saved, because it "still lords / Its strength for darkness, burrowing like a mole" (к, 467). From self-consciousness emerges the question of the self; the second section explores this topic in Keats and Yeats, showing that their concept of it demands relationship to the Other and so prefigures the interconnectedness of Being that is assumed in mythic consciousness (and is the subject of

1. Representative of this position is the anthology of essays edited by Harold Bloom, *Romanticism and Consciousness* (New York, 1970), containing in particular the studies by Geoffrey H. Hartman, "Romanticism and 'Anti-Self-Consciousness,' " pp. 46–56, and Bloom, "The Internalization of Quest-Romance," pp. 3–24. See also Richard Haven, *Patterns of Consciousness: An Essay on Coleridge* (Storrs, Conn., 1969) and Robert Langbaum, "The Mysteries of Identity: A Theme in Modern Literature," in *The Modern Spirit* (New York, 1970), pp. 164–84.

Although consciousness is not a theme expressly pursued in M. H. Abrams's magisterial *Natural Supernaturalism* (New York, 1971), his book is so vast in scope that it includes this theme and provides the most comprehensive context for it that Romantic scholarship has yet advanced. The work appeared after my own manuscript was completed. Keats plays a very minor role in Abrams's study, but some of our central themes are so similar that I can best describe their relationship through Wordsworth's metaphor: my own study is a side chapel to Abrams's larger edifice.

chapter 2). The present chapter ends with an examination of the faculty that the two poets employ in relating the self to the Other: a "greeting of the spirit." This faculty, an aspect of the Romantic concept of the imagination, is the agent of mythic apprehension.

I

"Curious Conscience"

Self-consciousness may be defined as an awareness of the separateness of the self from the world. Between these poles of the self and the world, the subject and the object, lies the range of consciousness and, consequently, several stages. The first is simple consciousness of the world itself, unreflecting animal awareness. At the second level human consciousness begins: a sense of the self and a separation of the self from the world becomes possible. I say "possible," because at this stage mythic thinking comes into play, the whole intent of which is to deny the separation without recourse to conscious reflection. At this stage, as Cassirer says, one *feels* a union of himself and the world, and that feeling response—the first element of mythic apprehension—holds in check the rudimentary consciousness of separation, transforming it through the dialectic of myths themselves. At a further stage the increasing pressure of the sense of self brings a consciousness of wider separation, and myth becomes religion. Here one is not necessarily yet possessed of a consciousness of personal and individual identity in our modern sense, but he is possessed of a consciousness of man's differentness and separation from the world. Finally we have that stage in which is born the individual in our post-Renaissance sense of the term, conscious of his personal uniqueness, his separation from fellow men as well as from nature. Tragically for us this sense became pronounced at the very moment that empirical philosophy was making it difficult to believe in a numinous Other (person or place) to which one could feel himself pro-

foundly related. So self-consciousness became that radical
sense of isolation and alienation common to the modern world.
If the earliest stage of consciousness sees the near disappearance of the self into the world, the extreme form of modern
consciousness sees the self existing alone; in this near solipsism, the world—because it cannot be reached, be related
to—for all practical purposes disappears.

The poles of consciousness, then, are represented by Wordsworth's "glad animal movements" on the one hand and on
the other by Arnold's Empedocles and Beckett's Murphy. Our
own situation at the latter pole is exemplified in our near
destruction of nature, modern Western man's sense that he
no longer lives with nature—in either harmony or tension—
but has, through technology, nearly absolute control over it.
Our present ecological crisis, however, coupled with the re-
animation of mythic thinking in the young, may lend new
validation to the mythic mode of thought and, while leading
us back to nature, lead us back to the sense of union for which
the Romantic poets quested.

In the meantime we have Murphy and a bitter paradox:
the self as a separate entity all but empty of self, a structure
of consciousness lacking any content. Hume's devastating insight is not merely an idea we ponder: it has become a situation we live. We find that the more consciously we insist on
a bounded identity of the self, the less self we have. Awareness of the self paradoxically becomes the absence of self. For
by insisting on specific individuality, we cut ourselves off
from any source for the self. If we cry "I am unique," we
imply there is an archetypal essence somewhere for our
uniqueness. That essence must reside in a transcendent realm,
or it must dwell within us. If it is transcendent, how can we
have it, be in touch with it, share it, or identify ourselves with
it, should we insist on the bounded limits of the temporal
self? Where is the stem of stress connecting the existential
"self" to this essence of self? Or, if we loosen the bounds of
identity to reach for this transcendent self which resides in
being, do we still have an individual self? Have we not
merged with something other? If, on the other hand, that

essential self dwells within us alone, of what can it consist, except, as Hume said, a bundle of sensations, memories, and perceptions? Duns Scotus's subtlety aside, there is almost no way out of this paradox. To insist on the integrity of the self is to insist on an entity which is indeed an existential possibility but is all but empty of being, in any of its more profound senses. And yet it is to experience that profound sense of being that we cry *I AM*. Hence the more we insist on the individual *I* and the more conscious we become of it as an entity, the less able are we to grasp or experience the *AM*, that fullness of being for which we thirst. The modern history of the self is a history of this irony. By mid-twentieth century, we have persons fully conscious of their own individuality yet desperately lacking in any sense of being; we have alienated, isolated men. Is not, then, Rimbaud's "long, immense, and deliberate *dérèglement des sens*" and all the following abandonment of rationality and reach for the irrational—what has been called the Dionysian thread in modern literature—a quest for being? Having trapped ourselves in the isolated self, devoid of being, we would abandon the self utterly for a taste of being.

This paradox of the self is almost always overlooked in general treatments of Romantic individualism. Romanticism, goes the common definition, is an emphasis on the individual, the affirmation of the self as an ultimate value; Byron's hero is taken as the paradigm. From this point of view Romantic humanitarianism seems contradictory. But this viewpoint is both inaccurate and oversimple, for the Romantic poets have a more profound grasp of the problem of the self than do many of their commentators, and what appears as contradiction to the latter is in reality necessary paradox.

The confusion results from thinking of the individual self as an end or aim of Romantic endeavor, as its purpose or value.[2] Instead the individual ego is merely the starting point.

2. This seems to me the error of Patricia M. Ball in *The Central Self: A Study in Romantic and Victorian Imagination* (London, 1968). She rightly sees that the Romantics do not regard identity as an ultimate

Soul Making

As Morse Peckham has observed, this was a consequence of the Romantic predicament. New philosophy had called all in doubt, the self as well as the world. Hence one had to start from the self. Value can be found only *through* the self (not merely "by means of" but "beyond"). It is no longer a given; it must be won, found (*made*, finally, in the poem itself). Until the self has been found and defined, there is no means of going beyond it. As Yeats said: "Before we can see objective truth we must exhaust subjective" (E, 483). This, then, is the meaning of Romantic individualism. The self is of value not so much in and for itself but as a starting point, as the only available testing ground of value. Like Descartes the Romantic can—indeed, has by Descartes himself been forced to—question all means of validation but his own experience. But the self is means, not end, and the Romantic exploration of it is not to affirm it as an end value but to establish its efficacy as a means to other values.

Coleridge, as usual, suggests the method of proceeding here. In the *Biographia Literaria* he defines the human soul as the first and lowest of "that class of Being . . . which is endued with a reflex consciousness of its own continuousness, and the great end and purpose of all its energies & sufferings is the growth of that reflex consciousness." Some pages further he says that "personality is a circumference continually expanding through sympathy and understanding, rather than an exclusive self-feeling."[3] Growth and expansion of the reflex (or self) consciousness: it is the program implied in the subtitle of Wordsworth's great poem, itself a mere prelude or starting point.

By means of an expansion of consciousness, the Romantic moves through the ego to the Self and through the Self to the Other. Coleridge says: "We begin with the I KNOW MYSELF, in order to end with the absolute I AM. We proceed from the

---

achievement. But she goes on to argue that "the Self is indeed the starting point . . . but it is also the goal . . . its realized possession both the motive and the reward for creative exertion," p. 64.

3. *Biographia Literaria*, ed. John Shawcross (London, 1907), 1: 202; 2: 20.

SELF, in order to lose and find all self in GOD."[4] One goes
through the individual self-conscious ego by relinquishing it,
thus freeing a deeper self that is paradoxically both the real
Self and the "not I"—what Rimbaud glimpsed in his cryptic
"Je est un autre," what Yeats called the universal self, the
Great Memory, or Personality as opposed to Character. In
this buried life, this profounder self than the ego, a man experiences Being—Coleridge's "one Life within us and abroad"
—and so not only knows the Other to be real but, having
access to it, feels himself related to it through Being. Through
this Self he can unite himself to the Other and transcend the
separation of the self and the world. To make the self, or know
the self, or have a self is therefore to make and possess the
means to transcend the self. Through knowing this deeper
self one knows being; then, convinced of its reality, he abandons the ego in order to join the self to Being. The way down
and the way up are paradoxically the same. The fall into
self-consciousness can be redeemed only by more consciousness. If we are to retain our humanity, self-consciousness cannot be obliterated; it can only be transformed. Self-transcen-
dence must be achieved in self-discovery. In Blake's terms one
must move from innocence *through* experience to "organized
innocence." Or, as Kleist wrote, we must eat of the tree of
knowledge again. Man falls from what Keats called "the infant or thoughtless Chamber" of consciousness into "the
Chamber of Maiden-Thought"; he is "impelled" to this "by
the awakening of the thinking principle" (L1, 280–81). Here,
in self-consciousness, "we see not the ballance of good and
evil. We are in a Mist." But there are chambers of consciousness beyond this, down passages presently dark, and "if we
live, and *go on thinking,* we too shall explore them" (italics
added). Through this comparison of "human life to a large
Mansion of Many Apartments," Keats describes the problem
of consciousness and foresees the solution—expansion of consciousness—explored in the two *Hyperions.* Expansion of
consciousness is, in fact, very much what Keats meant by

4. Ibid., 1: 186.

Soul Making

"philosophy" and "wisdom," "the continual drinking of Knowledge" (L1, 271) and "very gradual ripening of the intellectual powers" (L1, 214) so much on his mind in the spring of 1818. He believed that history showed "a grand march of intellect" from Milton to Wordsworth (L1, 282). Milton had explored Paradise Lost, the fall into self-consciousness and separation; Wordsworth had explored those dark passages leading to a wider consciousness and Paradise Regained.

In this question of consciousness there is an act of faith that separates the Romantic from the romantic egoist succeeding him in the nineteenth century. The Romantic retains faith in an order or realm of value external to the self, reached through a proper understanding of the self. When that faith is lost, solipsism begins, Beckett's Murphy is born, and the best remedy against despair is a disciplined hedonism. Pater is ambiguous because he marks the precarious point of passage from Romanticism to romantic egoism and our own predicament, to the affirmation of the self and its states of consciousness as ends in themselves. Though I think Pater has been misunderstood, it remained for Wallace Stevens to clarify Pater's method of proceeding and to make out of non-belief in transcendence a statement that is profoundly humanistic and related to the high Romantic claims for the imagination. And Stevens too, one notes, escaped no more than Pater from the charge of triviality, the charge of romantic egoism.

Central to the Romantic act of faith in an order or realm of value external to the self is an intense experience of divinity, the Other. Four general attitudes to this experience are possible. First, an attitude that denies or ignores the question of the Other: godhead is no more than the germ of idealized humanity waiting development in each man, a variation on Feuerbach's assertion that the divine is only a projection of human consciousness; what one has experienced is merely his own human potentiality. Second, the Gnostic belief that godhead is altogether transcendent. Third, the position that godhead is altogether immanent, in some variation descending

Chapter One

from Spinoza's pantheism (and very often looking, in effect, toward the first position). Fourth, the position of paradox: godhead is both immanent and transcendent, a mystery that Christianity shares, ironically enough, with much primitive faith.

Among the English Romantics only Coleridge and Blake seem to side generally with the last position, working out, of course, separate and often heterodox variations on this belief. Hence it is said with some insistence now that Romanticism is not really an attempt to explore the mystery of immanence and transcendence but is a movement away from that mystery to the first position, the self-deification of man.[5] There seems to me no way to settle this question either-or: as my study will show—the second chapter in particular—there is too much evidence available for both arguments, some of it looking in both directions at once, to the first position and the fourth. And evidence speaking directly of only the first position does not by necessity exclude the fourth, which may be assumed or implied. With this evidence the critic must recognize that he argues as his particular sensibility directs. The newer argument, when held single-mindedly, errs in making the Romantics too modern, too post-Nietzschean; my own

5. Harold Bloom writes, for example: "Different as the major Romantics were in their attitude toward religion, they were united (except for Coleridge) in *not* striving for unity with anything but what might be called their Tharmis or id component . . . the unfallen human potential for realizing instinctual desires. . . ." *The Ringers in the Tower: Studies in Romantic Tradition* (Chicago, 1971), p. 26.

Without the Freudian turn, this point is also argued about Yeats. Bernard Levine, for example, writes in *The Dissolving Image* (Detroit, 1970), p. 96: "Yeats, contrary to Cassirer's implication regarding apprehension of the Other . . . is too sophisticated to believe the god or daemon is separate from the most intimate projection of human consciousness." Levine believes that for Yeats the ideal "cannot be conceived to lie outside the human mind," p. 96.

Pursuing a similar argument, Frank Lentricchia, *The Gaiety of Language* (Berkeley, 1968), p. 73, believes that Yeats's very definition of creativity is a turning away from the Romantic concept of the imagination because it implies a greater power transcending itself to which the poetic will is subject. Yet he sees clearly that Yeats "would always be allured by those aspects of Romantic and symbolist theories which promised imaginative penetration of a world beyond time," p. 61.

argument, if misunderstood to mean that Yeats always assumed the fourth position, will err in making him too premodern, pre-Nietzschean. The truth, I think, is that Yeats and the Romantic poets before him moved in and out of several positions, not only the first but also, and just as often, the last.

The difference in the concept of the self held by the Romantic and by what I am calling the romantic egoist can hardly be overstated, because the difference is central in the Romantic attempt to unify the self and the world, to heal the wounds of consciousness. The difference is no less central to the unity of self and world affirmed by mythic consciousness, for that consciousness cannot be brought into play, cannot operate at all, if the ego insists on its uniqueness for its own identity. To see mythic consciousness in Keats and Yeats, then, it is necessary to see first their sense of self in which that consciousness is grounded.

II

"My Strong Identity, My Real Self"

Keats's major statements on the topic of the self are his speculations regarding soul-making and its seeming opposites, negative capability and the chameleon character of the poet. That he nowhere reconciles these speculations in a single statement is to me evidence that he saw little contradiction between them, that he took for granted the paradoxical nature of the self. It should be remembered, too, that the doctrine of soul-making is, in context, more an attempt to explain the necessity of "a world like this" than it is a statement about the nature of self. Whatever contradiction with his other speculations that the passage may imply is checked, I. think, by this consideration. At the same time, close attention to the text will reveal the double nature of the self which it proposes.

In his famous letter on the subject (L2, 102–104), Keats identifies man as an immanent extension of transcendent

deity. To him human beings at birth are "sparks of divinity . . . in short they are God": immediately he affirms that
the self is connected to (even mythically interchangeable
with) the Other. In saying next that these sparks of divinity
are, at birth, not souls but intelligences, "atoms of perception," he places consciousness at the very heart of man's
nature. Equally important, he does not grant men a priori
individuality; at birth one is merely a part of human consciousness, sharing this with all men and, in sharing divinity
with them, partaking of a deep and universal self grounded
in that divinity. Individual identity—our ordinary selfhood—
must, he says, be *acquired*, through the medium of experience
in the world.

Restating his argument, Keats adds to the elements of Intelligence and World a third element, Heart. He calls the
world a school and the heart the hornbook used in that school;
when an intelligence is able to "read" the heart, it is ready
to come into possession of a soul or Identity. He defines the
heart as "the Minds Bible" (echoing his earlier claim for "the
holiness of the heart's affections"); it is the mind's "experience," "the teat from which the Mind or intelligence sucks its
identity." The heart, in effect, is metonymy for sympathetic
intuition; Keats is saying here what he says elsewhere: discursive reason or even perception itself is insufficient for
knowledge, for experience, for identity. The mind must sub-
mit itself to the heart as the instrument of intuition; it must
act in cooperation with a feeling response to the world—Cassirer's first element in mythic apprehension—before identity
can be shaped by the world. This identity is the ordinary ego
of individual self-consciousness; but below it lies a deeper
self, the spark of divinity coupled with the heart, an intuitive
faculty.

Yeats is equally insistent on this participation of the deeper
self with the Other. In *Ribh Considers Christian Love Insufficient* his speaker asks how the soul can live at all till God
lives "in her blood," asks how there can be a physical world
for the soul to see or know until God makes that world, and,
moving in the soul, bids her to know that world. Yeats is af-

firming the divinity of man; at the same time, the poem is also insisting that godhead, if immanent, is also transcendent. Such close communication between God and the self did Yeats demand that he found Berkeley insufficient; for except in private journals Berkeley "dared not say that Man so far as he is himself . . . reflects the whole of God; his God and Man seem cut off from one another" (E, 408). Consequently Yeats was pleased to learn—and translated the Upanishads in the attempt to understand—that God is "the Spirit, the Self that is *in* all selves . . . the *source* of intelligence" (E, 461; italics added). The parallel with Keats is striking.

To make the distinction between the two levels of the self, Yeats employed the terms Personality and Character. Personality is the core of man, that general essence which the separate man shares with all men. Character on the other hand is identified with the individualizing traits of the specific man living in some one place at some one moment in history. Personality is amoral energy; Character is moral bounds for that energy, in the superficial sense of being bound to mores and customs. Personality is the expression of our deepest nature, Character the routine and daily habit of our quotidian life. Keats made a similar distinction, speaking of men of genius and men of action. Men of genius are like chemical catalysts: they act upon the "neutral" intellect of mankind but have not in themselves any individuality or "determined character"; these qualities of the self are reserved for men of power or action (L1, 184). The man of genius most deeply interesting to Keats was the poet, and he found him a "camelion," altogether lacking in the superficial self: "As to the poetical Character itself . . . it is not itself—it has no self—it is everything and nothing—It has no character" (L1, 387). In Yeats's terms Personality would dominate in Keats's man of genius, while Character would control his man of power.

The task of man is to reconcile and bring into harmony his ego and his deeper self, Personality and Character; in being this unified Self, he experiences Being and comes into relationship with the Other. Hence the task of the "pilgrim soul" (Y, 41) becomes the discovery and possession of the deeper self. Yeats "makes" the self by assuming the Romantic paradox of the self. He seeks Rimbaud's "I" that is an other—or, as he called it, the Mask.

The Mask is that personality opposite to what one is; it is not so much what the person would like to be, his ideal, as it is that which is necessary for him to assume, by an act of will, so as to contain and reconcile within himself opposites and thereby achieve full unity. Paradoxically this Mask is both outside and within the person. It is outside in the sense that it is no part of his conscious ego, is external to his ordinary self; and it is outside in the sense that one finds external to himself an image of it, often in some other person or persons. But at the same time it germinates in the deepest recesses of the self, at the very core of one's being. If this were not so, one's assumption of it would be false (as it is when the Mask is not rightly chosen or defined, when self-knowledge fails in its most difficult task; there are true and false Masks, as Yeats makes clear in *A Vision*). Self-discovery thus moves in two directions, outward to images of the Mask and inward toward the seed of it residing in the deeper self. When this seed flowers one comes into Unity of Being.

In both poets, then, we see the Romantic concept of the double self that is paradoxically one. Yeats's clear analysis of and programmatic approach to it must be seen as an attempt to unify the two selves which, across the nineteenth century, separate and lose all contact with each other.[6] This separation, heralded in *The Picture of Dorian Gray* and in Arnold's poem *The Buried Life*, is figured in *Dr. Jekyll and Mr. Hyde*, where the deeper self is made monstrous by the very horror of separation. Conrad's *The Secret Sharer* has its particular brilliance in making two persons of the two selves while yet affirming, at its end, their harmonious reunification in the one man. The story prefigures Lawrence's attempt to portray that

6. The fragmentation of the self in the nineteenth century is traced by Masao Miyoshi, *The Divided Self: A Perspective on the Literature of the Victorians* (New York, 1969); Byron and Shelley play important roles in his thesis. A more general work is by Robert Rogers, *A Psychoanalytic Study of the Double in Literature* (Detroit, 1970).

Soul Making

self residing below what he called the old stable ego of consciousness.

Yeats developed his body of beliefs slowly. In the poem *Adam's Curse* (1902) the doctrine is couched in terms of the discipline necessary to bring the self into fullness of being. The curse of Adam is precisely that fullness is not granted us *per se*; having lost it in the Fall, we must labor to redeem it. One of the women in the poem says, in reply to the poet, who has commented on her efforts: "To be born woman is to know . . . that we must labour to be beautiful." It is to this labor that a much later poem refers, wherein the adolescent Helen of Troy practices "a tinker shuffle" to perfect in the grown woman a beauty that men will remember forever (Y, 328). In *Adam's Curse* Yeats agrees with the woman and quickly replies: "It's certain there is no fine thing / Since Adam's fall but needs much labouring." If man's essence is potentially the most beautiful in nature, it is also the most difficult to bring to its proper pitch or form; it will not, as in lower animals, fulfill itself spontaneously. For the artist in particular the task is difficult; providing his created works with their proper pitch may drain his own energies and "dry the sap out of his veins," diminishing both the will and the energy required for the perfection of his life (Y, 91). Yeats, in fact, remarked that men must often "choose / Perfection of the life or of the work" (Y, 242). The sad irony acknowledged by the poet in *Adam's Curse* is that one has no assurance he will succeed in either task. The discipline required for successful art may not be at all the kind of discipline required for love and, applied to it, may leave the heart "as weary-hearted as that hollow moon."

In 1915 Yeats wrote *Ego Dominus Tuus*, cast into prose three years later in *Per Amica Silentia Lunae*. In both versions soul-making has developed into his doctrine of the Mask, even if that particular term is yet to come. The poem is familiar to most readers of Yeats, being of all his "system" poems probably the one most frequently anthologized. Yet its use of Keats in expressing its theme warrants discussion here. The burden of the poem is that no true artist—and, by im-

Chapter One

plication, no man—is ever granted Unity of Being by birth or
natural constitution; he must seek it. Ille (or, as Pound
punned, "Willie") says:

> By the help of an image
> I call to my own opposite, summon all
> That I have handled least, least looked upon.

Hic replies that he would find himself and not an image. But
Ille's point is that the self that can be known to the rational
discursive intellect is not complete and so cannot suffice; and
if one thinks it will suffice—as is "our modern hope"—then
"we are but critics or but half create"; such activity is all we
are allowed by the superficial self, whose chief component is
the intellect. Ille argues that even Dante—"chief imagination
of Christendom," of the unified sacramental vision—even
Dante "fashioned from his opposite / An image . . . Being
mocked by Guido for his lecherous life." Great art must come
from "tragic war," the dialectical struggle between the "self"
and the Mask, for Unity of Being. Even those "Impulsive men
that look for happiness / And sing when they have found
it"—men such as Keats—for them, too, their song will be but
a Mask, covering what they have seen when "awakened from
the common dream" of the superficial self and its life into
"dissipation and despair."

Ille says of Keats: "His art is happy, but who knows his
mind?"

> I see a schoolboy when I think of him,
> With face and nose pressed to a sweet-shop window,
> For certainly he sank into his grave
> His senses and his heart unsatisfied,
> And made—being poor, ailing and ignorant,
> Shut out from all the luxury of the world,
> The coarse-bred son of a livery-stable keeper—
> Luxuriant song.

Taken out of context the description is patronizing, no more
than a reflection of Victorian attitudes. In context, however,
the lines indicate that whatever Yeats may really have felt
about Keats, he is here using that Victorian distortion as an

image for the idea argued in his poem. Hence the lines are curiously commendatory. Only a man "poor, ailing and ignorant" could have found—both external to himself, imaged in a window, and deep in his unsatisfied heart—the Mask of such "luxuriant song." Yeats had seen Keats in these terms as early as 1901. Contrasting Keats and Shelley, he said then that there are poets like Keats who have, "so far as the casual eye can see, little personal will, but fiery and brooding imagination" (E, 328–29). This impersonal will is the central element or matrix of Personality, the very level of being that Yeats, in his poem, argues one must reach. This impersonal will or brooding imagination is "the voice of what is eternal in man" (E, 167).

Ille concludes the poem with the firm cry:

> I call to the mysterious one who yet
> Shall walk the wet sands . . .
> And look most like me, being indeed my double,
> And prove of all imaginable things
> The most unlike, being my anti-self. . . .

Certainly in 1915 the most obvious antiself to Yeats's poetry and thought was Keats, the sensuous and concrete qualities of whose work Yeats had "least handled, least looked upon." By implication, then, Yeats is saying that Keats, or qualities characterized by Keats and his work, is what he shall henceforth strive for.

In the poetry of his late years in particular, Yeats struggled to affirm both the given world and Personality, man's true being and passion, not the superficial traits of specific men. If, he felt, he could reach what Arnold had called "the buried life" (in Yeats's own phrase, "the buried self"), then poetry would have an audience; it would become an image of the audience, in which people could find their true nature expressed (A, 118–20). "Some thought of this kind," he wrote, "made Keats's lines telling how Homer had left great verses to a little clan seem to my imagination when I was a boy a description of the happiest fate that could come to a poet" (LY, 406). Those poets—and he said Keats was one—able to reach the level of the deeper self had the advantage that "everything they write is part of knowledge" (E, 329). In his Noh plays Yeats set out to learn the skill of expressing Personality without slipping into abstraction and vagueness, overgeneralized emotion lacking definition. If often failing in these plays, as in the early "beggar" poems of *Responsibilities*, he succeeded admirably in the later ballads and Crazy Jane poems.

Keats, too, sensed the growing split between the artist and society, the increasingly subjective movement of the arts that threatened to leave the artist isolated in his own consciousness. To avoid this road toward Beckett's Murphy, he determined to succeed first at epic then, if possible, at drama, considering his own lyric poems rather casually as exercises toward the larger forms. Like the mature Yeats, he subscribed to Wordsworth's definition of the poet as a man speaking to men, "the man who with a man / Is an equal, be he King, / Or poorest of the beggar-clan" (K, 499). Like Yeats he disapproved of the fashionable craving for originality, believing that each modern poet, like an Elector of Hanover, tried to rule the "petty state" of his particular ego (L1, 224). Neither poet had any use for the egotistical sublime. Late in life Yeats wrote: "I hated and still hate with an ever-growing hatred the literature of the point of view" (E, 511), an almost conscious echo of Keats's "we hate poetry that has a palpable design on us" (L1, 224).

"My character is so little myself," Yeats wrote in 1930, "that all my life it has thwarted me. It has affected my poems, my true self, no more than the character of a dancer affects the movements of a dance" (EX, 308). Again, almost consciously, he echoes Keats's belief that the poet "has no character"; rather, he is "everything and nothing" (L1, 387). "I am a crowd, I am a lonely man, I am nothing," Yeats cried, (E, 522), reaching for Personality, the deeper self related to all selves. In his prose Yeats said he sometimes felt that other voices must be speaking through him, as the Instructors of *A Vision* spoke through his wife. Keats knew a similar if less esoteric experience: "even now I am perhaps not speaking

Soul Making

from myself; but from some character in whose soul I now live" (L1, 388). Yeats imagined hovering near him a presiding Daimon, a manifestation arising from the *anima hominis*, itself a part of the *anima mundi*. Keats wrote to Haydon, "I remember your saying that you had notions of a good Genius presiding over you—I have of late had the same thought. . . . Is it too daring to Fancy Shakspeare this Presider?" (L1, 141–42)

For Yeats the source or home of these presiding figures was the *anima mundi* or, as he also called it, the Great Memory. He introduced the latter term in his essay "Magic" (1901), as part of three doctrines that he felt had been handed down from early times:

(1) That the borders of our minds are ever shifting, and that many minds can flow into one another, as it were, and create or reveal a single mind, a single energy.

(2) That the borders of our memories are as shifting, and that our memories are part of one great memory, the memory of Nature herself.

(3) That this great mind and great memory can be evoked by symbols. (E, 28)

The theory, almost identical to that "collective unconscious" Jung was shortly to posit, explains Yeats's concept of the double self and identifies the source of the deeper Self, of Personality and Mask. Furthermore it is also very similar to a belief held by Keats:

The Minds of Mortals are so different and bent on such diverse Journeys that it may at first appear impossible for any common taste and fellowship to exist between two or three under these suppositions—It is however quite the contrary—Minds would leave each other in contrary directions, traverse each other in Numberless points, and [at] last greet each other at the Journeys end. . . . Man should not dispute or assert but whisper results to his neighbor, and thus *by every germ of Spirit sucking the Sap from mould ethereal every human might become great*, and Humanity instead of being a wide heath of Furse and Briars with here and there a remote Oak or Pine, would become a grand democracy of Forest Trees. (L1, 232; italics added)

In the italicized lines Keats has described that journey to the

Chapter One

deeper self and its ground in the Great Memory by which
Yeats transformed the ego into the larger Self. Keats's "mould
ethereal" is analogous to Yeats's "great memory." Almost as
if he knew the Keats passage, Yeats wrote: "Certainly we
suck always at the eternal dugs" (LY, 731). The striking repetition of the identical verb offers evidence to validate the
belief they shared. Both men hoped that contact with the
deeper Self, grounded in Being, would transform Character
into Personality and so create "a grand democracy of Forest
Trees." Through knowledge enormous from the "mould
ethereal," every human might become great, as Apollo and
Keats become gods in the two *Hyperions*.

Yeats has himself described this transformation of the ego
into the Self: "A writer must die every day he lives, be reborn as it is said in the Burial Service. an incorruptible self,
that self opposite of all that he has named 'himself.' " (A, 277).
There could be no clearer statement of the concept of the self
shared by Romanticism, Yeats's doctrine of the Mask, and
mythic apprehension. Cassirer, for example, says that "mythic consciousness does not see human personality as something
fixed and unchanging, but conceives every *phase* of a man's
life as a new personality, a new self."[7] Eliade is even more
instructive: "the man of the primitive societies does not consider himself 'finished' as he finds himself 'given' on the natural level of existence. To become a man in the proper sense
he must die to this first (natural) life and be reborn to a
higher life. which is at once religious and cultural. . . . religious man *wants to be* other than he finds himself on the
"natural" level and undertakes to *make himself* in accordance
with the ideal image revealed to him by myths."[8] Eliade's
italics lead us back to that section of *The Tower* wherein
Yeats cries, "It is time to make my soul." Eliade also reminds
us that this mythic rebirth of the self underlies the initiation
rite. Before that event the man to be initiated is thought

7. *Language and Myth* (New York, 1946), p. 51.
8. *The Sacred and the Profane: The Nature of Religion* (New York,
1961), p. 187. See also Ernst Cassirer. *The Myth of the State* (New Haven, 1971), p. 40.

hardly to have a human identity. At initiation he is reborn with human identity, a member of the community, related to others. Initiation is suggested by Yeats's remarks and demonstrated by Keats's Apollo, who in *Hyperion* "dies into life." Keats himself is initiated before Moneta in *The Fall of Hyperion*. Through mythic consciousness Keats and Yeats transform the ego into the Self, and they are made gods precisely in the sense that they discover that the Self partakes of divinity. They are initiated into the mystery of Being, within us and abroad.

III

"A Greeting of the Spirit"

If the superficial self, the ego of self-conscious identity, must be transformed into the deeper self—if Character must give way to Personality—before one can discover, in the fullness of his own being, the ground of being of the Other—then one must ask what is the agent of this transformation. Keats gives the clue in his letter on soul making—that agent is the heart.

To Yeats and to Keats the heart, closer than the mind to the center of our being, guesses at truth which the mind does not grasp and reveals in intuition what the mind cannot know. The heart becomes a metaphor for the imagination and the faculty of mythic apprehension. Again and again Yeats returns to the revelatory function of the heart. *Heart* was, in fact, for both poets a favorite word; and Yeats believed as strongly as Keats in the "holiness of the heart's affections." In the very first poem of the *Collected Poems*, he wrote: "there is no truth / Saving in thine own heart" (Y, 7). And at the end of his career, the theme returns; feeling his intellectually constructed beliefs to have failed, he cries out that he must begin again where all intellectual beliefs begin, " in the foul rag-and-bone shop of the heart."

Both poets felt certain that, in Yeats's words, the heart or "the imagination has some way of lighting on the truth that

Chapter One

reason has not" (E, 65). Keats repeated again and again that
he could never accept a truth until he had experienced it, that
knowledge had to be known existentially to be known at all.
Yeats agreed: "We only believe in those thoughts which have
been conceived not in the brain but in the whole body" (E,
235). "Hands," he requested, "Bring the balloon of the mind
/ ... Into its narrow shed" (Y, 153):

> God guard me from those thoughts men think
> In the mind alone;
> He that sings a lasting song
> Thinks in a marrow-bone. ... (Y, 281)

Wishing himself to be as "ignorant" or instinctive "as the
dawn" (Y, 144), he exhorted women in particular, as if he
were Keats's thrush, not to spoil their instinctive being by the
abstract intellect. This theme persists from early poems on
Maud Gonne to its culmination in *Michael Robartes and the
Dancer* (1921); all but two or three poems in the volume
deal with this one concern, which is most fully realized in
the magnificent *A Prayer for my Daughter*.

In consequence of his belief in the heart, Keats valued
what he called "Negative Capability," the ability to trust in
intuition while the intellect accepts "uncertainties, Mysteries,
doubts, without any irritable reaching after fact and reason"
(L1, 193). If we can accept the feeling response of the heart
and its intuitive wisdom, we need "fret not after knowledge,"
just as the thrush of Keats's poem instructs, in its intuitive
knowledge of what is needful. Continually Keats's poems return to this theme of intuition, "unintellectual, yet divine"
(K, 504). Repeating the theme of *What the Thrush Said*, he
asks what seabird is a philosopher as it plunges in harmony
with the great waves (K, 504). In the sonnet *To Homer* the
theme finds full and brilliant realization. Keats reaffirms that
Homer's physical blindness, by freeing his intuitive vision,
allows him true insight into the meaning of natural processes.
"Aye, on the shores of darkness there is light," Keats cries, as
if he were himself the thrush in the other sonnet.

With this use of heart as metaphor for intuition and imagination and this belief in the efficacy of these faculties as agents of truth, we are taken to the major concern of my study: the structure of mythic apprehension underlying the Romantic solutions of Keats and Yeats to the problem of Adam's curse, self-consciousness.

At the center of the problem, both for the Romantic and the man of mythic consciousness, is that separation of the self and external world discussed at the opening of this chapter. Faced with this dichotomy, Wordsworth and Coleridge proposed a two-directional reconciliation inherited by their Romantic followers. Imagination, a faculty of feeling and intuition, when engaged with objects, either reveals a life ontologically within them or lends a coloring that gives them the semblance of the life felt within the perceiver. The Romantics hope the former to be true and often affirm that it is. Unable, however, to prove this position to materialists, they fall back on the latter. And even here they can argue for the first by saying that the feelings would have to be activated before one could perceive the vital life in objects, however "there" such life might be. In other words, if this vital life in objects may be merely a projection of the imagination, it is also true that such projection can never be proved, because this vital life, if it is there, cannot be perceived without the very faculty that may create it. At their most sanguine the Romantics believed that if noumenon could not be proved, it could not be disproved either. Often, however, this Kantian attitude seemed but cold comfort, and they doubted radically or tried to believe totally with Schelling that the noumenon was real and could be known. When they affirm this, the vital being shared by both subject and object—and revealed or provided by the imagination—becomes the ground in which subject and object, the self and the world, are reconciled. Hence imagination, the agent of this reconciliation, is placed at the pinnacle of man's faculties.

Here Romantic epistemology meets mythic consciousness, for one of the central elements of the latter, a sympathetic nonlogical response to the world, is also common to imagination. It is through feeling that we first apprehend the world.

Chapter One

Basing his position on general biological considerations, Cassirer writes: "States of feeling are not merely secondary and derived; they are not merely the qualities, modes, or functions of cognitive states. They are, on the contrary, primitive, autonomous, not reducible to intelligence, and able to exist outside it and without it."[9] Feeling, being prior to cognition at a biological level, is the very matrix of cognition and the first component in its earliest stages of operation. Hence, underlying Coleridge's brilliant description of the imagination is the simple fact, central to mythic thought, that external reality is engaged not merely by the mind but by the feelings. He says as much himself when, in *Dejection: An Ode*, he cries: "I see but cannot feel how beautiful they are." Wordsworth knew this truth and with it initiated Romantic epistemology in English poetry. "The affections lead us on," he says in *Tintern Abbey*, to that moment when "we see into the life of things."

Keats, too, understood this role of feeling in cognition. Unable to perceive how truth could be known by "consequitive reasoning," he wanted a "life of Sensations rather than of Thoughts" (L1, 185), meaning by "sensations" experience in which intense sensory stimulation activates deep feeling which, in turn, activates the intuition, the result being nonceptual, immediate, felt insights. The operation of "sensations" is all but synonymous with the sympathetic response of mythic apprehension. It relates the subject to the object in what Cassirer calls a feeling response. Because Keats could not *feel* the truth in Wordsworth's *Gipsies*, he spoke of the poem as a "sketchy intellectual landscape—not a search after Truth" (L1, 174).

In a somewhat puzzling letter (L1, 242–43), Keats attempted to set forth the Romantic position, a scale of being as being is determined by the feeling response essential to Romantic epistemology and mythic thought. The letter is puzzling because what he arranges into three classes are "ethereal things," and since he mentions objects possessing

9. *The Myth of the State*, p. 25; cf. pp. 23–26 and pp. 41–43.

empirical existence—sun, moon, clouds—it is difficult to know what he means by "ethereal."[10] He seems to mean objects that the mind is inclined to engage through feeling, for the classification turns on his introductory remark: "probably every mental pursuit takes its reality and worth from the ardour of the pursuer." "Ethereal things" are thus real, semireal, or "no things" according to the amount of feeling one must expend to uphold for them a reality in which the imagination as well as the intellect may be engaged. Some objects appeal so immediately to our feelings that we are not aware of expending any imaginative activity or labor in our response to them; they seem imaginatively informed by themselves, objects whose noumenon is powerful enough to be perceived independently of any imaginative response in the perceiver. These are real things, and they may be either natural ("Sun Moon & Stars") or man-made ("passages of Shakespeare").

Things semireal, on the other hand, "require a greeting of the Spirit to make them wholly exist"; their noumenon cannot be wholly known, their being wholly affirmed, independently of the perceiver, who must greet them with the active response of his spirit: his feeling, his imagination, his "sensations." Keats here comes to the center of Romantic and mythic epistemology, and his prefacing remark is now clear: semireal things take their "reality and worth from the ardour of the pursuer," from the perceiver himself and his feeling response. The thought has its parallel in Yeats: "Whatever flames upon the night / Man's own resinous heart has fed" (Y, 211). Things semireal may be either material

10. Writing to Haydon a year before this letter to Bailey, Keats did define his term: "the looking upon the Sun the Moon the Stars, the Earth and its contents as materials to form greater things—that is to say ethereal things—but here I am talking like a Madman greater things that our Creater himself made!!" (L1, 143) But the context here is less inclusive than that in the letter to Bailey. Here the subject is the artistic re-creation of reality, Coleridge's secondary imagination, rather than the perception of reality in general. It is true that the meaning of the term here does relate to that larger context. But to explore that relationship in the letter to Bailey would be to wander from the point Keats is making there, to which the secondary imagination is not central.

("Clouds") or immaterial ("Love"), objective or subjective. That love requires the participation of the imagination is clear; no critic, however, has bothered to explain why a greeting of the spirit is necessary for the existence of a cloud. Probably Keats means that it is only through our feelings and imagination that cloud shapes take the many resemblances we see in them, just as the beloved is created or defined by the feelings of the lover: the imagination grants identity to both, in a union of the perceiving mind and the perceived object.

No examples are given of "no things." By implication they exist as mental creations only, self-created by the imagination with no external object as direct stimulus. A yet unwritten passage of poetry in the mind of the poet, stimulated by imagination rather than immediate perception, would conceivably be a "no thing" until put down on paper (when it would become real or semireal, depending on the reader). Of all "ethereal things," "no things" demand the greatest expenditure of feeling, feeling transformed into imaginative energy, since, lacking any objective reality, they must be made as well as responded to.[11] They are "made Great and dignified by an ardent pursuit." Again Keats returns to his opening theme. Thinking, perhaps, that he is quoting Shelley's *Hymn to Intellectual Beauty*, he ends by saying that our minds " 'consec[r]ate whate'er they look upon.' " The phrase is indeed felicitous for the imagination's "greeting" with the object, the feeling response to the world shared by Romanticism and mythic apprehension. It looks back to a similar phrase in book III of *Endymion*, the fair copy of which Keats had finished a little over two weeks before. Endymion, greeting the moon—Keats's major symbol for the imagination—cries out: "Thou dost bless every where . . . / Kissing dead things to life" (lines 56–57).

---

11. Keats has this meaning in mind when he writes elsewhere of Lord Byron: "There is this great difference between us. He describes what he sees—I describe what I imagine—Mine is the hardest task" (L2, 200). Keats's culminating image for and attempt at that task will be his description of the face of Moneta in *The Fall of Hyperion*.

Soul Making

In Keats and Yeats the greeting of the spirit operates in contrasting modes. Here again Coleridge is helpful: "[Shakespeare] darts himself forth, and passes into all the forms of human character and passion, the one Proteus of the fire and the flood; [Milton] attracts all forms and things to himself, into the unity of his own ideal. All things and modes of actions shape themselves anew in the being of Milton; while Shakespeare becomes all things, yet forever remaining himself."[12]

Keats follows Shakespeare's method and Yeats follows Milton's. Keats "passes into all the forms" through empathy and his chameleon nature, enjoying fellowship with the essence or Self shared by all. Yeats "attracts all forms and things" to the bottom of his being, to that level where his ego is transformed into the Self, and the things are "shaped anew" as he discovers in them that same level of Being to which his ego is, in importance, a mere conscious epiphenomenon. The way *out* and the way *in* both lead to the Other.

As biographers and critics have shown, the empathic response was a natural and pervasive mode of Keats's imagination. Most readers will recall instances from his letters, the most famous, perhaps, being this: "if a Sparrow comes before my window I take part in its existence and pick about the Gravel" (L1, 186). Not often cited but most intensely empathic is his "listening to Rain with a sense of being drown'd and rotted like a grain of wheat" (L1, 273), reminiscent of two stanzas in *Isabella* (14, 35) in which Keats speaks of staring so intently at a grave that one comes to feel and picture the body beneath the sod.

The need for an empathic greeting of the spirit, if the Self is to join the Other, is perhaps the most basic theme in *Endymion*. There are, of course, numerous ways of reading the poem, but this necessity of surrendering the ego before the object seems to underlie them all. Endymion, having turned away from both nature and human society in his quest for a dream-goddess (book 1), must be taught to welcome nature

12. *Biographia Literaria*, ed. John Shawcross (London, 1907), 2: 20.

Chapter One

(book II) and sympathize with people (book III), loving an earthly woman before deserving the ideal (book IV).[13] In the opening of the poem Keats indicates what the melancholy Endymion's behavior should be:

> Apollo's upward fire
> Made every eastern cloud a silvery pyre
> Of brightness so unsullied, that therein
> A melancholy spirit well might win
> Oblivion, and melt out his essence fine
> Into the winds.   (lines 95–100)

It is in book III, however, through Glaucus (whose story is almost a double plot to his own) that Endymion comes to understand this sympathetic-empathic response as his salvation. Glaucus has been told he will not die *"If he explores all forms and substances / Straight homeward to their symbolessences"* (lines 699–700). Both men are saved by exercising a greeting of the spirit. In *Hyperion* (III, 99–102) Apollo cries out in the act of becoming deified that if he enters "any one particular beauteous star," he will "make its silvery splendour pant with bliss." In *The Fall of Hyperion* (I, 302–306) it is now Keats, rather than Apollo, who learns to see as a god sees, to "take the depth / Of things" through an intuitively active greeting of the spirit, just as the physical or "outward" eye pervades outward size and shape. In these passages Keats brings to fruition a theme that began in some of his earliest verse: "Objects . . . look'd out so invitingly / On either side. These, gentle Calidore / Greeted" (K, 14).

Keats's remarks on "real things" indicate that for each of the Romantic poets the exact nature of reality is differentiated by the ontological status predicated for the physical object through the operation of the imagination, his greeting of the spirit and feeling response to the object. Each of them,

---

13. This is my summary of an interpretation developed in convincing detail by Walter Evert, *Aesthetic and Myth in the Poetry of Keats* (Princeton, 1965), p. 175. Evert's reading should be compared with Charles I. Patterson Jr., *The Daemonic in the Poetry of John Keats* (Urbana, Ill., 1970), with which it shares my admiration. Both men, I think, are more nearly right about the poem than anyone else to date.

Soul Making

with perhaps the exceptions of Blake and Byron, moves at different times through a full range of positions in regard to the object, from Berkelean nonexistence through the vitalism described above to moments of despairing materialism; the polar positions are implied, if not directly stated. Such vacillation is very often the subject of their poetry, and at any given moment their ontological assumptions will be tied to a particular and changing relationship between imagination and intellect. This must be kept in mind when arranging the Romantic poets, according to their beliefs, in any epistemological or ontological scale. It is a caveat of particular importance when we relate Yeats to his Romantic forebears.

Because of the elements of Gnosticism found in his work, Yeats in placed by some critics with or near Blake, or Shelley, who is next to Blake. I do not deny that he has Gnostic moments throughout his career. But to insist on these moments is to distort the total picture of his work, especially the mature work, and to misdefine the central nature of his vacillating relationship to the world.[14]

Yeats, like Keats, affirmed in people, even in animals, an energy or power related to some divine source; this much is clear from his concept of the dual self. Unlike Keats, he rarely accepted, even provisionally, the existence of this force elsewhere in the material universe, except in trees (and very

---

14. Harold Bloom's *Yeats* (New York, 1970) is an ambitious study of the poet's relationship to his Romantic forerunners, especially Blake and Shelley. It is notable for the clarity with which Bloom shows those ways that Yeats is *not* like Shelley and, particularly, Blake—a much needed corrective. Bloom maintains that Shelley was the greatest influence on Yeats and traces that influence throughout the poet's career. My own study is not meant to throw Keats into competition with Shelley as an influence on Yeats but rather to complement the convincing picture Bloom draws of Yeats as a poet thoroughly attached to the Romantic movement. Since, however, I do see Yeats as a poet having more in common with Keats than is generally imagined, I think that Bloom's work should be read in conjunction with George Bornstein's *Yeats and Shelley* (Chicago, 1970). Bornstein argues well that the conscious influence of Shelley is seen in Yeats's pre-1903 verse dramas and the Rose poems; after 1923 Yeats is in conscious reaction against Shelley's influence. See also Dwight Eddins, *Yeats: The Nineteenth Century Matrix* (University, Alabama, 1971).

often in his work trees are more nearly emblems than objects whose noumenon he experiences). Over the course of the nineteenth century, science made difficult even a provisional acceptance of the high Romantic claim of Schelling, unless supported, as in Hopkins, by theological belief. The object, Yeats felt, was at best neutral, made vital only by a greeting of the spirit, an act of imaginative transformation. At the same time this very phrase indicates that the central thrust of his imagination was not the rejection of nature, as is sometimes argued. Such rejection was indeed a central intention of his youth, but not of his mature years. To make this clear, some chronology is in order.

When eighteen or nineteen Yeats was, he said, "in all things pre-Raphaelite" (A, 70) and took pleasure in the picturesque (E, 189). Then quite suddenly he "lost the desire of describing outward things" and "took little pleasure in a book unless it was spiritual" (E, 189). The immediate cause of this turning away from outward things was probably the necessary revolt against his father and the older man's love of the pre-Raphaelite. But the deeper reason was Yeats's belief that science and mechanistic rationalism had clipped an angel's wing and emptied the haunted air. Like Keats, he too mourned a golden age. "Descartes, Locke and Newton," he wrote, "took away the world and gave us its excrement instead" (EX, 325). The situation had grown so severe after Darwin, Comte, and Marx that Yeats, like the French symbolists, could not affirm even the beauty of the natural world, the outward things. To do so would be to put oneself in the enemy camp, with realism and, by extension, naturalism. No fate could have seemed less savory to a temperament like Yeats's, oriented toward spiritual realities. His discovery of Blake and Mallarmé and his love of Shelley offered, for a time, another path, away from Keats and outward things.

At the same time, however, Yeats was probably never more unhappy with his writing than in the 1890s, the very decade in which he wished to do away with outward things. He worked laboriously to effect change, both in his art and in his thinking. The change he made in the first fifteen years of the new century indicates that in one very real sense his whole career from 1900 can be described as a slow return to acceptance of the object, of outward things, until at last he could cry out, through his own greeting of the spirit, "Everything we look upon is blest." Though this change is difficult to summarize, involving as it does all the facets of his thought and personality, it can be put with some accuracy in this fashion. Early in his career Yeats believed that through symbolism he could retain transcendental realities. But—as he saw by 1900—symbols as he understood and used them, following Shelley and Mallarmé, were themselves a kind of abstraction, and so a surrender to those forces of scientific abstraction they were intended to combat. He came to realize that art can never dissociate itself from outward things and still be art: transcendental realities not firmly attached to physical realities are only another set of abstractions to place beside the mathematical abstractions of modern science. Hence he turned again toward the things of this world. "It is not possible," he wrote in 1906, "to separate an emotion or a spiritual state from the image that calls it up and gives it expression" (E, 286). He realized that genuine mystics could never be true poets because of their refusal to accept created things as symbol; they continually leap from the concrete, such as one beautiful woman, to some abstraction, such as Love itself (E, 150). The soul will not, of course, have real knowledge until free of time and place; "but till that hour it must fix its attention upon what is near, thinking of objects one after another as we run the eye or finger over them" (M, 358).

One must stress this shift in Yeats's poetics and the complexity it brought to his symbolism—symbolism traditionally Romantic as often as it is not—because of the wide influence of Frank Kermode's seminal study, *Romantic Image* (1957). Kermode's view is that the Yeats poem, like the Romantic poem in general, strives to be an aesthetic monad, a closed, formal, nondiscursive self-sufficient entity. As a definition of formal, rather than of ontological intent, I think this is accurate, and in this respect the Romantic poem, the Yeats poem, and the theories of much modern criticism share similar ambitions. But by failing to make adequate distinctions between nondiscursive and nonreferential, Kermode implies that the intent of the symbol within the poem—or of the whole poem considered as single symbol—is to become ontologically self-sufficient and thus nonreferential. This may be true of many of Mallarmé's symbols, but it is not true of the usual Romantic symbol. The Romantic symbol customarily remains attached to a referential reality outside the poem, which it attempts to reveal. If this revelation approaches totality, then the symbol seems to become one with the reality and in this sense achieves self-sufficient completeness; but it does not deny that it is merely emblematic of a reality grounded outside itself. It becomes reality only insofar as it embodies reality; it is not in itself reality, a closed system. Hence, though I am in complete sympathy with the historical thesis of Kermode's study—the interconnection of nineteenth- and twentieth-century poetry—I find his terminology over-simple and misrepresentative of Yeats. In this Yeats may speak for himself. Rereading Mallarmé in 1937, he wrote: "I find it exciting as it shows me the road I and others of my time went for certain furlongs. It is not the way I go now, but one of the legitimate roads" (DW, 135).

By 1906 Yeats was ready to announce two ways before literature: "upward into ever-growing subtlety, with Verhaeren, with Mallarmé, with Maeterlinck . . . or downward, taking the soul with us until all is simplified and solidified again" (E, 266–67). This, he says, is the choice of choices: "the way of the bird . . . or to the market carts." Some of the following sentences are ambiguous, but the whole "Discoveries" section of *The Cutting of an Agate* shows Yeats moving steadily to the market carts. Such was his culminating insight after the discontented 1890s: "Art bids us touch and taste and hear and see the world, and shrinks from what Blake calls mathematic form, from every abstract thing" (E, 292).

Blake's belief was not new to Yeats, even if he was only now beginning to apply it to his verse. In 1893, very early in his career, he wrote as part of his study of Blake that the imagination brings spirit to nature, entering into it so that nature "being revealed as symbol may lose the power to delude."[15] What is important here is Yeats's acceptance, even at this early date, of the reality of the object. He does not deny the existence of a material world or even speak of it Neoplatonically. He merely says it may delude. Presumably, he means that nature will deceive not by our accepting it as real but by our accepting it as lacking immanence altogether, by our denying its function as a vessel for transcendent forces. This denial is the limiting postulate of science and the error of the positivists. If the mirror of the mind becomes lamp and radiates a greeting of the spirit, nature can be redeemed and will provide us, as it provided Keats, with symbols of true reality (E, 276): "We should come to understand that the beryl stone was enchanted by our fathers that it might unfold the pictures in *its* heart, and not to mirror our own excited faces, or the boughs waving outside the window" (E, 163; italics added).

What is required is "right mastery of natural things," the subject of "Demon and Beast." The poem describes how the artist is momentarily seduced by the beauty and profusion of nature into relinquishing the imagination's task of shaping nature. Abandoned by the driving forces within his subjective self, the poet grows objective and passive before nature. At the same time, however, nature rouses his "whole being" into an "aimless joy" he would like to make linger for half a day. Hence he wishes not to repudiate nature itself, but merely to join his imagination to it once again, that his joy remain no longer aimless, unattached to transcendental meaning. As he said in the 1925 revision of *The Sorrows of Love*, he would have nature "compose man's image and his cry." The poet in particular is equipped with this power to transform nature, and we admire him because through him "nature has grown intelligible" (E, 509).

Yeats's way of making nature intelligible is not through Keatsian empathy, which it is doubtful that he really under-

15. Preface to volume 1 of the Yeats-Ellis edition of Blake, quoted by Ethel Cornwell, *The "Still Point"* (New Brunswick, N. J., 1962), p. 124.

stood. Given his own poor eyesight, he would probably have found this mode of greeting with the spirit to be, at least for himself, a surrender to passivity and confusion. To the extent that empathy is a response of the whole being to an object, he is in accord with Keats; of several paintings he said: "Neither . . . could move us at all, if our thought did not rush out to the edges of our flesh, and it is so with all good art, whether the Victory of Samothrace which reminds the soles of our feet to swiftness, or of the *Odyssey* that would send us out under the salt wind, or the young horsemen on the Parthenon" (E, 292). Empathy is not denied, but it is restricted to aesthetic objects, objects *already* made intelligible by the imagination of the artist; natural objects are excluded. With these Yeats is one who, in Coleridge's terms, "attracts all forms and things to himself." His thought may rush out to the edges of his flesh, but the outward movement really stops there; where Keats thrusts forward into empathy, Yeats stops and sinks into meditation. The Yeats poem becomes an act embracing the object of its concern through meditation; in this process both Yeats and the object (again in Coleridge's terms) "shape themselves anew." Both are drawn into "the unity of his own ideal"—that is to say, the unity of Being in which both are grounded. Whether his meditation is on the bust of Maud Gonne, the house at Lissadell or Coole Park, the churchyard at Drumcliffe, the lapis lazuli or sword from Japan, or the mosaics at San Clemente, Yeats in a characteristic poem is trying to capture through meditation on the concrete some glimpse of the transcendent.

Both Keats and Yeats know the separation of the self from the world and the separation of the divine from nature, the consequences of Descartes, Locke, and Hume. What they quest for is experience of the divine, of the *being* in which both self and world are grounded, in which they find their meeting. Keats's way is *out* and Yeats's way is *in*. But in both instances they employ the feeling response of mythic apprehension which, joined to the transforming power of the imagination, Keats called "a greeting of the Spirit." Faced with this problem of separation, both poets began their careers by asserting solutions which, if pursued, would have denied objective reality. But Keats had too much empathy with nature ever to deny her for long, and Yeats had too much sympathy with life to surrender to the disembodied.

Yeats, because of his historical situation, did sense the separation to be wider than Keats wanted to allow. Hence he seriously attempted on occasion to reduce reality to his imaginative terms and in this respect he is dissimilar to Keats, whose belief in immanence led him to adapt his imagination to reality. The transformations wrought by Yeats's imagination often approach and occasionally cross into the antinaturalistic; such crossings are evidence of his situation. He never tired of declaring that the mind must impose itself upon nature; the heroes of modern fiction, he thought, had minds "like photographic plates" (LY, 827). But within this insistence that a passive attitude toward nature did not make great poetry—an attitude implied in Keats's doctrine of the greeting of the spirit—he accepted the integrity of the object no less surely than did Keats.[16] His revolt was not against nature but against what he called "irrelevant description of nature."[17] This meant observing it "without ecstasy"—without an intense feeling response that could reveal the secrets of being in the heart of the beryl stone or the heart of man— and looking at it instead with that mere affection of a man in his back garden, "in the modern way . . . of people who have forgotten the ancient religion" (E, 177–78).

The "ancient religion," as Keats and Yeats well knew, was no longer a social reality. "Glory and lovliness have pass'd away," Keats prefaced his first volume. "The woods of Arcady are dead / And over is their antique joy." So Yeats be-

---

16. A similar position is taken by Priscilla Washburn Shaw in *Rilke, Valéry, and Yeats: The Domain of the Self* (New Brunswick, N. J., 1964). She sees Yeats affirming the integrity of both the self and the world, unlike, on the one hand, Rilke, who generally surrenders the self to the powerful and mysterious density of the world; and on the other hand, Valéry, who takes the world into his own consciousness, where it becomes an activity of consciousness rather than an entity with significant independence from the self.

17. *Oxford Book of Modern Verse* (New York, 1936), p. ix.

gan his own *Collected Poems*, bemoaning the Romantic situation. Both poets, as Keats says of Psyche in his ode, have come

> too late for antique vows,
> Too, too late for the fond believing lyre,
> When holy were the haunted forest boughs,
> Holy the air, the water, and the fire.

Keats here describes, briefly and poignantly, the essence of Yeats's "ancient religion": there was a time (that sad phrase of Wordsworth's) when the self perceived directly in the physical world that something which we call *the holy*. If this "ancient religion" cannot be found unselfconsciously operative in a culture, it can, nevertheless, be assumed by the individual through the exercise of imagination, through a greeting of the spirit. Keats therefore celebrates Psyche by his "own eyes inspired."

As many critics have suggested, Psyche in Keats's poem may indeed represent the imagination. But she represents a good bit more as well. She is the deep Self, what Yeats called Personality, that part of our being in touch with the Other, the divine, and one discovers her by surrender of the ego. In the poem this is accomplished by forgetting the ego, turning not inward but outward, to the surrounding landscape. Keats says he "wander'd in a forest *thoughtlessly*" (italics added), "And on the sudden, fainting with surprise, / Saw two fair creatures," and there follows the second stanza description of their union, Keats emphasizing the fact of union. The conscious self, surrendering its will, comes suddenly upon the deep Self, recognizes love, and thus figuratively is made ready to join with the Other, "To let the warm Love in!" The "bright torch" lighting the way to the Other is the imagination, originating in the heart, through which one has come to know first the Self. Unity of Being is not merely of the self; the unified Self is merely a step that reveals the unity of all Being. The Self, like God, is a circle whose center is everywhere and whose circumference is nowhere. Understanding these things, Keats wishes in the poem's close to let Psyche

herself into his own being. A complex symbol of his own unified being, of the powers that unify that being and so reveal
the ground of Being, and of the Great Memory through which
the Self is related to the Other, Psyche herself is the warm
love he invites into his mind and celebrates through mythic
apprehension.

Speaking of the Great Memory by its traditional name,
anima mundi, Yeats described it as "a great pool or garden
where it spreads through allotted growth like a great water
plant or branches more frequently in the air" (m, 352). He
might have been writing with Keats's poem in mind:

> Yes, I will . . . build a fane
>   In some untrodden region of my mind,
> Where branched thoughts, new grown with
>   pleasant pain,
>   Instead of pines shall murmur in the wind:
> Far, far around shall those dark-cluster'd trees
>   Fledge the wild-ridged mountains steep by steep;
> . . . .
> A rosy sanctuary I will dress
> With the wreath'd trellis of a working brain,
>   With buds, and bells, and stars without a name. . . .

Though Keats and Yeats may have come too late for the
"believing lyre," they will play upon it anyway, knowing in
its harmonies a mode of truth. Though they cannot return to
the original world of mythic apprehension, they can still employ its mode of thought to heal the strange disease of modern
life, transcending self-consciousness by transforming it.
Hence "even in these days so far retir'd / From happy pie-
ties," they take up that lyre and "see, and sing, by [their]
own eyes inspir'd."

Chapter Two
Unity of Being

I
"Energy" and "Essence"

According to Ernst Cassirer the first characteristic of mythic apprehension is a feeling response to the world. Sympathetic rather than utilitarian need first validates the object; hence order and unity in the cosmos is established not by logic but by feeling. If we miss this point, Cassirer says, "we cannot find the approach to the mythic world."[1] In this respect art resembles myth, and it emerges from this element in mythic apprehension, the feeling response operating through imagination and intuition. The preceding chapter considered this feeling response, this "greeting of the Spirit" as Keats called it, in which art and myth overlap. What lies before us is investigation of the characteristically mythic results entailed by this response as they are evidenced in the work of Keats and Yeats.

In mythic apprehension the most immediate and comprehensive result of this sympathetic response is a felt conviction of the solidarity of all life. The man of mythic perception by no means lacks the ability to grasp the empirical difference of things. But, says Cassirer, in his conception of nature these differences are ultimately subsumed in a more fundamental perception: "the deep conviction of a fundamental and indelible *solidarity of life* that bridges over the multiplicity and variety of its single forms. . . . The consanguinity of all forms of life seems to be a general presupposition. . . ." The mythic view is synthetic, not analytic: it does not divide life into classes and subclasses. Life is felt to be "an unbroken

1. *An Essay on Man* (New Haven, 1962), p. 82.

continuous whole which does not admit of any clean-cut and trenchant distinctions."[2]

In Keats and Yeats this "solidarity of life" is grounded, respectively, in the "mould ethereal" and the *anima mundi* or Great Memory. With these concepts the poets bridge the multiplicity and variety of life's single forms: the conscious ego and the physical world of objects and people. "Mould ethereal" and *anima mundi* manifest themselves in the physical world as that "something" in life's single forms which, when felt. we call *the holy*. With this term we are at the center of religion and myth as modalities of thought. While anthropological data show the content of religion—the *concepts* of the holy—to be multifarious indeed. underlying such content is the *experience* of the holy. This experience of an undifferentiated quality is the ground of mythic apprehension; in it myths originate, and out of it religions evolve. According to Cassirer, mythic apprehension takes its first step toward religion when the holy is differentiated and given names. The holy becomes the gods, and these in turn become God, no longer a power but the most powerful being, no longer a quality but an entity. Until one insists on these distinctions, his response to the holy is more nearly mythic than religious, centered on a feeling response to which categories and entities. the work of the intellect, are beside the point, if not actually alien.

Keats and Yeats remain in myth, in the sense that they believe the holy too great to be defined or explained by any single religious system. Christianity in particular they found limiting. Keats seems to have believed that Christian morality was life-denying. a theme developed in the sonnet *Written in Disgust of Vulgar Superstition*. The clergy outraged him, and his letters inveigh against "parsons" with a scorn worthy of Crazy Jane. Yeats. though he believed in all the Christian mysteries, rejected Christianity because it demanded the submission of the personal; it asked man to be passive, and passivity denied the artist and his creative powers. The saint's

2. Ibid., pp. 82, 81.

surrender of the self to God was one possible way the soul could reunite itself to God; but it could not be the way of the artist; the artist must actively search for God through imagination, finding Him in the stuff of the world. Christianity too often denied the worth and reality of that concrete stuff with which the artist must work.

Because of their mythic sense of the holy, both men sought what Keats believed he found in his doctrine of soul-making: "the Parent of all the more palpable and personal Schemes of Redemption, among the Zoroastrians the Christians and the Hindoos" (L2, 103). Yeats tried to trace religious ideas to their earliest appearance, "believing that there must be a tradition of belief older than any European Church" (A, 160). Keats's eclecticism with the holy is evidenced everywhere in his work; one may cite the Induction to *The Fall of Hyperion*. The description of the vast sanctuary, the strange vessels, and Moneta's temple fuses elements of medieval Christianity and Judaism with suggestions of the Egyptian and Druidic religions. Yeats himself perceived and admired this broad but deep religious character in Keats's work: "Supreme art is a traditional statement of certain heroic and religious truths, passed on from age to age, modified by individual genius, but never abandoned. . . . A great work of art, the 'Ode to a Nightingale' . . . is as rooted in the early ages as the Mass which goes back to savage folklore. In what temple garden did the nightingale first sing?" (A, 298). He felt that Keats's odes differed from the religious art of Giotto merely in accepting all rather than selected symbolism.

His own program was also acceptance of all the symbolisms: "Nor can a single image, that of Christ, Krishna, or Buddha, represent God to the exclusion of other images" (E, 433). Because we do so often take our single image to be exclusive truth, he insisted that we must "in hatred turn / From every thought of God mankind has had"; God, being the ineffable, the undifferentiated holy, cannot adequately be conveyed in any vain, parochial "trash and tinsel" of human thought or image (Y, 284). The presence of the holy we can know, and through the mediation of symbol Yeats records that presence. But the *being* of the holy remains a mystery impenetrable by the analytic intellect. He wanted to make his readers understand that "explanations of the world lie one inside another, each complete in itself, like those perforated Chinese ivory balls" (EX, 434). What he sought was the structure of mythic thinking itself, or a metaphor for it; and he believed he found one in the structure described in *A Vision*.

The undifferentiated holy is, in the term I have used, the Other: any phenomenon external to the self, which, experienced as exceptional, as different from its surroundings, seems to manifest power and hence arouses awe. Objects with such power and arousing such awe have *presence*. Anthropologists often refer to this quality as *mana*; and, as Cassirer points out. "students of ethnology and comparative religion have largely come to regard this conception not merely as a universal *phenomenon*, but as nothing less than a special *category* of mythic consciousness."[3] Following Rudolph Otto, he says it is by virtue of this predication that the holy is divided from the profane. Eliade follows suit, translating Otto's term "the holy" as *the sacred*. Another synonym is the *numinous*, and all of these terms, to Eliade, point to the term *being*. To him "*Being* and *the sacred* are one" in mythic apprehension; hence ontology is the content of mythic epistemology.[4] The mythic mind, in its sympathetic response to the world, *feels* in the cosmos the unity of being, the solidarity of life.

Eliade's work is built not only on Cassirer, whom he curiously never mentions, but on G. Van der Leeuw, whose phenomenological analysis of religion is a twentieth-century classic in the study of religion. To Van der Leeuw, the key synonym for *mana* is Power; it is in consequence of Power felt within an object that it seems a departure from the ordinary.; it is before this Power that one feels awe. His remarks are revealing: "Power is never personal. It becomes a universal Energy, whether. in the psychological sense and in direct application to humanity, or on the other hand as cosmo-

3. *Language and Myth* (New York, 1946), p. 64.
4. *The Sacred and the Profane* (New York, 1961), p. 210.

Chapter Two

logical. In the first instance Power becomes Soul, but a superpersonal Soul closely akin to Power; in the second it assumes the form of a divine agency immanently activating the Universe."[5] Here in summary is the subject of the present chapter, the universal Energy or Power that is the ground of the "solidarity of life" discussed by Cassirer. The preceding chapter traced Van der Leeuw's first instance, the psychological manifestation of universal Energy as "a superpersonal Soul": Keats's "mould ethereal," Yeats's *anima mundi*—the concept of the deep Self shared by both poets. The present chapter explores Van der Leeuw's second or "cosmological" instance, the predication by Keats and Yeats of the Universal Energy in creatures and objects external to the self.

A sense of numinous power immanently within things is by no means unique to Keats and Yeats. It is one of the central elements of Romantic poetry and contributes much to making that poetry so closely allied to mythic apprehension. Wordsworth and Coleridge record the experience in their poetry and often discuss it there; they do not, however, have any single name to give it. Probably Hopkins's term *instress* is the most familiar name for it in English literature, and I think it useful to recall this expression before turning to Keats and Yeats. They, too, like Hopkins, have terms. Yeats's "energy" is clearly analogous to instress, and I shall shortly argue that Keats's terms *essence* and *beauty* are synonymous for the Energy or Power that characterizes the holy, itself the object of mythic consciousness.

Hopkins defines *instress* as the force which keeps a thing in existence, by which "all things are upheld" and without which they are meaningless.[6] It is an intensification of *stress*, "the making a thing more, or making it markedly, what it already is; it is the bringing out of its nature."[7] In another

5. Gerardus Van der Leeuw, *Religion in Essence and Manifestation* (New York, 1963), 1: 30.

6. *The Journals and Papers of Gerard Manley Hopkins*, ed. Humphrey House and Graham Storey (London, 1959), p. 127.

7. *Further Letters of Gerard Manley Hopkins*, ed. Claude Colleer Abbott, 2nd ed. (London, 1956), p. 327.

context he speaks of "the sensible thing so naturally and gracefully utttering the spiritual reason of its being,"[8] a phrase Yeats would surely have admired, describing as it does that intuitive bodily wisdom he predicated for women and for persons of low or high station who were bred in tradition. Hopkins's first use of the word is in an undergraduate essay on Parmenides' concept of Being; he makes the term, in fact, all but synonymous with Being.

To Hopkins all natural objects radiate this instress or vital force, Being in the act of upholding itself. "What you look hard at seems to look hard at you"[9] as its "self flashes off frame and face."[10] In No. 57, "Kingfishers catch fire" and "dragonflies draw flame." The birds seem to burn with their own inexhaustible energy, and in the act of being themselves they catch the sun's rays on their bodies; the flame of Being and flame of the sun (the flame of the sun's own radiating being) mingle and flash forth to the poet's eye; the insects, too, draw the sun's flame on the air. In the poem *Spring*, the thrush "through the echoing timber does so rinse and wring / The ear, it strikes like lightnings to hear him sing." In No. 57, dropped stones send forth their own sound, each bell and plucked string its own tune:

> Each mortal thing does one thing and the same;
> Deals out that being indoors each one dwells;
> Selves—goes itself; *myself* it speaks and spells,
> *Crying What I do is me: for that I came.*

People, too, flash forth their instress: "They rain against our much-thick and marsh air / Rich beams, till death or distance buys them quite" (No. 40).

Though Keats does not, like Hopkins, speak of this inner quality of natural objects as flashing or flaming out, he does

8. *Journals and Papers*, p. 261.
9. Ibid., p. 204.
10. *Poems of Gerard Manley Hopkins*, ed. W. H. Gardner and N. H. Mackenzie, 4th ed. (London, 1967), p. 98. Henceforth poems by Hopkins will be cited in the text, identified by the number assigned them in this edition.

see an inner power moving through them. Objects to him are
upbursting. upmounting, pulsing, budding, blooming, and
especially *teeming* and *swelling,* just as they are in Hopkins's
nature sonnets. He uses as verbs *plump, brim,* and *flush*; *leaf*
becomes a verb as it does in Hopkins. This power brings objects to fullness of being. *Full,* in fact, is one of his favorite
epithets; objects to him are *full-brimmed, full-ripen'd, full-
blown, full-leav'd, full-flowering, full-hearted,* often *over-
brimm'd* or *o'er flowing.* Eliade would see here a direct reflection of mythic consciousness: "whatever is perfect, 'full,'
harmonious, fertile—in short, whatever is 'cosmicized,'
whatever resembles a Cosmos—is sacred."[11] Observing immanence in nature. Keats feels "every sense / Filling with spiritual sweets to plenitude, / As bees gorge full their cells"
(*Endymion,* III. 38–40). It is with human beings more often
than with objects that Keats feels the radiance of Being expanding beyond rather than to the edge of the object's physical limits. On numerous occasions he speaks of another person's "identity" being so strong that it presses upon him,
often to his discomfort. Generally, however, he experiences
this vital power *within* the object, while Hopkins sees it coming outward. It is a difference merely of focal length.

Though Yeats does not directly speak of power in non-an-
imate objects, he does imply that material objects (like the
lapis lazuli and Sato's sword in his poetry) have some kind of
intimate relationship with the divine.[12] In his study of East-
ern thought, he was pleased to find that the Indian—unlike
the European mystic who is indifferent to if not afraid of
nature—

speaks continually of the beauty and terror of the great mountains, interrupts his prayer to listen to the songs of birds, remembers with delight the nightingale that disturbed his meditation
by alighting upon his head and singing there, recalls after many

11. *Myth and Reality* (New York, 1963), p. 32.
12. Only in *A Vision* does he say that all things have a Daimon.
Helen Vendler, *Yeats's Vision and the Later Plays* (Cambridge, Mass.,
1963), p. 58, has a valuable discussion of this point, drawing the parallel
to Hopkins. I find the passages in *A Vision* to be, however, more ambiguous than Mrs. Vendler does.

Unity of Being

years the whiteness of a sheet, the softness of a pillow, the gold
embroidery upon a shoe. These things are indeed part of the
"splendour of that Divine Being." (E, 431)

Tom the Lunatic and Ribh affirm as much in the *Supernatural Songs*.

It is in animate nature that Yeats sees a radiating energy
with transcendent power—what Hopkins called "that energy
or instress with which the soul animates and otherwise acts
in the body."[13] From Berkeley, Yeats quotes a passage that
imagistically relates to Hopkins's instress:" 'In the *Timaeus*
of Plato,' writes Berkeley, 'there is something like a net of
fire, and rays of fire in the human body. Does this not seem
to mean the animal spirit flowing, or rather darting, through
the nerves?' This fire is certainly that energy which . . . is
distinguished from will" (E, 440). The passage repeats the
same concept that Yeats had employed in a very early poem
on Maud Gonne: "The fire that stirs about her, when she
stirs / Burns but more clearly" (Y, 76); the image, though
borrowed from seventeenth-century convention, is nevertheless borrowed to express a felt quality of being. This same
élan, life as energy, finds rich expression through a different
metaphor in *Ancestral Houses*:

> Life overflows without ambitious pains;
> And rains down life until the basin spills,
> And mounts more dizzy high the more it rains
> As though to choose whatever shape it wills
> And never stoop to a mechanical
> Or servile shape, at others' beck and call.
>
> . . . .
>
> Homer had not sung
> Had he not found it certain beyond dreams
> That out of life's own self-delight had sprung
> The abounding glittering jet. . . .
> (Y, 198)

"Energy," in fact, was Yeats's name for the physical manifestation of the divine; he quoted Berkeley: "The Spirit—*the*

13. *The Sermons and Devotional Writings of Gerard Manley Hopkins*, ed. Christopher Delvin (London, 1959), p. 137.

active thing—that which is soul. and God" (E, 407, italics added).

So much did Yeats value this Energy that his vacillating attitude toward inanimate nature is probably accounted for by science having thoroughly emptied inanimate nature of this quality, reducing it to dead matter understood only in mathematic terms. This vital energy of power that Yeats would like to have read into all creation is, I think, the theme of the puzzling early poem *Who Goes with Fergus?* Ruler of the wood, the sea, the stars, Fergus is the personification of a numinous power that "drives" his "car" through all things, calling us to surrender to him, to drive with him, leaving abstract brooding "upon love's bitter mystery."

Yeats felt that many men of action have, like the hawk or leopard, a power of calculation and daring, "an energy of swift decision . . . of sudden action, as if their whole body were their brain" (E, 343). "Those riders upon the Parthenon had all the world's power in their moving bodies," he wrote, praising "exaltation of the body, uncommitted energy" (v, 276). He called this energy "innocence," an unself-conscious instress such as Hopkins saw in animals (No. 58). Perhaps his most moving tribute to this life sustaining force is the conclusion to *The Man and the Echo*. There, much beset by abstraction and self-centered feelings of remorse, he is suddenly distracted from his thought by the stricken cry of a rabbit, just seized by a descending hawk or owl. The rabbit's cry, affirming life, is the final answer to the negating rocky voice of Echo; at the end of life—for the rabbit and the old poet Yeats—life triumphs.

Keats saw a similar energy or power in men and animals: "I go among the Fields and catch a glimpse of a stoat or a field mouse peeping out of the withered grass—the creature hath a purpose and its eyes are bright with it—I go amongst the buildings of a city and I see a Man hurrying along—to what? The Creature has a purpose and his eyes are bright with it. But then as Wordsworth says, 'we have all one human heart'" (L2, 80). Even he himself, in his labor at poetry, was "pursueing the same instinctive course as the

veriest human animal you can think of." Such a conclusion
caused him to ask:

> May there not be superior beings amused with any graceful
> though instinctive attitude my mind m[a]y fall into, as I am
> entertained with the alertness of a Stoat or the anxiety of a
> Deer? Though a quarrel in the streets is a thing to be hated, the
> energies displayed in it are fine; the commonest Man shows a
> grace in his quarrel—By a superior being our reasoning[s] may
> take the same tone—though erroneous they may be fine—(L2, 80)

Keats's "energies displayed" are synonymous with Yeats's; to
mythic consciousness, stoat and man display, in Yeats's
words, "all the world's power in their moving bodies" (V,
276) because that power is the universal Energy.

In mythic thought this Energy or Power is unattended by
moral value. As Van der Leeuw points out, "*Mana* resides
alike in the poisoned arrow and in European remedies. . . . It
is simply a matter of Power, alike for good or evil."[14] So it is
in Keats's quarrel in the streets and in his mistress's "rich
anger" in the *Ode on Melancholy*:

> Or if thy mistress some rich anger shows,
> Emprison her soft hand, and let her rave,
> And feed deep, deep upon her peerless eyes.

"What shocks the virtuous philosopher, delights the camelion
Poet" (L1, 387). Yeats's last poems are often criticized for
this amoral response to energy and power. These lines are
representative:

> You that Mitchel's prayer have heard,
> 'Send war in our time, O Lord!'
> Know that when all words are said
> And a man is fighting mad,
> Something drops from eyes long blind,
> He completes his partial mind,
> For an instant stands at ease,
> Laughs aloud, his heart at peace.
> (Y, 342)

14. *Religion in Essence and Manifestation*, 1: 26.

Chapter Two

They show, too, how closely tied is universal Energy to discovery of the deeper self, of Personality. The sheer beauty of energy, perceived without ethical consideration, leads Yeats to see men reaching their highest pitch in moments of proud defiance: Robert Gregory, a crazed girl, and those celebrated in *Beautiful Lofty Things*.

Through perception of this Energy at sufficient distance, objects and persons, no matter how trivial or mean, become fit subjects for poetry, apart from all moral considerations but one: a forgiveness that comes over the perceiver. "Great literature," Yeats wrote, "is, indeed, the Forgiveness of Sin" (E, 102), "that untroubled sympathy for men as they are" (E, 106). One agent of that sympathy is love: "It does not desire to change its object. It is a form of the eternal contemplation of what is" (DW, 114–15). Yeats believed that "if you liberate a person or a landscape from the bounds of motives and their actions, causes and their effects, and from all bonds but the bonds of your love, it will change under your eyes, and become a symbol of an infinite emotion, a perfected emotion, a part of the Divine Essence . . ." (E, 148–49). Such forgiveness is the subject of his poem *Paudeen*. Yeats, "indignant at the fumbling wits, the obscure spite" of the common Irish shopkeeper, stumbles outdoors where the unself-conscious curlews crying in the wind overhead suddenly bring the revelation that

> on that lonely height where all are in God's eye,
> There cannot be, confusion of our sound forgot,
> A single soul that lacks a sweet crystalline cry.

As Keats can bless the lowly stoat for the energy it displays, so Yeats can forgive the spiteful Paudeen. At least once, in *No Second Troy*, he was able to look on Maud Gonne's political passion with the same forgiving eye. Sometimes such forgiveness must be given to the self, if one is to move beyond the confines of his own ego. Yeats comes to this self-forgiveness in *Demon and Beast*, discussed in the previous chapter, and in the great *Dialogue of Soul and Self,* to be considered in the next chapter. This perception of morally neutral energy, says Keats, concluding his discussion of the quarrel in the streets, "is the very thing in which consists poetry" (L2, 80–81).[15] He is, I think, correct. Poetry as well as myth seeks to embody that apprehension of Power called by Eliade *being* and characterized by Van der Leeuw as *energy.* This is true, at least, of Romantic poetry, where Cassirer's felt solidarity of life is so frequently affirmed. Keats had said as much two years before this letter when he wrote in *Sleep and Poetry* that "A drainless shower / Of light is poesy; 'tis the supreme of power" (lines 235–36). Yeats would have agreed, for he believed that images of "the wild," images full of power like "an eagle on the wing . . . make the Muses sing" (Y, 316).

It is not surprising, then, that on several occasions Yeats wrote that in man the universal Energy is particularized as the power of creativity. He prophesied that after 1927 "Men will no longer separate the idea of God from that of human genius, human productivity in all its forms" (V, 299). In high Romantic fashion he believed that "imagination was the first emanation of divinity" (E, 112). His sentences accord with Eliade's description of creation in mythic apprehension: "Every creation springs from an abundance. The gods create out of an excess of power, an overflow of energy. Creation is accomplished by a surplus of ontological substance." Hence the inspired poet is, as Yeats said, "a vessel of the creative power of God" (E, 202). Keats would have agreed, feeling that his own identifying energy or Personality was the urge

---

15. He hastens to add: "and if so it is not so fine a thing as philosophy—for the same reason that an eagle is not so fine a thing as a truth" (L2, 81). He means, of course, that morals must play some part in the scheme of things. Neither Keats nor Yeats was fully consistent in his valuation of amoral energy. Yeats, pushing the matter to extremes, may have written in his last years some poems dangerously close to being antihuman. But these should not distort the picture of his usual sense of tragedy before violence: beauty it might bring to birth, but it could be a terrible beauty.

to write poetry; he wondered, in fact, if he had any identity or Character at all beyond that. Poetry was his purpose and his eyes were bright with it. Both men find the nature of their deeper selves to be the power of creation. This concept led Yeats to define genius as the entrance into our daily lives of that outside power residing in us in our buried selves (A, 164). Eliade is again apropos: "every creation . . . represents an irruption of creative energy into the world."[16]

For the sense of presence in things—their particularization of Power or universal Energy—Keats used two terms: *essence* and *beauty*. Both are what he tried to express in that large category of words centering around the word *full* and the prefix *up-* when attached to words of motion. The first of these terms, *essence*, has engaged the attention of many critics; the second, *beauty*, has gone generally unglossed. A brief look at the first will serve well to conclude this section; the second will require a section to itself.

The central text for Keats's term *essence* is that controversial passage in *Endymion* (1, 777–815) that, for fifty years, has been used as a key in interpreting not only the poem itself but very often Keats in general. Until the mid-1940s critics usually accepted "essence" in its metaphysical sense and interpreted the passage in question and the whole poem as an allegory dealing with Neoplatonic ascent to realms of purity beyond sensual beauty and pleasure. But in 1947 Newell F. Ford published two articles, developed later in his book *The Prefigurative Imagination of John Keats*, that take a view radically opposed to traditional opinion, arguing through word collation in Keats's poetry and prose that *essence* in Keats's usage has no transcendental or Neoplatonic meaning. The negative aspect of Ford's argument has been quite persuasive; almost all interpretations of the passage published since have accepted some kind of empirical denotation as prior to or coexistent with transcendental connotations in the term.

Ford is accurate, I believe, in saying that "essence" is a "loose name for entities attractive to the aesthetic sense, enti-

16. *The Sacred and the Profane*, p. 97.

ties both of the objective world and of the imagination."[17] But he goes too far when he empties the word of all transcendental meaning, saying it "signified to Keats no wedding of finite mind with Infinite Being."[18] For it is precisely "Infinite Being" that Keats sees moving in the object when the object has first been aesthetically apprehended, met by a greeting of the spirit. Ford, in restoring to us one half of the term, throws out the other half. It is indeed a *thing* of beauty to which Keats responds; he remains attached to the concrete object. But what is the *beauty* of the thing? Ford would have it mean the Pythagorean harmony of parts within a whole. But it is not merely—or, as I shall argue in the next section, even primarily—the harmonious interplay of parts within a thing that stirs Keats's response. Instead, it is the beauty or numinous quality he finds welling within the object—its essence, its manifestation of Being—that his spirit greets.

I share Ford's discontent with those interpretations that would have Keats follow Plotinus' *via negativa*; such renunciation of the sensuous is manifestly alien to his temperament. At the moment of Keats's insight, the light of his senses does not go out; even in the actual darkness surrounding him in the *Ode to a Nightingale*, he must imagine physical, concrete beauty. Ford also has my sympathy insofar as Keats's Neoplatonic critics argue for what could be called a doctrine of transsubstantiation, a metamorphosis of matter into spirit alone or an abandonment of matter. But Neoplatonism, one of the covering Cherubs in Romantic poetry, is considerably complex, woven of many ambiguous and often contradictory strands. Plotinus himself, for example, was outspoken in his condemnation of the Gnostics and advocated the contemplation of nature (*Enneads*, 5, i, 2), and Proclus believed matter distinctly not evil. Ford oversimplifies the doctrine he finds wanting and so ends in an error opposite to that of those critics he corrects. In Neoplatonism there is a strand of consubstantiation, as it were, a belief in transcendent spirit or

17. Newell F. Ford, *The Prefigurative Imagination of John Keats* (Hamden, Conn., 1966), p. 15.
18. Ibid., p. 15.

Chapter Two

power made immanent in matter. It is along this paradoxical
and sometimes pantheistic strand that Keats is to be located,
along with Coleridge during that period of his greatest poetic
achievement.

Essence, then, signifies to Keats the vital energy or latent
power of an object; in this respect it is temporal and non-
transcendent; but this same *essence* partakes of a transcendent universal Energy or power and in this respect is Neoplatonic. It is apprehended through a feeling response that, in
Keats's case, is empathic. In objects apprehended through a
greeting of the spirit, the concrete and the ideal are seen as
one; "the energies displayed" in man or stoat become active
evidence of an immanent, universal power which, in mythic
consciousness, is the ground of all Being, the guarantee of the
solidarity of all life. In man this power is specifically a part
or aspect of the divine and is the center of the Self, what Yeats
called the Personality. In natural objects this universal Energy can be equated with the leaven in the magnificent Hymn
to Pan:

> be still the leaven
> That spreading in this dull and clodded earth
> Gives it a touch ethereal—a new birth:
> Be still a symbol of immensity. . . .
> *(Endymion,* 1, 296–99)

By means of this leaven, Keats wrote a few lines earlier, "the
mass / Of nature's lives and wonders puls'd tenfold" (lines
104–105); it is an image repeated later, in the *Epistle to
Reynolds,* where the items of a landscape "seem a lifted
mound / Above some giant, pulsing underground." Bruce
Miller has defined this leaven as "an emanation of the sustaining and perfecting Pan-Spirit . . . supernature manifested
in nature."[19] Substitute *anima mundi* for "Pan-Spirit" and
the phrase is perfectly applicable to Yeats. Wordsworth was
more nearly right than he knew: the Hymn *is* a pretty piece
of paganizing; it is mythic apprehension at its most genuine.

19. Bruce Miller, "On the Meaning of Keats's *Endymion,*" *KSJ 14*
(1965): 39.

"Beauty in All Things"

In his *Autobiography* Yeats wrote: "Yet is not ecstasy some fulfillment of the soul in itself, some slow or sudden expansion of it like an overflowing well?" (A, 286) The sentence looks back to Keats's cluster of *full-* words, used to express a similar apprehension of Energy; and it parallels Van der Leeuw's definition of the psychological operation of that Energy, when it "becomes Soul, but a superpersonal Soul closely akin to power." Yeats then adds: "Is not this what is meant by beauty?" My argument in this section is that the universal Energy apprehended in mythic consciousness is indeed what Keats and Yeats meant by *Beauty*. The word is synonymous with Keats's term *essence* and with the term *energy* found so frequently in Yeats, and it is one meaning of *passion*, a term common to both poets. All these terms attempt to define the "holy," "sacred," or "numinous" quality in things that is perceived in mythic consciousness. In every "thing of beauty," every "shape of beauty," Keats sees this universal Energy; foreshadowing Yeats's image of the overflowing well, he calls it "An endless fountain of immortal drink / Pouring into us from the heaven's brink" (K, 66).

The problem one faces with Keats's use of the term Beauty is its frequent conjunction with the word Truth. To define the first it is necessary to define the second, and the critic finds himself immediately entangled in one of the most controversial topics in the study of Keats. Not only do the closing lines of the *Ode on a Grecian Urn* tease one out of thought, but so do several other collocations of the terms appearing in the letters. Although the literature on the topic is now enormous, all of it seems to me marred by incompletion: too often critics have explained only one of the terms or one side of the famous equation that ends the *Ode*, remaining reticent about the other. What is needed are equivalents for the terms Beauty and Truth that explain their paradoxical convertibility more adequately than heretofore.

Chapter Two

The first text for the theme is the now notorious letter to Bailey written November 22, 1817 (L1, 183–90). While I am not of the party who believe this letter the central document in understanding Keats, I do not think its contents contradicted by other evidence, however much its assertions may be qualified by the maturing Keats. I begin with it because it is the first use of the term Beauty in Keats's letters. He announces:

> I am certain of nothing but the holiness of the Heart's affections and the truth of Imagination—What the imagination seizes as Beauty must be truth—whether it existed before or not—for I have the same Idea of all our Passions as of Love they are all in their sublime, creative of essential Beauty.

The final statement is the key to the whole passage: all our passions—and by implication the imagination is in some way a passion—create "essential Beauty" just as the particular passion love does. The significant questions to ask, then, are three: "What is "passion"? In what way is the imagination a passion? What is "essential Beauty"? These questions answered, the way will be clear to the question of Beauty and Truth.

By "passion" Keats means emotional and spiritual energy, through the active expenditure of which we express our being and uphold and sustain ourselves in being. Though he does not couch his thought in these terms, only a definition of this sort will explain, on the one hand, how all the particular passions can create beauty and, on the other, how imagination can be, like love, a passion. The passions create "essential Beauty" in two respects. Their active play in a person causes him to be beautiful to the beholder, just as in the *Ode on Melancholy* the mistress is beautiful in her anger and in *Hyperion* (I, 34–36) Thea is beautiful in her sorrow. On the other hand, it is through his own passions and because of them that the artist attempts to express the beautiful.

Further evidence of this interpretation of passion as creative of Beauty can be found in book I of *Endymion*. Immediately following the famous section on "a fellowship with essence," Keats writes an extended and remarkable passage on the power of human love (lines 816–42), which is, quite simply, to energize the universe. Endymion says that although love is thought to be mere physical passion, he believes it produces "more than our searching witnesseth," such as a revelation of immanent Being. He questions whether earth would ever bloom and fructify or objects have their own nature at all if humans did not love. Keats is saying, unwittingly perhaps, that the activity of love is the first manifestation of universal Energy; it is the most basic operation of that Energy, not only in man but in the whole world. The passion Love, when it is more than physical passion (when, as the letter says, it is "sublime"), can reveal the aspect of the holy that Keats calls "essential Beauty." In book III of *Endymion* he writes:

> O Love! how potent has thou been to teach
> Strange journeyings! Wherever beauty dwells,
> In gulf or aerie, mountains or deep dells,
> In light, in gloom, in star or blazing sun,
> Thou pointest out the way, and straight 'tis won.
>   (III, 92–96)

Keats's letter says that imagination is likewise a passion. The assertion seems quite odd, but the syntactic logic clearly points to it; the word "for" (meaning "because") makes "imagination" in the first clause parallel to "our Passions" and "Love" in the second. In explaining this assertion it is helpful to recall Keats's letter on "real things," also written to Bailey, four months after the letter in question. (For a fuller discussion, see chapter 1, section 2). Keats writes: "Every mental pursuit takes its reality and worth from the ardour of the pursuer" (L1, 242). What he calls in this letter "a greeting of the Spirit" validates empirical and imaginary things by revealing the numinous quality through which they partake of universal Being. The imagination, in other words, is "the ardour of the pursuer"—the passion—from which "every mental pursuit takes its reality and worth." When the pursuit is a Pursued—a person or an object—imagination operates as an act of love that discovers (or figuratively "creates") the essence of the beloved.[20] Hence the imagination is the intuitive passion or energy; it is the feeling response or greeting of the spirit, through which one perceives ("seizes") beauty in the material Other or in the non-material images of the mind. It is the faculty of apprehension through which the particular passions are seen as beauty and beauty is rendered artistically. Yeats's phrase is apropos: "Excited, passionate, fantastical / Imagination" (Y, 192).

Keats says that all our passions create "essential Beauty." Because he was not altogether careful in his use of abstract words, it may seem sophistic to think he here uses "essential" in its root sense. I do not see any other reading possible, however, since "necessary or requisite" would be meaningless in context. He means either "the essence of Beauty" or "the Beauty of essence"; and when, as explanation of his meaning, he refers to book 1 of *Endymion* (containing the "fellowship with essence" passage), it is not unreasonable to assume that the essence of Beauty *is* the beauty of *essence*. Or, in terms of his letter, passion is the essence of Beauty. For Keats, Beauty is a vital inner life in objects, radiating in man metaphorically from the heart ("the heart's affections") and manifesting an immanent Power that is possibly God (though Keats never specifies it as such), thus being a "holiness." It is all but synonymous with Yeats's *energy* or Hopkins's *instress* and may generally be said to be Being itself, "from which the Mind or intelligence sucks its identity" (L2, 103).[21] The

20. This, it seems to me, refines W. W. Beyer's accurate but overgeneral "Beauty and Love are ultimately one," *Keats and the Daemon King* (New York, 1969), p. 140. Beyer has a valuable discussion of the love-beauty conjunction, pp. 142–44, 306–308.

21. Three readings suggestive of my interpretation are those by Leonidas M. Jones, "The Ode to Psyche: An Allegorical Introduction to Keats's Great Odes," *KSMB* 9 (1958): 22–26; Glen O. Allen, "The Fall of Endymion: A Study in Keats's Intellectual Growth," *KSJ* 6 (1957): 37–57; and Bernard Blackstone, *The Consecrated Urn* (London, 1959), pp. 340–41. Jones believes Beauty to be a temporal reflection of divine truth, Truth being that divine or absolute Truth itself. Allen, with a definition of Truth I shall deal with later (a fusion of pain and pleasure), implies that Beauty is inspired intensity. Blackstone speaks of statistical truth, "the congruence of statement with brute fact," and living truth, "the congruence of a part with its whole . . . one is the intellectual beau-

following Spring, writing of the only things for which he feels genuine humility, he juxtaposes "the Principle of Beauty" with "the eternal Being" (L1, 266).

A year after the 1817 letter to Bailey, Keats writes of his "love of beauty in the abstract" (L1, 373), introducing yet another of those troubling general terms which he repeats with frequency in his letters. Though this is not the occasion to argue the evidence, a check of all his uses of this word indicates that he usually means by it "imaginary" or "pertaining to imagination."[22] The word occurs again in an even more revealing passage, written to the George Keatses: "The mighty abstract Idea I have of Beauty in all things stifles the more divided and minute domestic happiness—an amiable wife and sweet Children I contemplate as part of that Beauty. But I must have a thousand of those beautiful particles to fill up my heart" (L1, 403). Very often in Keats, imagination is intimately connected with intuition as a mode of immediate knowledge, and that burden is present in this use of "abstract." He is saying, I think, that he holds it as a principle that instress, the inner active power of being, can by intuition be found in all created things. The concept is also "abstract" in the sense that, though he is not always able to experience this quality in all created things, he nevertheless affirms its

---

ty, the beauty of form [Truth?] and the other is temporal beauty, the beauty of phases [Beauty?]."

Walter J. Bate's interpretation in *The Stylistic Development of Keats* (New York, 1962) is quite suggestive, but we do not attach our definitions to the same terms. What I read as Beauty he reads as Truth, "the joint 'identity,' character, reality, and beauty of a phenomenon," p. 45. The coalescence of Beauty and Truth he calls the "potentially dynamic revelation of being and individuality," p. 50, which I would restrict to Beauty alone. With Beauty he is less specific; in *From Classic to Romantic*, p. 182, he says that it "would be viewed as a sort of by-product which attends the fulfillment by a creature, object or . . . aesthetic form, of its distinctive and individual function, significance, and nature," but the "by-product" is never clearly defined as form or some other quality. Throughout his definitions Bate obviously has in mind the qualities Hopkins meant by instress, but his application of this quality to Keats's Beauty and Truth requires, I think, sharper focus.

22. Newell F. Ford conveniently collects them in the appendix to his book, along with other key words, but he makes no inference of the term's meaning for Keats.

Chapter Two

existence in them as an intellectual belief. The position is thus related to the concept set forth in the field mouse passage (L2, 80) and dramatized by Yeats in *Paudeen*. The passage from Yeats's prose quoted to gloss that poem is equally pertinent here: "If you liberate a person or a landscape from the bounds of motives and their actions, causes and their effects, and from all the bonds but the bonds of your love, it will change under your eyes, and become a symbol of an infinite emotion, a perfected emotion, a part of the Divine Essence" (E, 148–49). Keats would greet Beauty wherever he meets it and bless when he understands: "Beauty, in things on earth, and things above / I swear!" (K1, 480). A year and a half later he brings together the previously separated phrases: "I have lov'd the principle of beauty in all things" (L2, 263).

When he tells Fanny Brawne that "I cannot conceive any beginning of such love as I have for you but Beauty" (L2, 127), he again seems to have in mind an inner vital power, expressive of the transcendent, which, for him, she radiates. There is, he says, a type of love, of less intensity one assumes, for which he has "respect and can admire *it in others*" (italics added); again love becomes a synonym for essence and for Beauty within the other person. But this less intense essence has not the "richness, the bloom" that his own heart desires. "Bloom," with the connotations accruing through its use in the poetry, becomes the key word here, a metaphor for the vital, fulfilling quality of essence.

He adds immediately another epithet, "the full form," a noun used a week earlier in speaking of his "devotion to so fair a form" (L2, 123). The same noun is used for the beautiful Grecian urn: "O Attic shape . . . silent form." Thus it might seem that Keats means by Beauty not instress but form, the harmonious articulation of parts within an object, rather like Hopkins's *inscape*.[23] For some years I myself felt this

23. David Perkins, *The Quest for Permanence: The Symbolism of Wordsworth, Shelley, and Keats* (Cambridge, Mass., 1959), p. 209 n., uses Hopkins's term *inscape* as a synonym for *essence*. My own text indicates a finer distinction in terms which I think must be made. Though Hopkins never defined the term *inscape*, it is generally assumed to refer to the

most likely to be his meaning. Certainly it expedites interpretation of the *Ode*'s concluding lines, which would then be paraphrased: Beauty, the form of the physical urn, is a reflection of Truth, the eternal and absolute Form of things; and this Truth is Beauty because it temporally manifests itself in objects that partake of eternal Platonic Form and hence are deemed beautiful. This reading accords with the Pythagorean aspects of Coleridge's definition of beauty. But it also presupposed a sophistication in formalist aesthetics more nearly modern than Keatsian; almost always in Keats feeling has precedence over form.[24] Furthermore, this reading, however successful for the *Ode*, will not translate successfully the passages in the letters where Beauty is mentioned.

If Beauty and Truth are to be read, both in the letters and the poems, as proceeding from some conceptual consistency, however loosely articulated in Keats's consciousness, the referents for these terms must be rephrased. Beauty is instress, the active vital power manifesting universal Energy, and Truth is the transcendent principle of Form, the harmonious relationship among parts of the whole, and it may remain in abstraction or may manifest itself in concrete objects (empirical or imaginary) and philosophical propositions.[25] Keats's meaning for Beauty accords with Plotinus' concept of beauty; it is vital spirit, power, energy, the numinous. His meaning for Truth accords with Pythagorus' concept of beauty; it is symmetry, form, syntax.

---

pattern or formal relationship of qualities in one object or among objects, which, aesthetically apprehended, grants insight into the being or inner life (instress) of the object or objects. Instress and inscape or interpenetrating aspects of an entity. They correspond to Keats's "Beauty" and "Truth."

24. Compare, for example, the following in a bantering tone: "I have not time to elucidate the forms and shapes of the grass and trees; for, rot it! I forgot to bring my mathematical case with me; which unfortunately contained my triangular Prism so that the hues of the grass cannot be dissected for you" (L1, 162).

25. A. C. Bradley, "Keats and 'Philosophy,'" in *The John Keats Memorial Volume*, ed. G. C. Williamson (London, 1921), p. 45, also sees Truth as form: "whatever is felt, perceived, imagined, as beautiful, would, if adequately expressed in an intellectual form, be found a reality truly conceived." He does not, however, define Beauty.

Syntax, however, is meaningless, insignificant, dead, unless the perceiver feels it to be *informed* by immanent power. Thus Keats wrote that he could "never *feel* certain of any truth but for a clear perception of its Beauty" (L2, 19; italics added). This immanent power or Beauty that grants life to syntax or Truth cannot be apprehended by the intellect alone; it must be perceived through imagination, intuition, feeling. These must operate with the senses in a greeting of the spirit to realize the vital beauty in material objects. Keats offers an illustration: "A year ago I could not understand Raphael's cartoons—now I begin to read them a little." He implies that he perceived the form or formal relationships in Raphael's paintings but that this form seemed artificial or empty to him because uninformed by feeling, energy, a vital living power. The truth of the form became meaningful truth to him only when he perceived Beauty within the form. Unable to find this beauty in a painting by Benjamin West, he said: "There is nothing to be intense upon; no woman one feels mad to kiss; no face *swelling into* reality" (L1, 192; italics added).[26]

On the other hand, if the instress of Beauty is felt, even in the "no things" of the imagination, then "whatever the imagination seizes as Beauty must be truth," because beauty is a true reality, a manifestation of the highest reality, Being itself. Furthermore, the forms that this imagined beauty takes must symbolically reflect some aspect of eternal Form, regardless of whether the imaginings have any "true" correspondence to empirical reality. So, too, what the imagination seizes as Beauty and embodies as art will be truth, even if it is a kind of creation never existing before, because Truth is the formal syntax that contains Beauty in its extramental existence and without which it would dissipate itself. It is in light of these definitions that "the Imagination may be compared to Adam's dream—he awoke and found it truth."

Newell F. Ford is wrong, then, in saying of "Beauty must

26. Compare Yeats: "What had been a beauty like the burning sun fades out in Vandyke's noble ineffectual faces" (v, 295), a criticism he made of Sargent's portrait of Woodrow Wilson (A, 175).

be truth" that the verb "must" indicates that "Keats's faith
seems to rest on an ardent wish." The verb does not indicate
"an element of wishfulness"[27] but, by definition of the inseparable connection between Beauty and Truth, an element
of necessity. While both Beauty and Truth may exist and
have meaning as separate intellectual concepts, imaginative
or empirical constructs not partaking of both are, if not impossible, altogether without value. Ford would separate form
and content, thus denying a central intention of Romantic
metaphysics. Endymion's beloved Cynthia may be, when he
first sees her, no more than an imaginary vision; but she is a
vision of fulfilled Truth and Beauty, of perfect inscape and
essence, form and energy; and Endymion mentions them in
that order:

> Whence that completed form of all completeness?
> Whence came that high perfection of all sweetness?
> Speak, stubborn earth, and tell me where, O where
> Hast thou a symbol of her golden hair?
>
> (1, 606–609)

Yeats, like Keats, saw the inseparable relationship between
Beauty and Truth and defined beauty in Keatsian terms. In
1903 he wrote: "The close of the last century was full of a
strange desire to get out of form, to get to some kind of disembodied beauty, and now it seems to me the contrary impulse has come. I feel about me and in me an impulse to
create form, to carry the realization of beauty as far as possible" (LY, 402). The passage clearly indicates that Yeats
thought of beauty as a quality distinct from form, which
might or might not embody it. "The realization of beauty" is
beauty realized in form, beauty and truth become one. A year
earlier, in *Adam's Curse*, he had written that "we must labour
to be beautiful": we must labor to find a form that will contain the beauty of instress. Without it, beauty is dissipated;
with it beauty embodies truth. The dance and the dancer become one. In 1929 Yeats wrote to Sturge Moore that he understood beauty "as including all the natural *expressions* of . . . a

27. Ford, p. 22.

body, its *instincts, emotions*, etc. Its value is in part that it excludes all that larger modern use of the word and compels us to find another word for the beauty of a mathematic problem or a Cubist painting. . . ."[28] Clearly he saw a distinction between the beauty of instress and the Pythagorean beauty of form, wishing to reserve the term Beauty for instress alone.

Yeats shared with Keats the concept of truth as form or syntax, either empty of or filled with a vital spiritual power. It is as syntax that he saw the entire system of *A Vision*: its parts he regarded as "stylistic arrangements of experience comparable to the cubes in the drawing of Wyndham Lewis and to the ovoids in the sculpture of Brancusi" (v, 25). The specific geometric forms employed, the Great Wheel and the interpenetrating gyres, were syntactic forms, having only a symbolic relation to spaceless reality (v, 69). To ask if Yeats believed in the system is thus all but meaningless: one does not believe or disbelieve in forms themselves, he merely perceives them or he does not. Yeats "believed" in the system to the extent that, as a form able to order coherently his otherwise disordered speculations and intuitions about absolute reality and its relations to temporal reality, it seemed a form filled with spiritual life. Any other system or form that could have contained that reality to his satisfaction he would likewise have "believed." He did not believe in it as final truth; he accepted it as viable metaphor. Absolute truth itself was not the system but what the Indian calls *Samadhi*, "an ideal form" or syntax all but unattainable here on this earth (e, 463), resembling "that last Greek number, a multiple of all numbers because there is nothing outside it" (e, 462).

Like Keats, he found "In all poor foolish things that live a day, / Eternal beauty wandering on her way" (y, 31). In *The Rose of the World* he writes that before God made either

---

28. *W. B. Yeats and T. Sturge Moore: Their Correspondence, 1901–1937*, ed. Ursula Bridge (London, 1953), p. 144 (italics added). Compare "Art bids us touch and taste and hear and see the world, and shrinks from what Blake calls mathematic form, from every abstract thing, from all that is not a fountain jetting from the entire hopes, memories, and sensations of the body" (e, 292–93).

archangels, men, or the physical world, there "lingered by His seat" perfect beauty, and to express that beauty He made the world, "a grassy road / Before her wandering feet." A woman who preens before a mirror is striving through physical form to express or symbolize that "face I had / Before the world was made," desiring her lover "love the thing that was / Before the world was made" (Y, 266). Persons who possessed this beauty, informed with an instress uniquely their own, he called *Beautiful Lofty Things*. In that poem he shows people in situations, frames, that reveal their being—Maud Gonne at Howth station, like "Pallas Athene in that straight back and arrogant head"—or he shows them making spontaneous gestures that uphold their identity:

> Augusta Gregory seated at her great ormolu table,
> Her eightieth winter approaching: "Yesterday he
> threatened my life.
> I told him that nightly from six to seven I sat
> at this table,
> The blinds drawn up."

In the poem *A Crazed Girl*, another person is cited who adds to the qualities of spontaneity and defiance a deep, irrational passion. These beautiful lofty beings, so full of unique power, are things "never known again." The sheer force of their being puts to shame the poet's attempt to express such instress within artistic form:

> The poets labouring all their days
> To build a perfect beauty in rhyme
> Are overthrown by a woman's gaze
> And by the unlabouring brood of the skies. . . .
>   (Y, 64)

As Yeats grew older and saw the women around him growing old, he wrote on occasion as if their beauty had been nothing more than form all along, rather than some inner, immanent quality of being. It is Maud Gonne's physical form he remembers and celebrates in *A Thought from Propertius*, and in *For Anne Gregory* the speaker says that only God can love Anne for her inner being and not her yellow hair. As early as 1910 he had entertained the possibility that beauty is only form. In *The Mask* he questions if the woman really does contain the inner beauty of being that is indicated by the external beauty of her physical form. Both judging him and asking him to forget the question, she answers: "It was the Mask that engaged your mind. . . . Not what's behind." The man can only conclude that in such case she is probably his enemy. But the woman, wiser than he, replies: "What matter, so there is but Fire / In you, in me?" She is saying what Keats might have said, that if man brings his greeting of the spirit to the object with beautiful form he will find it to have, if only because he so endows it, a beautiful inner vitality, life, being.

At the end of his life, however, Yeats returned to his first concept of beauty. In *Young Man's Song* (1929) the youth believes that if we truly perceive the instress of another being, that perception will sustain the other's beauty through the fading of its external inscape and physical form. Yeats agrees. Having a *Quarrel in Old Age*, he wonders where the woman's earlier "sweetness" has gone; but at the end he affirms that

> Somewhere beyond the curtain
> Of distorting days
> Lives that lonely thing
> That shone before these eyes
> Targeted, trod like Spring.
>   (Y, 248)

Her physical beauty of form, "targeted" in his eye during the short period when it was in conjunction with (targeted with) her inner beauty of energy, "trod" on his heart and the world with the freshness, vitality, and suddenness of Spring. That physical beauty has faded. But the lines affirm that the true perfection of the beloved's physical form is, like her unique inner beauty, eternal. The question of youthful and aged bodily form is most clearly formulated in *A Bronze Head* where Yeats, looking at the bust of the old Maud Gonne and remembering the young, *"her form all full"* (italics added), asks: "who can tell / Which of her forms has shown her substance right?" He immediately posits a tentative answer:

"maybe substance can be composite." She is both "human, superhuman," and her "human" substance is carried in the bodily form that blooms and decays; but her "superhuman" substance, still visible "as though a sterner eye had looked through her eye," has no earthly form of its own but that borrowed earthly form whose moment of perfection and bloom is an analogy of its own form resident in eternity.

The conceptual distinction between Beauty and Truth allowed Keats and Yeats to formulate criticism of their own and other art. Keats's "love of beauty in the abstract" made him a severe critic of his own work (L1, 373); in his imagination he had a general or ideal concept of beauty, of instress, and if his works were not persuasive of that power they failed as Raphael's paintings first seemed to fail, being merely "a sketchy intellectual landscape, not a search after truth" (L1, 174), as he said of Wordsworth's "Gipsies." (Here "truth" seems to mean "beauty fully realized in form.") Asking Reynolds to criticize *Hyperion*, he had such an idea in mind: "put a mark × to the false beauty proceeding from art, and one ‖ to the true voice of feeling" (L2, 167). False beauty is mere form, empty of instress; true beauty is shape informed with feeling, energy, essence. Yeats, too, made similar distinctions:

> True art . . . makes every form . . . every gesture, a signature of some unanalysable imaginative essence. False art is not expressive, but mimetic, not from experience but from observation. . . .
> True art is the flame of the Last Day, which begins for every man when he is first moved by beauty, and which seeks to burn all things until they become "infinite and holy." (E, 140)

False art or beauty does not express essence and does not arise from feeling ("experience"); it is merely mimetic of external form, a sketchy intellectual landscape. In *The Circus Animals' Desertion* Yeats passed judgment on the false beauty in his own work, a judgment as severe as that which Keats passed on himself before Moneta's altar. Yeats admits in the poem that the task of shaping life into coherent patterns can become for the artist more exciting than life itself; "Players and painted stage took all my love / And not those things that they were emblems of." The poet masters disorder through creation of images that, "complete," grow in "pure mind." But so purified, these images threaten to have no relationship to existing things or suffering reality and so become mere forms, "the false beauty proceeding from art." Realizing this, Yeats descends to the rag-and-bone shop of the heart in which these images are grounded, there to gain passion, energy—in a word, Beauty—to fill the forms of "pure mind" with life. The descent has its parallel in *The Man and the Echo* where, at the bottom of a pit, Yeats's thought is returned to Beauty by the stricken cry of the rabbit.

The priorities in this discussion, it should be said, are but the priorities of analysis. At a level beyond the analytic intelligence, Beauty and Truth are interpenetrating aspects of the same reality, but in perception of this reality one or the other quality may take precedence. Though Keats, for example, is struck first by Fanny's beauty, he is led to speak of her "full form"; the phrase expresses the coessential nature of reality. Similarly, when he writes in the letter on Raphael of "magnificence of draperies beyond any I ever saw," he speaks of their instress first, followed by their inscape: they have "the most tender feeling . . . making up a fine whole." But the perception of inscape could precede the felt perception of instress. He speaks of "the shape of beauty" (K, 65, 473), "that *shape*, that fairness, that sweet minor *zest*" (K, 474; italics added), "of fit *mould* and *beauty*, *ripe* and *rare*" (K, 395; italics added).

Thus when Keats concludes the *Ode on a Grecian Urn* with the paradox "Beauty is Truth, Truth Beauty," he means exactly what he says. His assumption is that in transcendent reality one of these aspects of the Whole cannot exist without the other; they become, in effect, identical. They are so separated in this life, first because this life is a state of separation and contraries, and second because the discursive intellect, by nature analytic, does not know how to apprehend or adequately define that synthetic Whole of which beauty and truth are interpenetrating aspects; the best it can do is struggle for names. Yeats named the Whole the Thirteenth Cone or a Sphere and called its temporal manifestation in living matter *Unity of Being*. Keats had no single noun for the Whole, but its temporal manifestation he called *essence* or *beauty*, especially as these qualities exist in the *truth* of form. Because of its paradoxical reconciliation of being and form, the urn teases us out of thought as does eternity, whose reconciliations are not available to the discursive intellect. The urn is like the Elgin marbles that bring "dim-conceived glories" to the brain; it is "a shadow of a magnitude." Offering us only its "silent form," a silent music of inscape, the urn asks us to intuit its instress, residing beyond time, through a greeting of the spirit, an outgoing of our own instress. The poem's action traces the greeting that Keats proffers and the vision of instress operative in eternity that he reads upon the urn. Beauty as I define it is found in the lovers and their passion and in the lowing heifer and the trees; truth or inscape is in the abstract syntax of the unheard melodies and the geometry of the town empty of living beings, the latter a good transition to "O Attic shape!" and "silent form." Empathizing in fellowship with the urn, Keats reaches a point of self-surrender that is too self-destroying and, as in the letter to Fanny, is forced to withdraw to a middle distance from which the urn is seen not as a possible reality on earth—Keats does not confuse art and reality—but as a paradigm and artifice of eternity, like Yeats's golden bird.

At the end of the *Ode* the urn is saying: "Being is Form and Form is Being. Through the artistic perfection of my material form and the intensity of being that you intuit in the legend thereon, you are able to apprehend this paradox. It is the only one of heaven's reconciled paradoxes that, being mortal, you can ever fathom; it is all of heaven you can know on earth. But this reconciliation, when experienced, is sufficient proof that in heaven or eternity all other paradoxes are resolved; thus it is all of heaven that you need to know."[29]

29. Jones, p. 25, writes: "Beauty perceived imaginatively is the only realization of the divine that we can achieve on earth. . . . But that is enough to know about divinity. . . ." Earl Wasserman, *The Finer Tone* (Baltimore, 1953), p. 16, makes a correlative point: "what the symbolic

Chapter Two

Future generations may acquire this wisdom through a fellowship with the essence of the urn, for the urn is like Sato's sword and its embroidered sheath in Yeats's poetry, a "gift" that may moralize / My days out of their aimlessness" (Y, 200).

Beauty is Truth and Truth is Beauty when the numinous element of the holy, an aspect of Power or universal Energy, is embodied in a form so organized that it reveals that Beauty to a feeling response, a greeting of the spirit. Eliade's remarks on the sacred object, though they differ slightly from the interpretation given above, corroborate its mythic dimension: "The object appears as the receptacle of an exterior force that differentiates it from its milieu and gives it meaning and value. This force may reside in the substance of the object or in its form."[30] The metaphysical assumptions underlying the aesthetics of Keats and Yeats are not merely Romantic, they are mythic as well. When *beauty*, *essence*, or *energy* is perceived, there follows, in Cassirer's terms, "the deep conviction

---

drama ultimately discovers is the way in which art relates man to that region" where opposites are reconciled. Albert S. Gérard, *English Romantic Poetry* (Berkeley, 1968), follows suit: "the main theme of the *Ode* is . . . the function of art in life," p. 225. "Not until he reaches a better world will man be able to know more and to elucidate the strange interconnection of the ideal and the actual. But in this world art is man's highest endeavor . . ." p. 235.

I should add that I do not support my interpretation of Beauty and Truth by offering a close reading of the entire *Ode* because I do not believe the poem sufficiently delimits noninterchangeable meaning for these terms, prior to its final statement that in a particular kind of experience these qualities do become nondiscursively one. The experience of the poem convinces me that this nondiscursive unity is real. But when the urn affirms this unity for two qualities which it chooses to specify by name, one must ask what, in the context of the poem, these qualities represent. That context allows and will support all too many meanings for the terms, my own included. Thus any interpretation of those terms will remain, so far as the poem as context is concerned, to a large extent a priori. The context defining Truth and Beauty becomes, not the poem itself but, as I have tried to indicate, Keats's letters.

30. *Cosmos and History: The Myth of the Eternal Return* (New York, 1959), p. 4. Cassirer, *Language and Myth*, p. 65, is suggestive here: "the more one tries to 'determine' [mana], i.e., to interpret it in the categories of distinctions and contradictions familiar to our thinking, the more widely one misses its true nature."

of a fundamental and indelible *solidarity of life* that bridges over the multiplicity and variety of its single forms." From "mould ethereal" and the "anima mundi," Keats and Yeats affirm the unity of Being.

Chapter Three
The Vast Idea

Four characteristics of mythic apprehension exhibit the same intention of consciousness; they affirm the felt solidarity of life discussed in the preceding chapter. Each functions to support that central intention of mythic thought, and each may be said to reveal that intention by its own means. The first characteristic is metamorphosis: if everything is connected to everything else, anything may change into anything else. The second is a particularization of the first: the interconnection and reciprocity among the four natural elements and among the four seasons. The third is related to the second: a particular apprehension of time in which, on the one hand, the present moment is invested with the dimension of the past, of the future, or of both; and in which, on the other hand, linear progression of time is denied or cancelled: time bends back on itself, as it were, in an eternal return to its beginnings. The fourth is the refusal to admit the fact of death, a characteristic that is really no more than the solidarity of life in a different perspective and to which the first three characteristics are instruments. Though Cassirer considers these four elements separately, never pointing to their fundamental similarity, that similarity of intention is not obscure.

These elements are similar not only to each other but to the structure of mythic narrative as well. They display in their activity what Lévi-Strauss found in the activity of myth itself: a movement through opposites to a mediation of those opposites; often they are the mediating agent itself. In particular they attempt to mediate two of the most difficult pairs of opposites confronting the mind: the One and the Many, and Permanence and Change. When mythic thought has mediated these paradoxes to its satisfaction, by means of the characteristics peculiar to it, the solidarity of life is recognized and hence the separation of the self and the world is overcome. That moment of mediation—what Yeats called "the Great Moment"—is the subject of chapter 4. The present chapter considers, in separate sections, each of the characteristics of mythic apprehension that contributes to the Great Moment.

----------------------------------- I -----------------------------------

"From Feathers to Iron"

In mythic thought, apprehension or expectation of metamorphosis is coexistent with the solidarity of life: when all is felt to be connected, everything may suddenly turn into every other thing. According to Cassirer, "If there is any characteristic and outstanding feature of the mythical world, any law by which it is governed—it is this law of metamorphosis."[1] Once again poetry and mythic consciousness overlap, for Coleridge believed this "Protean self-transforming power" to be at the heart of the creative process: "To become all things and yet remain the same, to make the changeful God to be felt in the river, the lion, and the flame—that is true imagination."[2] Cassirer would insist that it is mythic apprehension as well; and indeed, as I have pointed out before, Coleridge's "imagination" is very much a faculty of mythic thinking. Here it is so through his insistence on metamorphosis and on "the changeful God," analogous to the *Power* or universal Energy perceived in mythic consciousness. Likewise, his famous definition of symbol—it "partakes of that reality which it renders intelligible"—is analogous to the same structure of mythic thought. One wishes he had made a thorough analysis of metaphor, for it is most certainly the major link between poetry and myth, through the metamorphosis of objects it entails. An analysis of metaphor might very well reveal its structure to be the structure of myth dis-

1. *An Essay on Man* (New Haven, 1962), p. 81.
2. Quoted in René Wellek, *A History of Modern Criticism* (New Haven, 1955), 2: 163.

covered by Lévi-Strauss. Suggesting such a speculation is Charles Pierce's undeveloped remark: "The sense of a symbol is its translation into another symbol."

From the evidence of Keats's work, metamorphosis seems to have been not merely a concept acquired through his schooling in Ovid but a mode of perception innate to him. Related to a schoolboy's literary fancy is the earliest extended example in his poetry. He sees his friend George Felton Mathew changed from a flower to a fish of gold, thence to a swan and then into a human being. With *Endymion* he has grown more serious, and the poem is filled with examples of metamorphosis suggesting an ultimate ground of sacred power, the waterfall passage in book II (613–26) being the best known. Cynthia becomes the Indian Maid and then reveals herself to be Cynthia at the same time, a mediation between the human and divine, the real transformed to the ideal. Much of *Lamia*'s meaning turns on the interpenetration of human and the divine realms. Lamia's transformation from snake to woman is magnificently handled, and the description of her marriage hall—a subtle interchange of stone, wood, and plant—draws from Keats some of his best writing in that poem. Apollo becomes a God in *Hyperion*, a theme symbolized in my epigraph from Malraux. Keats himself confessed in the *Ode to Psyche* the organic, metamorphic character of his thinking: "In some untrodden region of my mind / . . . A rosy sanctuary will I dress . . . / With all the gardner Fancy e'er could feign, / Who breeding flowers, will never breed the same. . . ." G. Wilson Knight's observation is especially well taken: "His interiors are fertile growths, his ethereals solid, his solids fluid, his light weighty, yet with each object remaining its particularized self."[3]

It is interesting that his letters written during the revision of *Endymion* return on several occasions to the idea of metamorphosis. The Reynolds sisters, visiting by the sea, "find out resemblances between waves and Camels—rocks and dancing Masters—fireshovels and telescopes—Dolphins and Madonas" (L1, 150). In a more serious vein he told Reynolds that "when

3. G. Wilson Knight, *The Starlit Dome* (London, 1964), p. 277.

The Vast Idea

Man has arrived at a certain ripeness in intellect any one grand and spiritual passage serves him as a starting post toward all 'the two-and thirty Pallaces' " (L1, 231); the allusion has never been satisfactorily identified, but the passage is indicative of a mode of perception whereby one is led rapidly from item to item by intuited relationships between them. To Bailey he expressed a similar idea: "Eve[r]y point of thought is the centre of an intellectual world—the two uppermost thoughts in a Man's mind are the two poles of his World he revolves on them and everything is southward or northward to him through their means—We take but three steps from feathers to iron" (L1, 243). Keats felt, rightly, that his own letters moved in this fashion: "If I scribble long letters I must play my vagaries . . . I must play my draughts as I please, and for my advantage and your erudition, crown a white with a black, or a black with a white, and move into black or white, far and near as I please—" (L1, 279). An earlier letter to Reynolds well expresses his metamorphic perception: "Would we were a sort of ethereal Pigs, & turn'd loose to feed upon spiritual Mast & Acorns—which would be merely being a squirrel & feed[ing] upon filberts. for what is a squirrel but an airy pig, or a filbert but a sort of archangelical acorn" (L1, 223). To the George Keatses he wrote: "I feel more and more every day, as my imagination strengthens, that I do not live in this world alone but in a thousand worlds—" (L1, 403).

Yeats very often saw metamorphosis as the problem of the One and the Many, its philosophic or discursive counterpart. Like Empedocles he thought that "all things are a single form which has divided and multiplied in time and space" (v, 212). "Only one symbol exists, though the reflecting mirrors make many appear and all different" (v, 240). He spoke of images that seemed "mirrored in a living substance whose form is but change of form" (m, 346).

In the world of Yeats's early verse, where so much is "wandering," fluid, "drifting," four poems present human metamorphosis. Instances will be remembered from *The Wanderings of Oisin*. In *Fergus and the Druid* the title characters

Chapter Three

"From change to change . . . have been many things," the Druid a raven and a weasel, Fergus "A green drop in the surge, a gleam of light / Upon a sword, a fir tree . . . An old slave . . . A king . . ." In *The Song of Wandering Aengus* the speaker catches a fish which turns into a "glimmering girl" whom he spends his life pursuing. The speaker of *He Thinks of His Past Greatness When a Part of the Constellations of Heaven* has been a hazel tree, a rush, a man, and—one assumes from the outrageous title—a star. These poems preface Yeats's mature speculations on reincarnation in *A Vision* and the metamorphosis in the later poems. In *Easter 1916* a terrible beauty is born in the transfigured patriots. In *Mohini Chatterjee* the Brahmin admonishes Yeats to contemplate his previous existences as king, slave, fool, rascal.

Between the early and the late poem, shortly before the turn of the century, Yeats came to feel that his early reliance on metamorphosis, if seeming to grant unity, was more often in effect an example of the very dispersal he feared, the sense of flux and chaos he felt threatening him. When he came to write *A Vision* he defined this ambiguous nature of metamorphosis, especially its role in his own phase. At Phases Eleven and Twelve, when Unity of Being begins to be possible, "every emotion begins to be related to every other as musical notes are related. It is as though we touched a musical string that set other strings vibrating" (v, 88). Yeats is possibly echoing his father's metaphor for Unity of Being: to his son's image of the perfectly proportioned human body, John Butler Yeats preferred "a comparison to a musical instrument so strung that if we touch a string all the strings murmer faintly" (A, 117). At Phase Seventeen, Yeats's phase, Unity of Being "is now more easy than at any other phase" (v, 141). On the other hand, the Body of Fate at Phase Seventeen is Loss, which, if ascendent, will cause dispersal of that unity for which the Will (simplification through intensity) ardently strives (v, 141–42).

Just before the turn of the century, Yeats's Body of Fate for several years held sway. "A conviction that the world was now but a bundle of fragments possessed me without ceasing"

The Vast Idea

(A, 117). If everything flows into everything else, what permanence is possible?

Now image called up image in an endless procession, and I could not always choose among them with any confidence, and when I did choose, the image lost its intensity, or changed into some other image. . . . I was lost . . . astray upon the Path of the Chameleon, upon *Hodos Chameliontos.* (A, 163)

He was, he wrote, as helpless to create artistic order as the hero of his novel *John Sherman* had been to create philosophic order (A, 226). Not until a few years later, at Coole Park, did "the first few simple thoughts that now, grown complex through their contact with other thoughts, explain the world, [come] to me from beyond my own mind" (A, 226–27), from the *anima mundi.*

The disappearance of the diatonic into the totally chromatic was painfully felt, at one time or another, by both Keats and Yeats. The state is one of being "unmeridian'd," to use a favorite word of Keats in the fall of 1819. Image calls up image in confused procession, as Yeats says. His *Hodos Chameliontos* is similar to Keats's "Things all disjointed" in the *Epistle to Reynolds.* The poem opens with a lengthy stream of disconnected images: "Two witch's eyes above a Cherub's mouth, / Voltaire with casque and shield and habergeon . . ." A day before composing the *Epistle,* Keats wrote a letter to James Rice in the same mood, showing himself unable to "keep in the check rein—Or I should stop here . . . You will see however I am obliged to run wild, being attracted by the Loadstone Concatenation" (L1, 255). Yeats, criticizing one of Dorothy Wellesley's poems, also used the rein metaphor: "I don't like the other so much, it runs on from one association to another, and you never pull at the bit" (DW, 157). When structure or pattern is lost, the intervals between items disappear, chromaticism results, and a sense of harmony between the One and the Many is impossible. Yeats, though he restructured harmony through *A Vision,* never felt that any system of temporally understood harmony could satisfactorily explain final reality. "I think," he wrote in 1930,

Chapter Three

"that two conceptions, that of reality as a congeries of being, that of reality as a single being, alternate in our emotion and in history, and must always remain something that human reason . . . cannot reconcile" (EX, 305).

If "Concatenation" and "Hodos Chameliontos" are fundamentally a problem in metaphysics, they are, at a more immediate level, a problem in aesthetics: how does one arrest blur and drift in imagery? Keats wrote to Hayden of "the innumerable compositions and decompositions which take place between the intellect and its thousand materials before it arrives at that trembling delicate and snail-horn perception of beauty" (L1, 264–65). In Milton he found one solution, "what may be called his *stationing*."[4] According to Keats, Milton customarily fixed or stationed his subjects—people or animals—in a background; not content merely to name the subject, he generally attached to the name a phrase positioning the subject in space, thus creating foreground and background as in painting. As early as *Sleep and Poetry* Keats was making efforts at such stationing:

> Things such as these are ever harbingers
> To trains of peaceful images: the stirs
> Of a swan's neck *unseen among the rushes*:
> A linnet starting *all about the bushes*:
> A butterfly, with golden wings broad parted,
> *Nestling a rose.* . . .
> (lines 339–44; italics added)

It is through stationing, as critics have noted, that Keats's human figures acquire that statuesque or sculptural quality so often common to them.

Keats's characters also seem very often to be processional figures, fixed yet moving, as in a Greek frieze. Yeats's figures are similar. Apprehending personalities he knew as figures of mythic dimension, Yeats freezes them in some unself-conscious, often heroic gesture, in relief against a specific background; they move past as if members in an Elizabethan progress. One sees them thus in the first great poem of his

4. Quoted in W. J. Bate, *John Keats* (Cambridge, Mass., 1963), p. 246.

maturity, *In Memory of Major Robert Gregory*, where he mastered the technique he later frequently employed. Others appear in *The Tower*, and the two Coole Park poems are structured through the background of place. The Gore-Booth sisters are "stationed" at Lissadell, Crazy Jane at the blasted oak or on the road. *Beautiful Lofty Things* is a chime of such stationed figures: "My father upon the Abbey stage . . . Standish O'Grady supporting himself between the tables . . . Augusta Gregory seated at her great ormolu table . . . Maud Gonne at Howth station waiting a train" (Y, 300).

Yeats acquired this habit during his days as an art student: "I could not compose anything but a portrait and even today I constantly see people, as a portrait painter, posing them in the mind's eye before such and such a background" (A, 50). Such stationing contributed to that "simplification through intensity" which he sought as Mask, to oppose the Body of Fate (loss or dispersal) in Phase Seventeen, where images "now flow, change, flutter, cry out, or mix into something else" (V, 141).[5] Once he rejected an elaborate metaphor of a breaking wave which, if functional as a symbol, damaged the poem's texture "because it spoilt the simplicity" (EX, 392–93). Again and again Yeats makes the point that mere naturalism, with its wealth of detail, robs a poem of architectural coherence, leaving "fragmentary sensuous beauty" (E, 353); art is deliberate creation and must involve the leaving out of "some element of reality as [in] a Byzantine painting" (E, 243). Thus he simplifies his images by sheering from them concrete detail, hoping by this to focus them through intensity, that they may bear symbolic or suggestive weight: "certain words must be full and numb. Here and there in correcting my early poems I have introduced such numbness and dullness, turned, for instance, 'the curd-pale moon' into the 'brilliant moon,' that all might seem, as it were, remembered with indifference, except some one vivid image. (A, 263). Aesthetic intention, rather than some consistent meta-

5. He remarks that in Phase Fourteen, Keats's phase, "images were separated from one another that they might be subject to knowledge" (V, 141).

Chapter Three

physical distaste for the concrete, accounts for the spare, unadorned nature imagery in his work.

Stationing is, finally, analogous to another characteristic of mythic thought: numinous or sacred space. In mythic apprehension there is a "difference between two *provinces* of being: a common, generally accessible province and another, sacred precinct which seems to be raised out of its surroundings, hedged and guarded against them."[6] If in most poets stationing is merely aesthetic, in Keats and Yeats it contributes to the creation of sacred space because it exists in a context of other mythic elements. Eliade indicates its connection with myth: "to organize a space is to repeat the paradigmatic work of the gods."[7] Cassirer writes: "Every mythically significant content, every circumstance of life that is raised out of the sphere of the indifferent and commonplace, forms its own ring of existence, a walled-in zone separated from its surroundings by fixed limits. . . ."[8]

Keats's obsessively repeated "bowers" come immediately to mind and are perhaps the most obvious example of sacred space in Romantic poetry. Recent study of them obviates any further commentary here.[9] Yeats, though he has no bowers, has a very strong sense of sacred place. Although he does not, like Keats, render whole landscapes in detail, his mature work does reflect his early conviction that poetry should hold, "as in a mirror, the colours of one's own climate and scenery" (E, 5), an omission he thought damaging in Shelley's *Prometheus Unbound* (E, 350).

Places have for Yeats a quality of *mana*, and his poetry is particularly rich in examples of sacred space, even as early

6. *Philosophy of Symbolic Forms* (New York, 1955), 2: 85. Cassirer discusses at some length this marking off of numinous sacred space, pp. 83–104. He is followed in this by Eliade, nearly every one of whose books has a lengthy discussion of it, often with a wider range of examples than Cassirer.
7. *The Sacred and the Profane* (New York, 1961), p. 32.
8. *Philosophy of Symbolic Forms*, 2: 103. In connection with this sense of a thing being "raised out of its surroundings," one should compare the literal meaning of "ecstasy": a standing forth, or out.
9. See Morris Dickstein, *Keats and His Poetry* (Chicago, 1971), passim.

in his career as *The Lake Isle of Innisfree*. Later we see not woods but a blasted oak, not the "dim sea" of the early poems but the river running past Thoor Ballylee. His tower itself is emblematic of the cosmic axis Eliade has discussed: "Communication with heaven is expressed by one or another of certain images, all of which refer to the *axis mundi*: pillar . . . mountain, tree, ladder . . . around this cosmic axis lies the world . . ."[10] "For the pole to be broken denotes catastrophe,"[11] just as Yeats's broken tower presages a declining civilization.

Very often in Yeats's poems persons are stationed in a numinous environment with which they have a reciprocal relationship. A very moving example is *Coole Park, 1929*: *this* place and *its* past, *this* company and *these* people are seen in sacred or mythic closure, walled-in and standing out from the common world. In 1902 he said of Arnold's "On the Study of Celtic Literature": "I do not think he understood that our 'natural magic' is but the ancient religion of the world, the ancient worship of Nature and that troubled ecstasy before her, that certainty of all beautiful places being haunted" (E, 176). To exemplify this sense of "places being haunted," he pointed to passages in the *Mabinogion* and Keats.

As an aesthetic device, stationing is an attempt to mediate the claims of the One and the Many. Sacred space works to the same end. Eliade writes: "Revelation of a sacred space makes it possible to obtain a fixed point and hence to acquire orientation in the chaos of homogeneity. . . ."[12] Those spaces walled-in or lifted above the ordinary environment have uniqueness and singularity. At the same time, they display a common element, *mana*, and this joins them to each other. In some instances *mana* may be felt to reside permanently in a place; but in other instances a heretofore common place may suddenly seem possessed of *mana* and become sacred. Metamorphosis is again at work, contributing to the mythic sense of life as a continuous whole. Yeats, very late in life, wrote movingly of this mystery: "You must feel plunged as I do

10. *The Sacred and the Profane*, p. 37.
11. Ibid., p. 33.
12. Ibid., p 23.

into the madness of vision, into a sense of the relation between separated things that you cannot explain, and that deeply disturbs emotion" (DW, 135–36).

———————————— II ————————————

"An Interchange of Favors"

The apprehension of metamorphosis in Keats and Yeats finds fullest poetic expression in repeated images expressing change in the natural world. For this manifestation David Perkins, discussing Keats, used the term "myth of process."[13] In Perkins's phrase the word "myth" bears connotations that are not related to my own use of the word. But the term "process" is useful for two of Cassirer's characteristics of mythic thought taken together: metamorphosis and its particularization, the interconnection and reciprocity among the four natural elements and the four seasons. It points to the fact that in Keats's

13. Perkins, *The Quest for Permanence* (Cambridge, Mass., 1959), p. 197. Both Perkins and Bernard Blackstone, *The Consecrated Urn* (London, 1959), see this myth of process as the informing center of Keats's poetry. Blackstone's interpretation is through "Growth and Form," terms certainly correlative to my own. But these terms, and Blackstone's reading of the poems through them, are not employed in any clearly defined thesis, excepting his insistence that Keats's thought was "rooted in Hermetic soil" and Thomas Taylor's translations. Believing as I do that Keats exhibits the natural mythic mode of consciousness, I do not find it necessary or profitable to insist on sources, especially those it seems unlikely Keats knew.

More recently Walter Evert, *Aesthetic and Myth in the Poetry of Keats* (Princeton, 1965), has made equally bold but well substantiated claims, believing the myth of process to be a fully developed, conscious, and consistent pattern to which all Keats's poetry through *Endymion* conforms. Although the principle of analogy Evert sees operating in Keats bears some resemblance to what I discuss as metamorphosis, our treatment of myth is otherwise dissimilar.

Margaret Sherwood's early essay in *Undercurrents of Influence in English Romantic Poetry* (Cambridge, Mass., 1934), is still perhaps the most seminal study of Keats's myth making. But her belief that Keats used myth to interpret the processes of nature I would invert; it is my belief that Keats interpreted the processes of nature through his mythic consciousness, only then turning to myth in the narrative sense to embody what the mythic consciousness had already grasped.

poetry flux, growth, decay, and permanence are not presented as discontinuous aspects of nature but, on the contrary, as parts of one continuous pattern that, perceived, grants meaning to mutability and death.

Process is common in Romantic literature, being perhaps the central factor by means of which nature appears organic rather than mechanical. Its evidence is so frequent in the work of some poets that it seems to have been for them a structure of apprehension. In this respect their work is mythic, as Lévi-Strauss defines myth. To him myth is an algebra of analogy (a : b : : c : d) by means of which natural entities are interchangeable one with another; the origin of this algebra is the structurally determined operation of the mind. "Myth starts from a structure by means of which it constructs a set" of objects.[14] This transformational grammar in myth has its own analogy in Romantic poetry in the transformational interchange of natural elements by means of process. Some poets, like Wordsworth and Yeats, were highly conscious of process as a mode or structure of cognition; Yeats, for example, believed the process of the seasons to be "the symbolical syntax wherein we may write the History of the World" (E, 471). Other poets, like Keats, were less conscious —sometimes hardly conscious at all—of its operation. What distinguishes Keats and Yeats is the insistence with which this sense of process informs the poetry. These poets seem to echo Cassirer: "contemplation is directed not toward the mere content of change but toward its pure form."[15]

With Keats this sense of process was, I think, the "vast idea" that rolled before him in *Sleep and Poetry* (lines 284–300). The young poet admits that he has neither "spanning wisdom," nor knowledge of the history of ideas, nor "minist'ring reason." Yet he has, he says, a "vast idea" which, in showing him "the end and aim of poetry," grants him the "liberty" to begin his career as a poet in spite of the educational liabilities he cites. What this "vast idea" is, Keats does

14. "The Structural Study of Myth," in *Myth: A Symposium*, ed. Thomas A. Sebeok (Bloomington, Ind., 1965), p. 83.
15. *Philosophy of Symbolic Forms*, 2: 111.

not say. But while insisting that " 'Tis clear / As anything most true," he gives two examples of true clear things which, in themselves, are emblematic of process:

> as clear as that the year
> Is made of the four seasons—manifest
> As a large cross, some old cathedral's crest,
> Lifted to the white clouds.

The first instance is a direct reference to process. The second reveals the deep religious feeling associated with process, as if the myth of process were itself, like the labor of "soul-making" which illustrates it, "the Parent of all the more palpable and personal Schemes of Redemption" (L2, 103). The myth of process exemplifies those "heroic and religious truths, passed on from age to age" (A, 298), which Yeats felt rooted Keats's work "to the early ages of religion before the Mass;" he saw in Keats's odes "the symbolism in day and night, and winter and summer, spring and autumn, once so great a part of an older religion than Christianity" (E, 149–50).

Keats concludes the passage with the vision of "an ocean dim, sprinkled with many an isle," which "spreads awfully before me." What toil, he cries, what desperate turmoil to explore its wilderness. "Ah, what a task!" The archetypal image of the everchanging, generating sea embodies the idea of process. Just as living is a continual tension between growth and decay, so the elements of the sea and land, ocean and islands, form a harmonious pattern. The young poet has an intense, intuitive awareness of this clear truth. He will trace the myth of process which, as he says of its god Pan, will be "Dread opener of the mysterious doors / Leading to universal knowledge" (*Endymion*, I, 288–89). His task will be to explore and so come to image this knowledge, as he finally does in the face of Moneta.

The first door to this knowledge is a sense of awe before the natural elements, before their power and the sense of presence within them. In Keats and Yeats the many occurrences of the elements have not only purposes defined by the context of the specific poem but also reference, through an undercurrent of significance, to their presential noumenon itself. Whatever the immediate purpose of their employment, the deeper purpose is expression of the mythic awe before their power. Each element, by its own mode of existence and the characteristics peculiar to it, reveals some aspect of the sacred. As Eliade says, "the gods manifested the different modalities of the sacred in the very structure of the world."[16] The sky, for example, reveals transcendence and eternity by simple awareness of its infinite height. To the mythic mind, the natural characteristics of things reveal the sacred. Eliade calls these revelations *hierophanies:* "a modality of the sacred expressed through a specific mode of existence in the cosmos."[17]

Keats's mode of viewing the elements is analogous to if not identical with that of the man of mythic consciousness. In his first volume of poetry he wrote that there are times for certain persons when "A sudden glow comes on them, naught they see / In water, earth, or air, but poesy"; poesy, as I noted earlier, he defines in this same volume as "the supreme of power." He wrote in *Endymion* (III, 30–35):

> A thousand Powers keep religious state,
> In water, fiery realm, and airy bourne;
> And, silent as a consecrated urn,
> Hold sphery sessions for a season due,
> Yet few of these far majesties, ah, few!
> Have bared their operations to this globe.

To the poet in particular are these operations bared. For Homer

> Jove uncurtain'd Heaven to let thee live,
> And Neptune made for thee a spumy tent,
> And Pan made sing for thee his forest-hive.
> (K, 463)

Though blind, Homer was one of those few who had a "triple sight" into these operations. "Such seeing . . . as it once befel / To Dian, Queen of Earth, and Heaven, and Hell" (K, 463).

16. *The Sacred and the Profane*, p. 119.
17. Ibid., p. 155.

Chapter Three

Through the vision of process he is granted a kind of god-head, just as Keats is when he sees Moneta's face.

Keats continually finds mythical significance or noumena in the separate elements, especially air and water, Of the four elements, fire alone is slighted in his work. In the early sonnet *To my Brothers* he speaks of flames playing "Like whispers of the household gods." In the *Song of Four Fairies* Salamander sings of the metamorphic, chiming shapes which are her nature:

> Let me see the myriad shapes
> Of men, and beasts, and fish, and apes,
> Portray'd in many a fiery den,
> And wrought by spumy bitumen.
> (K, 444)

Throughout his career, but especially in the early verse, air is for Keats a source of vision. On first looking into Chapman's Homer, Keats "felt . . . like some watcher of the skies / When a new planet swims into his ken." Poetry itself, he says in *Sleep and Poetry*, is a "wide heaven," a "drainless shower of light," and he speaks of "the secrets of some wond'rous thing / That breathes about us in the vacant air . . . shapes of light, aerial limning . . . a faint-heard hymning" (lines 30–34). In *I Stood Tip-toe* he is brought "Shapes from the invisible world, unearthly singing / From out the middle air" (lines 186–87). In the *Epistle* to his brother George he says that "what we, ignorantly, sheet-lightning call" is really "the swift opening" of the "wide portal" to realms of "gay Knights" (lines 29–40; cf. *Sleep and Poetry*, lines 125–54); thunder accompanying this lightning is the "trumpet clear" of the warder who announces the opening gate, "tones that reach naught on earth but Poet's ear." The passage recalls that in *Hyperion* (I, 276–83):

> Sweet-shaped lightnings from the nadir deep
> Up to the zenith,—hieroglyphics old,
> Which sages and keen-eyed astrologers
> Then living on the earth, with labouring thought
> Won from the gaze of many centuries:
> Now lost, save what we find on remnants huge

The Vast Idea

Of stone, or marble swart; their import gone,
Their wisdom long since fled.

In *Endymion* (III, 23–28) he speaks of "throned seats un-scalable / But by a patient wing" (again the godhood image) where the wise can "poise about in cloudy thunder-tents / To watch the abysm-birth of elements." The poet, as creator, shares in the everlasting process of natural creation, whose observer he can become.

Water, especially the ocean, draws Keats's feeling response even more than airy space. Its meaning for him, however, has less in common with its customary significance as a source of life than with its more complex significance in mythic thought. There, as Eliade points out, water is not so much a symbol for life, which exists in forms, as it is the preformal, amorphous "stuff" from which the living forms are differentiated. It is "the reservoir of all the possibilities of existence," and "one of the paradigmatic images of creation is the island that suddenly manifests itself." Here, I believe, is the vast idea behind Keats's oceans and their islands, and here is the significance of the imagery in the "vast idea" passage:

> An ocean dim, sprinkled with many an isle,
> Spreads awfully before me. How much toil!
> How many days! What desperate turmoil!
> Ere I can have explored its wideness.
> Ah, what a task!

A month or two before writing this passage, in the sonnet on Chapman's Homer, Keats used the discovery of a new ocean as the culminating vehicle for the moment of vision, and the "wild surmize" it elicits is the same emotion he feels in the "vast idea" passage when he sees the ocean and isles spread "awfully before me." Cortez, like Keats, stares in awe at the reservoir of all the possibilities not merely of existence but of creation; in the octave of the sonnet, creations—works of literature—are symbolized as islands. (In the sonnet directly addressed to Homer, the ocean and the islands recur.) Seeing Lake Winander from two different views, Keats wrote his brother Tom: "—they make me forget the divisions of life;

Chapter Three

age, youth, poverty and riches; and refine one's sensual vision into a sort of north star which can never cease to be open lidded and steadfast over the wonders of the great Power" (L1, 299). The parallels to *Bright Star* have often been noted. One may add the parallel to the "eagle" stare of Cortez, silent on a peak in Darien. In dissolving "the divisions of life" and revealing "the wonders of the great Power," the vision of water is exemplary of mythic interconnectedness and of the Great Moment, the subject of the next chapter.[18]

Just as the eternal motion of the sea is part of its meaning, so moving into and out of it accounts for its complexity in mythic thought. Eliade must be quoted at length: "Immersion in water signifies regression to the preformal, reincorporation into the undifferentiated mode of pre-existence. Emersion repeats the cosmogonic act of formal manifestation; immersion is equivalent to a dissolution of forms. This is why the symbolism of the waters implies both death and rebirth."[19] Endymion's plunge into the ocean in book III bears this mythic implication. Underwater, his self-centered being suffers a sea-change, and he is reborn as a man with sympathy for his mortal kind. Keats's account of the origin of myth itself in *Endymion* involves immersion in and emersion from water. A poet passes "a sleeping lake" which contains "a ditty / Not of these days," passed to it by a forest which, in turn, had it from a cavern wind:

> in it he did fling
> His weary limbs, bathing an hour's space,
> And, after straight, in that inspired place
> He sang the story up into the air,
> Giving it universal freedom. (II, 835–39)

Myths are born from immersion of mythic consciousness in the reservoir of all the possibilities of existence—that is, the

18. There is a similar meaning to the ocean metaphor in the sonnet *To Homer*, the *Ode to a Nightingale*, the verse *Epistle to Reynolds*, and *Hyperion*. Because these poems are discussed at length in chapter 5, their use of the metaphor is not repeated here.

19. *The Sacred and the Profane*, p. 130. Compare Yeats's description of the sea as "part of some indefinite and passionate life, which had begun to war upon our orderly and careful days" (M, 280).

reservoir of Being itself, symbolized as water and "mould ethereal."

Two months before the sonnet on Chapman's Homer, Keats wrote of the sea in terms that anticipate its future metaphoric uses:

> The ocean with its vastness, its blue green,
> Its ships, its rocks, its caves, its hopes, its fears—
> Its voice mysterious, which whoso hears
> Must think on what will be, and what has been.
>
> (K, 39)

In the last line the sense of temporal process emerges clearly, as it does in the first two lines of the sonnet *Time's Sea*: "Time's sea hath been five years at its slow ebb; / Long hours have to and fro let creep the sand." A year later, in the sonnet *On the Sea*, he requests us to sit near a cavern's mouth and "brood / Until ye start, as if by sea-nymphs quired!" The shock given Cortez's men is again suggested. At the same time, water, like air, is informed with harmonious cosmic music, hence is "a mighty Minstrell" (L1, 158).

The work of this minstrel-priest Keats saw a summer later on the Scottish walking tour, when he visited the sea cavern at Staffa (K, 493–94). Neither Aladdin nor the wizard of the Dee nor Saint John when he saw churches built in heaven "gaz'd at such a rugged wonder"; natural processes themselves are wonders far exceeding images brought by magic or Christian vision. To this "Cathedral of the Sea" dolphins come, like "palmers" to "pay devotion due." In the cavern the poet discovers Lycidas, who has been for the place "the pontiff-priest . . . Proteus is my Sacristan." But, Lycidas says, "the stupid eye of mortal," comprehending nothing but a geological phenomenon, has so desecrated the cavern that he has decided to "soon unweave / All the magic of the place," leaving it "free to stupid face, / To cutters and to Fashion boats."

In book II of *Endymion* Keats writes of the ocean as if it were the *anima mundi* feeding the conscious memory: "Wide sea, that one continuous murmur breeds / Along the pebbled shore of memory!" (ii, 16–17) The lines are strikingly similar to Yeats's observation on the relationship between consciousness and the *anima mundi*: "Our daily thought was certainly but the line of foam at the shallow edge of a vast luminous sea; Henry More's Anima Mundi, Wordsworth's 'immortal sea which brought us hither . . . and near whose edge the children sport' " (M, 346).

Yeats was undoubtedly most influenced by the water imagery of Blake, and particularly of Shelley—"Water is his great symbol of existence and he continually meditates over its mysterious source" (E, 85). Yet he understood well enough this high Romantic image and Keats's relationship to it to speak of the earlier poet's islands and to say in *A Vision* that Phases Eight through Fifteen (Keats is Phase Fourteen) are associated with water "because there the image-making power is at its height" (v, 93). He himself meditated over its mysterious source. "What's water but the generated soul?" he asks in *Coole Park and Ballylee, 1931*, a poem structured by images of stream and lake. "Yet is not ecstasy some fulfillment of the soul in itself, some slow or sudden expansion of it like an overflowing well?" (A, 286). It is a remarkably felicitous image for the Great Moment (here called ecstasy); and seven times in his poetry he refers to "the abounding glittering jet" of the soul. In *The Celtic Twilight*, in the persona of an old peasant whose belief he is repeating, he writes with startling Keatsian parallels:

> He thinks that if we sent our spirits down into the water we would make them of one substance with strange moods of ecstasy and power, and go out it may be to the conquest of the world. We would, however, he believes, have first to outface and perhaps overthrow strange images full of a more powerful life than if they were really alive. It may be that we shall look at them without fear when we have endured the last adventure, that is death.[20]

Here come together Endymion's plunge, Keats's fascination with death, and his struggle before Moneta's naked face as he

20. *The Celtic Twilight and a Selection of the Early Poems*, ed. Walter Starkie (New York, 1962), p. 77.

becomes godlike in his grandest attempt to image the Great Moment. A religious awe before the natural elements is, then, the first door leading to universal knowledge. The elements function, in Philip Wheelwright's apt term, as mythoids.[21] Positing, like Cassirer, a stage of human consciousness prior to the formulation of mythic narrative, Wheelwright calls the product of this stage a mythoid. It is an "incipient myth," a situation that may develop into narrative. The sense of presence is perhaps its most important feature; as the perception of *mana* is succeeded by the conception of "separate spirits or daemons," mythoid becomes myth. As examples of mythoid Wheelwright points to recurring groups of related images. The four elements compose such a group, as do the seasons, and their interaction Keats spoke of as an "interchange of favours" (κ, 6). The phrase occurs in *I Stood Tip-toe*, with which Keats chose to open his first volume, and if this wandering poem has any subject as such it is an affirmation of the identity of natural process, myth, and poetry which the work of his maturity will clarify.

The second door to universal knowledge is perception of the mythoidal "interchange of favours" among elements in which, if all changes, all nevertheless remains. "There is," Keats wrote, "a continual courtesy between the Heavens and the Earth—the heavens rain down their unwelcomeness, and the Earth sends it up again to be returned to morrow" (L1, 273–74). Underlying the vast idea of process is this paradoxical balance between the One and the Many. The day before Keats sent his verse *Epistle to Reynolds* (there deeply perplexed by life's inequities and the nature of the imagination), he wrote to James Rice on the question:

As there is ever the same quantity of matter constituting this habitable globe—as the ocean notwithstanding the enormous changes and revolutions taking place in some or other of its demesnes—notwithstanding Waterspouts whirpools and mighty Rivers emptying themselves into it, it still is made up of the same bulk—nor ever varies the number of its Atoms—And as a

21. *Metaphor and Reality* (Bloomington, Ind., 1968), pp. 136–38.

certain bulk of Water was instituted at the Creation—so very
likely a certain portion of intellect was spun forth into the thin
Air for the Brains of Man to prey upon it—You will see my drift
without any unnecessary parenthesis. That which is contained in
the Pacific [can't] lie in the hollow of the Caspian—that which
was in Miltons head could not find Room in Charles the seconds—

(L1, 255)

Just as Yeats's interpenetrating cones contain fixed sums of
qualities whose proportions to each other shift as time pernes
along their length, so Keats affirms the fixed sum of an element—water or intelligence—which, in the process of time,
shifts into and out of vessels of unequal capacity.

Concomitant with this balance between the One and the
Many is the paradoxical relationship between Permanence
and Change, the second factor underlying the vast idea of
process. Life and Death are but knowable halves of a whole
which, qua whole, is unknowable to the analytic intellect.
Living and dying complement each other as systole and dia-
stole, halves of a whole that is Process; between them they
create a second kind of "interchange of favours." Intuitive
understanding of this equal interchange grants explanation
of perceived inequities in nature, a theory of compensation
through which one can accept those inequities. A clear example in Keats's work of this process and of compensation is the
Indian Maid's song in the last book of *Endymion*:

> O Sorrow,
> Why dost borrow
> The natural hue of health, from vermeil lips?—
> To give maiden blushes
> To the white rose bushes?
> Or is't thy dewey hand the daisy tips?
>
> O Sorrow,
> Why dost borrow
> The lustrous passion from a falcon-eye?—
> To give the glow-worm light?
> Or, on a moonless night,
> To tinge, on syren shores, the salt sea-spry?

(IV, 146–57)

Cassirer summarizes these first and second stages in mythical apprehension: "From the rhythm and periodicity which can be felt in all immediate life and existence the mind of man now rises to the idea of the temporal order as a universal order of destiny, governing all reality and all change."[22] The early work of Keats is rich in examples of the interchange of favors. In *I Stood Tip-toe* the interchange is not only announced but exemplified (lines 43–46): the bubbling stream may "haply mourn" that clusters of blue-bells "should be rudely torn / From their fresh beds. . . . By infant hands, left on the path to die." The "haply mourn" may be little more than worn eighteenth-century convention, but the following antitheses (torn—fresh, infant—die, path as progress —path as terminal point) show supporting depth of observation. Similar images in *Endymion* are more assured: "plunder'd vines, teeming exhaustless" (III, 927); "the ripe grape is sour" (IV, 35). *Calidore* presents a view of "*swelling* leafiness" colored by the "*setting* sun"; in the scene are "*drooping* flowers . . . *fresh* from summer showers" (italics added). The latter perception anticipates the second stanza of the *Ode on Melancholy*, just as the musical interchange of *The Grasshopper and the Cricket* sonnet anticipates the musical interchange of spring and autumn in the ode *To Autumn*. Seen from the view of process, "The poetry of earth is never dead."

Keats's sense of process does not stop with *Endymion* but runs right through Oceanus' speculations in *Hyperion* and the Induction to the *Fall of Hyperion* to the ode *To Autumn*. Like the song of the Indian Maid, these later instances build toward acceptance of life's inequities through recognition of the compensation inherent in process. Oceanus, almost echoing an Elizabethan notion of the great chain of being, asks his fellow Titans in *Hyperion*:

> Say, doth the dull soil
> Quarrel with the proud forests it hath fed,
> And feedeth still, more comely than itself?
> Can it deny the chiefdom of green groves?
> Or shall the tree be envious of the dove
> Because it cooeth, and hath snowy wings

22. *Philosophy of Symbolic Forms*, 2: 111.

Chapter Three

> To wander wherewithal and find its joys?
> We are such forest-trees, and our fair boughs
> Have bred forth, not pale solitary doves,
> But eagles golden-feather'd, who do tower
> Above us in their beauty.... (ii, 217–27)

He would transfer the Titans' attention from their personal loss to the larger process of which that loss is only a part. He uses, as Keats almost always did, images from the process in nature to make his human point.

Keats employs the same analogy in his sonnet *Four Seasons*:

> Four seasons fill the measure of the year;
> There are four seasons in the mind of man
> . . . .
> He has his Winter too of pale misfeature,
> Or else he would forego his mortal nature.

The subject of the poem is not, as it might seem to be, physical mortality; rather it is the reciprocity between body and soul: as the body declines toward death, the soul or spirit moves to greater wisdom, and the second compensates for the first. The vast idea of process has been for Keats the discovery that, as David Perkins puts it, "it is only through time that things can work out their latent potentiality."[23] This discovery is the theme of the sonnet *After Dark Vapours*, the sestet of which blends into one process the cycles of human and natural life:[24]

> The calmest thoughts come round us—as of leaves
> Budding,—fruit ripening in stillness,—autumn suns
> Smiling at eve upon the quiet sheaves,—
> Sweet Sappho's cheek,—a sleeping infant's breath,—
> The gradual sand that through an hour-glass runs,—
> A woodland rivulet,—a Poet's death. (K, 458)

The natural cycle of the first tercet (foreshadowing the imagery of *To Autumn*) is paralleled by the human cycle of the

23. Perkins, p. 197.

24. See Paul R. Baumgartner, "Keats: Theme and Image in a Sonnet," *KSJ* 8 (1959): 11–14, for a most astute reading of this sonnet.

The Vast Idea

second. The repetition implies that although the Great Year of the one thing closes, that closing is itself only part of a succeeding cycle, some Greater Year. Through the perception of process, mortality can be accepted. "How fever'd," then, "is the man who cannot look / Upon his mortal days with temperate blood" (к, 469). So begins one of the two sonnets *On Fame*. Keats says that to struggle against mortality is unnatural and self-destructive: "It is as if the rose should pluck herself, / Or the ripe plum finger its misty bloom." The rose and the plum accept their place in process and the time allotted to them. "Why then should man, teasing the world for grace, / Spoil his salvation for a fierce miscreed?" The concluding phrase is perplexing, for nothing in the poem's context delimits possible meanings for the "fierce miscreed." The title, however, suggests that it is fame, the struggle to win against mortality by the immortality of fame.

Such fame Keats had rejected a year before when, fearing an early death before his writing or his love for Fanny had been fulfilled. he found "salvation" in accepting his place in cosmic process: "on the shore / Of the wide world I stand alone, and think / Till love and fame to nothingness do sink" (к, 462). The sea again serves as metaphor for a *sub specie aeternitatis* perspective on events. And though process is not a direct theme of the poem, it is implied by the connotations of the sea metaphor that accrue in its occurrences elsewhere in Keats's poetry.

"A fierce miscreed," then, is the struggle to deny mortality through means that are unnatural. either fame or, possibly, organized religion. One can only speculate here, but the very conjunction of "salvation" and "miscreed" suggests that the latter is any religion asking us to alter our natural bodily movements in order to win the salvation of an abstract heaven. Keats found organized religion to be life-denying, as the sonnet *Written in Disgust of Vulgar Superstition* shows. The sonnet *On Fame* is evidence that for him the mythic apprehension of process was a better vision of salvation. Although he never abandoned the attempt to discover the transcendent, that quest became in his mature work, as in the mature work of Yeats, fully rooted in earth. One could say of Keats what Yeats said of himself, Lady Gregory, and Synge:

> All that we did, all that we said or sang
> Must come from contact with the soil, from that
> Contact everything Antaeus-like grew strong.
>
> (Y, 318)

―――――――――――――― III ――――――――――――――
"Time Annihilate"

When permanence and change are seen as interpenetrating factors with rhythm and periodicity, a particular apprehension of time ensues. Cassirer, finding it in mythic thought, calls it "a kind of biological time, a rhythmic ebb and flow of life" preceding apprehension of a "properly cosmic time."[25] He defines one manifestation of it, Eliade another.

According to Cassirer, the man of mythic apprehension is not aware of time as a set of discrete coordinates, past, present, and future; rather, time is for him a fluid field within which the solidarity of life is witnessed. It is only in post-mythic consciousness that the periods of time are believed to be distinct, through operation of the analytic intellect which wishes to station events singly. In mythic consciousness these periods of time are simply not *felt* to be single and so have not gained meaningful separation. Cassirer writes: "Present, past, and future blend into each other without any sharp line of demarcation."[26] "The magical 'now' is by no means a *mere* now, a simple, differentiated present, but is . . . laden with the past and pregnant with the future."[27] Time itself, in other words, is metamorphic; its structure, like that of the elements of the cosmos, involves transformation.

25. *Philosophy of Symbolic Forms*, 2: 109.
26. *An Essay on Man*, p. 83.
27. *Philosophy of Symbolic Forms*, 2: 111.

The Vast Idea

Cassirer's "biological time, a rhythmic ebb and flow of life" probably refers, like his discussion of the feeling response, to the biological processes of the human body. But when biology is thought of as the seasons, his phrase is also introduction to Eliade's discussion of mythic time. Eliade believes that the man of mythic consciousness has his sense of time determined for him largely by observation of the seasons and the moon: both provide evidence for believing that the linear aspect of time is illusion, for both show that at some point time bends back on itself and begins again. This empirical evidence accords with psychological need: it arrests, even cancels the linear drift through mutability and decay to eventual death. Most myths and rituals, according to Eliade, are attempts to return *in illo tempore*, "to those days" in which everything began, came into being. This moment of beginning is the sacred moment: first, the gods are then manifest, for it is through the direct activity of the gods that all things and all meaningful states of things (such as man's being sexed or his social institutions) came into being; second, while the gods are thus involved and present there is no time-as-linear-progression. Hence, "this eternal return reveals an ontology uncontaminated by time and becoming."[28] In Eliade's analysis of mythic thought, this apprehension of time is the central factor, sharing its preeminence only with perception of the numinous. The eternal return, in fact, is a structure through which the numinous is revealed.

These two manifestations of the mythic sense of time are central to Keats and Yeats. So central, in fact, is this mythic sense of time that the other aspects of mythic thought often occur in their work in conjunction with it. This conjunction, however, initiates in the poets an experience which itself deserves special study; hence examination of it must be postponed to the next chapter. Here, through discussion of examples that occur in relative isolation, I will do no more than introduce the mythic sense of time in Keats and Yeats, that this aspect of mythic thought may take its place among the

28. *Cosmos and History: The Myth of the Eternal Return* (New York, 1959), p. 89.

single aspects of mythic apprehension that are the subject of this chapter.

In discussing Keats's concept of time, several critics have used terms analogous to Cassirer's definition of mythic time, even though Cassirer and mythic thought are not mentioned. One critic, for example, has spoken of Keats's "interwoven time."[29] Two often cited examples are "ripe October's faded marigolds" (*Endymion*, II, 397), and the magnificent image from the *Ode on Melancholy* in which pleasure is "Turning to poison while the bee-mouth sips." Both exhibit Cassirer's magical "now": the present of an object or event is seen merely as a momentary point in the fluid field of temporal process. The *Fairy's Song* contains an excellent example: "Young buds sleep in the root's white core." Some images proceed chronologically through the temporal periods: "the birth, life, death / Of unseen flowers" (*Endymion*, I, 234–35); "new flowers at morning song of bees, / Bloom'd, and gave up . . . honey to the lees" (*Lamia*, I, 142–44). Others promise the eternal return: "There is a budding morrow at midnight" (K, 463). One example that I have never seen cited is the most startling of all; as Isabella's brothers set out with her lover, Keats writes: "So the two brothers and their murder'd man / Rode past fair Florence" (stanza 27). That Keats was conscious of this mode of apprehension is evidenced in his review of Edmund Kean's acting: "There is an indescribable gusto in his voice, by which we feel that the utterer is thinking of the past and future, while speaking of the present."[30] This mythic apprehension of time, as my final chapter will argue, becomes perhaps the central element of his sensibility, the theme of some of his major poems, and all but a synonym for his mature conception of "melancholy."

In Yeats the mythic sense of time manifests Eliade's eternal return more often than Cassirer's time fusion, though this is

---

29. Hubert Heinan, "Interwoven Time in Keats's Poetry," *TSLL* 3 (1961): 382–88. See also Robert Wooster Stallman, "Keats the Apollonian: The Time and Space Logic of His Poems as Paintings," *UTQ* 16 (1947): 143–56.

30. Quoted in Bate, *John Keats*, p. 245.

The Vast Idea

not absent. First to mind is the whole system of *A Vision* and its basic metaphors of the revolving wheel and perning interpenetrating gyres. In his system Yeats allows a Great Year for all entities, giving "to the smallest living creature its individual year" (v, 202). Each of these Great Years is a microcosm of the single Great Year which is the cosmos: "a Greatest Year for whale and gudgeon alike must exhaust the multiplication table" (EX, 396). Yeats explains: "It is as though innumerable dials, some that recorded minutes alone, some seconds alone, some hours alone, some months alone, some years alone, were all to complete their circles when Big Ben struck twelve upon the last night of the century" (v, 248). In his account of historical cycles, any period which is Phase One for a particular cycle is, at the same time, Phase Fifteen for some other cycle. Hence Yeats's schemes record not merely a wearying succession of birth, maturity, and death; they affirm the simultaneity of these events. Past and future impregnate the present, as in Keats.

Process is the very structure of the Yeatsian universe, its syntax of truth, just as it is in the Keatsian, explaining the course not only of individual human experience but also of civilization. The difference is not so much in kind as in degree. Yeats is self-conscious to the highest degree, systematizing process in the staggering detail of *A Vision*; Keats is intuitive to the highest degree, presenting process in the concrete imagery of his poetry. Yeats gives us a cyclical theory of history; Keats gives us *Hyperion* (one theme of which, as I shall show, is similar). What Keats reads in Moneta's face, Yeats reads in Heraclitus' maxim, which he so frequently cited; he wrote to Ethel Mannin: "To me all things are made of the conflict of two states of consciousness, beings or persons which die each other's life, live each other's death. That is true of life and death themselves" (LY, 918).

If Yeats's poems are not rich in Keatsian observations of natural processes, the vast idea of process nevertheless dominates many of them. Behind *The Wandering of Oisin* lies his reading in Boehme and others, from whom he learned that Oisin's journey was, in Thomas Whitaker's words, "a sym-

Chapter Three

bol for the alchemical rota or opus circulatorium, the cyclical
transformation of the four elements, the four seasons, and
other quaternities."³¹ One of his minor lyrics, *The Wheel*,
uses the seasons to make a human point in much the same
fashion that Keats uses them in the *Four Seasons* sonnet. In
his mature poems Yeats exchanges mythic apprehension for
the "embroideries / Out of old mythologies"(y, 125) that
often merely decorate his early poems.

In *The Road at My Door*, the poet takes from natural process consolation for the horrors of civil war. A "brown Lieu-
tenant and his men"—men of war on errands of war—stop
by his house. We are not told their errand—tension is kept
implicit; probably it is one of query for suspected enemies in
the neighborhood. The poet speaks to them casually of the
foul weather, as if to avoid the subject of war. But he mentions "a pear-tree broken by the storm," and talk of the physical storm, casually begun, suddenly seems emblematic of the
violent storm of war. Nature has provided a bitter commentary on man's folly; hence talk of the storm no longer avails
to hold the war at bay. As if to redeem nature he begins at
once to count, silently to himself, the young offspring
which a moor-hen "guides upon the stream." The act, he says,
is "to silence the envy in my thought," an envy for the full,
unobstructed flow of their lives, generation succeeding generation, parent helping child along the stream in the harmonious process of life—unlike the process of his own life and
society, broken by the self-destruction of war, brother set
against brother. If nature breaks the pear-tree, she also gives
the moor-hen her young, new life to redeem the old. But the
poet's own immediate human world holds no such consoling
image of life to balance death. There are only the soldiers, so
he turns aside, "caught / In the cold snows of a dream." Ire-
land in the civil war is unreal, a dream, cut off from instinctive health and growth, caught in the cold snow of violence
and death. Reality is the moor-hen guiding her young upon
the water.

31. *Swan and Shadow: Yeats's Dialogue with History* (Chapel Hill,
N. C., 1964), p. 26.

The Vast Idea

The theme is continued in the succeeding poem, *The Stare's Nest by My Window*. As the war proceeds, homes and houses fall, deserted ruins. But the natural cycle, oblivious of man's destruction, continues uninterrupted; the honey bees and birds build in the loosening masonry. Yeats says his own wall is loosening; and in one of his most poignant refrains, begs the honey bees "come build in the empty nest of the stare." Through cyclical process of sacred living things, he reveals his sense of loss, his sense of anguish—and his hope for some consolation.

Yeats's insistent theme of age is a particularization of the mythic apprehension of process. In *His Phoenix*, an old man thinks of his beloved when she was young and takes grudging consolation from process, from knowledge that "there'll be that crown, that barbarous crown [of beautiful women] through all the centuries." Several of his greatest poems dealing with age regard process not as decay or death balanced by new life but as the mystery of youth and age seen simultaneously as One, in the mythic sense of time. The speaker in *Girl's Song* asks: "When everything is told, / Saw I an old man young / Or young man old?" It is the same question that perplexes Yeats in *Among School Children* and *A Bronze Head*. In the former poem this simultaneous perception, should a mother have it of her new-born son, would be an agony as painful as the expression of Moneta's face, whose eyes behold a similar if vaster perception of process. In *A Bronze Head* simultaneous memories of the young and the aged Maud Gonne lead the poet to think "substance can be composite . . . in a breath / A mouthful held the extreme of life and death." "Who can tell," the poem asks, "Which of her forms has shown her substance right?" a question applicable to Keats's Cynthia-Indian Maid and to Lamia.

In the first of *Two Songs from a Play* and in *The Gyres* Yeats writes of history as cyclical process. When in the former poem Dionysus is slain, "all the muses sing / of Magnus Annus at the spring, / As though God's death were but a play"—which, with the rebirth of another god in another cycle, it might very well be thought. In *The Gyres*, with too

Chapter Three

forced a bravado, Yeats accepts the "Irrational streams of blood . . . staining earth" in the twentieth century because the end of an era is at hand and can only by followed by the return of an age valuing those Yeatsian ideals so sadly lacking in the poet's own time. The present is seen as a repetition of the past: "Empedocles has thrown all things about; / Hector is dead and there's a light in Troy" (Y, 291).

Early in the century, while developing his mature metaphysics, Yeats recognized his commitment to the apprehension of process:

The poet must not seek for what is still and fixed, for that has no life for him. . . . [He must] be content to find his pleasure in all that is forever passing away that it may come again, in the beauty of woman, in the fragile flowers of spring . . . he must endure the impermanent a little, for these things return. . . . Is it that all things are made by the struggle of the individual and the world, of the unchanging and the returning . . . and that the poet has made his home in the serpent's mouth?   (E, 287–88)

"The mirror-scalèd serpent," as he explained years later, "is multiplicity" (Y, 283), the unalterable fact of the Many, which pass away to return, a cycle symbolized by the serpent with its tail in its mouth. The poet, living in the serpent's mouth, accepts "the ring where everything comes round again" (E, 287).

Keats, too, announcing his poetic maturity in *Endymion,* celebrated process in what is perhaps the most magnificent passage in the poem, the Hymn to Pan. Pan, the traditional god of earth, becomes for Keats the god of process and of the poetry of earth, drawing from him his instinctive sense of mythical time:

> O thou, to whom
> Broad leaved fig trees even now foredoom
> Their ripen'd fruitage; yellow girted bees
> Their golden honeycombs; our village leas
> Their fairest blossom'd beans and poppied corn;
> The chuckling linnet its five young unborn
>
> . . . .
>
> yea, the fresh budding year
> All its completions—   (I, 251–60)

The Vast Idea

Rising to its climax, the Hymn asks Pan to tease us out of thought, as does eternity, with his mystery of process that can be intuited but never fully understood, while the life force in process, the kind of *power* discussed in chapter 2, renews itself perpetually:

> Be still the unimaginable lodge
> For solitary thinkings; such as dodge
> Conception to the very bourne of heaven,
> Then leave the naked brain: be still the leaven,
> That spreading in this dull and clodded earth
> Gives it a touch ethereal—a new birth:
> Be still a symbol of immensity;
> A firmament reflected in a sea;
> An element filling the space between;
> An unknown—   (1, 293–302)

"Immensity . . . firmament . . . sea": the words echo that "ocean dim sprinkled with many an isle" which spread awfully before Keats when he first announced his vast idea. And the Hymn itself repeats the celebration of the fusion of poetry and nature which he made in *Sleep and Poetry*:

> Sometimes it gives a glory to the voice,
> And from the heart up-springs "Rejoice! rejoice!"
> Sounds which will reach the Framer of all things. . . .
>   (lines 37–39)

When we perceive the syntax of process, "All about us," as Yeats wrote, "there seems to start up a precise inexplicable teeming life, and the earth becomes once more, not in rhetorical metaphor, but in reality, sacred" (EX, 369).

---------------------------- IV ----------------------------

"The Finer Tone"

Cassirer points out that in mythic thought the feeling of the solidarity of life—Yeats's unity of being—is so strong that it defies, even denies, the fact of death: "In a certain sense the whole of mythical thought may be interpreted as a constant

Chapter Three

and obstinate negation of the phenomenon of death."[32] As the previous sections of this chapter have shown, the chief instrument in this negation is metamorphosis, particularly in its several manifestations of process. There is, finally, the metamorphosis of life into life after death. In mythic consciousness, as Eliade says, "Death is another modality of human existence."[33] Mythic thought makes no clearer distinction between life and death than between sleeping and waking, relating them, as Cassirer notes, "not as being and nonbeing, but as two similar, homogenous parts of the same being."[34] Eliade's summary is, to the point: "Generation, death, and regeneration (=rebirth) were understood as three moments in a single mystery, and the entire spiritual effort of archaic man was exerted to show that there must be no intervals between these moments."[35]

Keats and Yeats, like the majority of men, share this refusal to admit the fact of death. In their thought, however, it takes a particular turn. They see that in a world structured by process, death is very often the simultaneous companion of fulfilled being. Keats implies, for example, in *After Dark Vapours* and the *Four Seasons* sonnet, that the moment of temporal death is also the moment of highest spiritual fulfillment possible within time. Placing supreme value on intensity (a topic of the next chapter), Keats and Yeats were able to see death, if met with lived intensity, not as a moment of final failure but as a moment of final success. It is in this sense that "Death is Life's high meed" (K, 470), a "luxury" to brood over like beauty (L2, 133). And it is in this sense that Keats's being "half in love with easeful death" is not the death wish that detractors of Romanticism are wont to call it.

Yeats sees that the very energy of being, the fire that sustains things, is also the source of their undoing; "beauty dies of beauty" (Y, 291).

32. *An Essay on Man*, pp. 83–84.
33. *The Sacred and the Profane*, p. 148.
34. *Philosophy of Symbolic Forms*, 2: 36–37.
35. *The Sacred and the Profane*, pp. 196–97. Eliade's concept of mythic time here becomes structurally analogous to Cassirer's.

The Vast Idea

> The painter's brush consumes his dreams;
> The herald's cry, the soldier's tread
> Exhaust his glory and his might:
> Whatever flames upon the night
> Man's own resinous heart has fed.
>
> (Y, 211)

The very activity and motion by which things express their essence will eventually lead on to the destruction of the form containing that essence. Things thus "unselve" themselves.

At the same time, however, their metamorphosis in death gives them even fuller being, for "being is only possessed completely by the dead" (E. 226). "What else can death be," Yeats asks, "but the beginning of wisdom and power and beauty?" (M, 115). The idea is embodied in *All Souls' Night*. The burden of the poem is that, compared to the dead, the living are incomplete. Yeats calls up those dear friends who spent their lives trying to learn what the dead know, those whose "elements have grown so fine" now that the mere fume of wine can give their palates sharpened by death an "ecstasy / No living man can drink from the whole wine" (Y, 226). For Yeats as for Keats, death is life's high meed.

In another of his poems Yeats accepts the mythic attitude to death defined by Cassirer and Eliade. The lower animals, he points out in *Death*, have no knowledge of death; but if a man understands metamorphic process ("Many times he died, / Many times rose again"), then he also "knows death to the bone"—knows, in other words, that "man has created death" (Y, 230); death is merely an idea in the mind of man. The same assertion occurs in *The Tower*:

> Death and life were not
> Till man made up the whole,
> Made lock, stock and barrel
> Out of his bitter soul. . . .
>
> (Y, 196)

Since wisdom, as Yeats said in *Blood and the Moon*, "is the property of the dead, / A something incompatible with life" (Y, 234), the living man is bitter in his incomprehension of the Whole. When he tries to "make up" the Whole, all he can

know are its parts ("lock, stock and barrel"), the halves of
life and death into which the Whole falls for the temporal intelligence. The lines imply that these seemingly opposite
halves are illusion, nonexistent except to the analytic intellect. The lines following are difficult: "And . . . being dead,
we rise, / Dream and so create / Translunar Paradise." But
in light of Yeats's concept of the stages of death (the dead
have only partial knowledge until the soul has fulfilled its
dreaming back and, come to full understanding, is then released into the Thirteenth Cone beyond life and death), they
imply that the newly dead, having only partial knowledge,
"dream" as those in life "dream"; they too must speculate
about the nature of the Whole. Hence the idea of paradise
held by the dead is similar to that held by the living, and in
both instances is "made up" of the only possible materials:
our highest moments, here in time. Of these great moments
"Man makes a superhuman / Mirror-resembling dream" (Y,
196–97), as Yeats says elsewhere. The idea is very similar
to that put forth by Keats in the last line and a half of the
Ode on a Grecian Urn: what, from the urn, we are able to
intuit or "dream" of the Whole is all we know on earth; yet it
is all we need to know to be assured that there is a "Translunar Paradise."

The mirror that the dream of Paradise resembles is our
own temporal existence at its finest moments. "I am orthodox," Yeats wrote, "and pray for the resurrection of the body,
and am certain that a man should find his Holy Land where
he first crept upon the floor" (E, 297). One of Keats's favorite
speculations took this bearing: "We shall enjoy ourselves here
after by having what we call happiness on Earth repeated in
a finer tone and so repeated" (L1, 185). Such a finer tone,
with its complement of beauty, is "the grandeur of the dooms
/ We have imagined for the mighty dead" (K, 65).

In *Broken Dreams* Yeats affirmed that "in the grave all, all
shall be renewed." Twenty years later that "all" is made even
more specific when Tom the Lunatic, seeing death in nature,
cries out against it:

The Vast Idea

> Whatever stands in field or flood,
> Bird, beast, fish or man,
> Mare or stallion, cock or hen,
> Stands in God's unchanging eye
> In all the vigour of its blood;
> In that faith I live or die. (Y, 264)

Keats generously grants immortality to all of nature in the ode *Bards of Passion and of Mirth*; heaven will contain trees, lawns, deer, flowers, birds. His favorite earthly analogue for heaven is the bower that contains these items. Yeats also thought the bower or garden one of man's favorite images for the mirror-resembling dream:

> Quattrocento put in paint
> On backgrounds for a God or Saint
> Gardens where a soul's at ease;
> Where everything that meets the eye,
> Flowers and grass and cloudless sky,
> Resemble forms that are or seem
> When sleepers wake and yet still dream,
> And when it's vanished still declare,
> With only bed and bedstead there,
> That heavens had opened.
> (Y, 342–43)

In Keats's heavenly garden, "the rose herself has got / perfume which on earth is not"; all things are repeated in a finer tone that makes death life's high meed. "Natural and supernatural with the self-same ring are wed . . . For things below are copies, the Great Smaragdine Tablet said" (Y, 283). Here, as Eliade says, there is no interval between life and death.

Yeats carries to its logical conclusion Keats's speculation on our earthly happiness being repeated in a finer tone: man will enjoy in heaven sexual as well as spiritual intercourse. His speaker Ribh, in a moment of vision, sees that "Godhead on Godhead in sexual spasm begot Godhead" (Y, 284). Pythagoras and Plotinus learn on landing in heaven that "nymphs and satyrs / Copulate in the foam" (Y, 324). Heaven is, indeed, "an improvement of sense—one listens to music, one does not read Hegel's logic" (LY, 781):

Chapter Three

When such bodies join
There is no touching here, nor touching there,
Nor straining joy, but whole is joined to whole;
For the intercourse of angels is a light
Where for its moment both seem lost, consumed.

(Y, 282)

Keats never goes so far, after the awkward eroticism of *En-dymion*. Yet the sexual passion depicted on the Grecian urn, itself an earthly analogue of a hoped for finer tone, makes it not unfair to say that Yeats's conviction never ceased being a part of his favorite speculations.

Chapter Four
The Great Moment

I
"There All the Gyres Converge in One"

When the elements of mythic apprehension operate simultaneously, a particular experience results, for which one can most easily use Yeats's term "the Great Moment" (E, 260). In this experience the self joins or is made ready to join the Other—either nature, art, or man—because the mode of apprehension employed reveals that eternal and sacred quality (or substance, perhaps), that unity of Being in which the subject and the object are embraced. In mythic thought the mode of apprehension through which the Great Moment occurs is metamorphic process, discussed in the preceding chapter. Awareness of process is the very agent of the experience in question, a field of vision in which all is seen as changing and, through recurrence, remaining, the Many paradoxically One. When the world is fully *felt* or intuited in this fashion, an intense sense of its harmonious operation results, accompanied by a moment when the whole of process is stationed, stopped in its passage through time: "All things hang like a drop of dew / Upon a blade of grass" (Y, 249).

Such moments require for their occurrence a paradoxical mood of both intensity and disinterestedness or stillness. They result not merely in a revelation of the solidarity of life but, through process, in an acceptance of life's inequities and so a fusion of joy and pain that Keats called "melancholy" and Yeats termed "tragic joy." Yeats said, and Keats would have agreed with him: "To me the supreme aim is an act of faith and reason to make one rejoice in the midst of tragedy" (DW,

12). For them, mythic apprehension allowed that act of faith, that kind of reason.

In communicating this experience the poems of Keats and Yeats will sometimes draw attention to or specify the particular elements of mythic thought; sometimes the poems specify only the structure that these elements share, a mediation of opposites. The poems will, in other words, make particular reference to process, metamorphosis, time, and the numinous; or they will simply speak of a moment or experience in which opposites of some kind are reconciled. The poem successfully rendering this Great Moment is structurally analogous to mythic narrative in Lévi-Strauss's definition, for such a poem, like a narrative myth, "always works from the awareness of opposition towards [its] progressive mediation"; its purpose is to provide a "model capable of overcoming a contradiction."[1] Myths create this model of mediation, says Lévi-Strauss, by their very *praxis*, the structure of action within them. In the Romantic poem this intention of mythic consciousness is generally achieved through image, through fellowship with the essence of some person, natural object, or work of art which has become a symbol for and seems to partake of the reality beyond time where contraries are permanently reconciled.

The experience of the Great Moment is not unique to Keats and Yeats, having been a commonplace in Christian and Buddhistic writers for centuries. In the Romantic period Blake called it the "Pulsation of the Artery," and Wordsworth spoke of such experience as "spots of time," "unknown modes of being." In Coleridge's theories of the symbol and of imagination occurs a similar reconciliation of opposites. Later in the century Browning spoke of "the infinite moment" and "the good minute." More influential, if less understood, was "the privileged moment" of Pater, himself the chief figure linking Keats and Yeats. In the twentieth century T. S. Eliot has called a generally similar experience "the still point," and

1. Claude Lévi-Strauss, "The Structural Study of Myth," in *Myth: A Symposium*, ed. Thomas A. Sebeok (Bloomington, Ind., 1965), pp. 99, 105.

one thinks at once of Joyce's concept of the epiphany.[2] That the Great Moment occurs in one mode or another in so much Romantic and modern literature suggests two things: the close relationship of Romantic poetry to mythic consciousness and the close relationship between much modern and Romantic literature.

In the Great Moment the chief antinomy overcome is that which has been central to my study: the separation of the subject and the object, the self and the world, generated by self-consciousness. In Keats and Yeats, however, there is a host of other contraries consequent upon this one. Since the Great Moment in their work represents a mediation of these opposites, it is not out of place to review them as background to that experience itself. Such review will lend greater point to seeing Lévi-Strauss's definition of mythic structure behind the Great Moment.

When Keats began writing, his use of contraries was little more than exercise in eighteenth-century antithesis; at that time he affirmed the muse would not "condescend / Mid contradictions her delights to lend" (K, 29). But a year later the reconciliation of opposing modes of perception was figured as a task necessary for Endymion's salvation, and the Cave of Quietude passage is more replete than any other in Keats's

2. Northrop Frye, *A Study of English Romanticism* (New York, 1968), pp. 158–59, distinguishes between the epiphany of Joyce and Wordsworth on the one hand and Keats on the other: "Keats's odes are epiphanic in a narrower and more traditional sense. They are not concerned with objects or experiences found at random, but with icons or presences which have been invoked and evoked by a magical spell, and held as a focus for meditation." Yeats is to be grouped with Keats in such a distinction. See Edward C. Jacobs, "Yeats and the Artistic Epiphany," *Discourse*, 12 (1969), 292–305.

Ethel Cornwell, *The "Still Point"* (New Haven, N. J., 1962), pp. 6–7, discusses Eliot's concept; her book explores in Coleridge and a group of twentieth-century writers a mode of apprehension somewhat similar to the Great Moment. See also Morris Beja, *Epiphany in the Modern Novel* (Seattle, 1972). The concept of epiphany is likewise central to James Benziger's *Images of Eternity* (Carbondale, Ill., 1962); he carries his argument on the topic to specifically Christian interpretation or, stopping short of that with Keats and Yeats, nevertheless argues for implicit Christianity, a position I find somewhat dubious.

work with oxymoron and verbal self-contradiction. By the time he wrote *The Eve of St. Agnes* his use of contraries had become one of the distinguishing characteristics of his imagery and diction. Three months later contraries became the structural components of the great odes, followed that summer by *Lamia*, into which, as in no other of his poems, the full gamut of contraries is structured: the immortal and the human, imagination and intellect, poetry and philosophy, permanence and change, dream and reality, love and ambition, contemplation and action, passion and thought, pleasure and pain, pursuit and satiety.

The list reads like one drawn from Yeats, in whose work we find inspiration and labor, the spontaneous and the studied, imagination and intellect, naiveté and sophistication, folk art and coterie art, the peasant and the aristocrat (generally sharing the same qualities), body and soul, character and personality, self and mask, the sordid present and the heroic past, contemplation and action or saint and swordsman; the list could be extended indefinitely.

At the turn of the century Yeats began to believe in the necessity of these contraries. In 1898 he wrote that "only imperfection in a mirror of perfection, or perfection in a mirror of imperfection, delights our frailty" (E, 150). In 1910 he was of the opinion that "all noble things are the result of warfare . . . the divisions of a mind within itself" (E, 321). When he came to formulate his thought in *A Vision* he wrote that the whole system was founded upon "the belief that the ultimate reality, symbolized as the Sphere, falls into human consciousness . . . into a series of antinomies" (v, 187); "human life is impossible without strife between the *tinctures*" (v, 79). "Every phase," he wrote at the end of his life, "has characteristic beauty—has not Nicholas of Cusa said reality is expressed through contradiction?"[3] If in the end, as chapter 1 has indicated, he gave the balance of his allegiance to the swordsman who lives in this world, against the saint who

---

3. *The Oxford Book of Modern Verse* (New York, 1936), p. xxxiii. The belief that "every phase has characteristic beauty" looks back to the subject of chapter 2.

would live in another, it was, as he said, "not without vacillation," and that vacillation was itself "perhaps the sole theme" (LY, 798).

In his prose Yeats was willing to concede that all contraries are necessarily a part of truth; but many of his greatest poems are loyal to one opposition at a time.[4] In Keats's mature work, by contrast, the loyalties vacillate so ambiguously that we cannot with authority assign any single belief to any single poem. (*Lamia* is a good example.) Richard Harter Fogle is surely correct in saying that "No poem contains all modes of experience, or even two experiences or ideas projected with equal force. The reconciliation of equal opposites is a theoretical, not an actual process; it would be colorless, odorless, tasteless, faceless,"[5] like Yeats's Thirteenth Cone or Shelley's deep truth that is imageless. At the same time there is still a disconcerting latitude of contraries in a late Keats poem. This fact makes one think that the exploration of conflict as the syntax of temporal existence was becoming for Keats—as it did become for Yeats—of equal interest with the reconciliation of opposites to be realized in a given poem.

The emotional mood prerequisite for the Great Moment is itself a reconciliation of opposites, of intensity on the one hand and disinterestedness or stillness on the other. The first term was a favorite in Keats's speculations and finds its parallel in Yeats's cry "intensity is all" and in his insistence on passion, to him "the essential" (LY, 791). Intensity or passion, when seen in others, is evidence of that energy or essence through which they partake of mythic Power; when felt within the perceiver, it puts him in touch with his Personality. Through passion, Yeats wrote, "men become conjoint to their buried selves" (A, 165), to the deepest source of their being. Intensity or passion is evidence of Being. When

---

4. At the same time his mature aesthetic, like his metaphysic, was the attempt to reconcile opposites. This position has been argued quite convincingly by Edward Engelberg, *The Vast Design: Patterns in W. B. Yeats's Aesthetic* (Toronto, 1964), who shows that no single contrary can be taken alone as final explanation of Yeats's attitude to a given aesthetic element.

5. "Keats's 'Ode to a Nightingale,'" *PMLA* 68 (1953): 214.

stillness is also felt, Being is contemplated and, these contrary emotional states experienced at once, the Great Moment is possible. "If your passion is but great enough"—and if it is coupled with contemplation—"it leads you to a country where there are many cloisters" (E, 181). "An individual with great emotional intensity might . . . give to all those separated elements and to . . . abstract love and melancholy, a symbolical, a mythological coherence" (A, 119). Intensity is a force for fusion through which the world, perceived as process and stationed at timeless moments, has mythological coherence.

Yeats portrays just this kind of vision through intensity in *An Irish Airman Foresees His Death*. Robert Gregory, swept up with the intensity of flying, is carried to an almost Olympian disinterestedness wherein he sees that death, in relationship to the intensity of the present, is no more than the fulfillment of life. The mythic sense of time comes into play.

> I balanced all, brought all to mind,
> The years to come seemed waste of breath,
> A waste of breath the years behind
> In balance with this life, this death.

The present moment is invested with past and future; neither equals the intensity of the airman's present flight; hence they are but "years" compared to the duration of the Great Moment —"this life"—which, by being so full, will become in self-exhaustion "this death." The intensity of the experience makes the airman ready for a union with that which lies beyond time and mortality. Yeats had prefigured the theme in a poem published five years earlier, *That the Night Come* (Y, 123):

> She lived in storm and strife,
> Her soul had such desire
> For what proud death may bring
> That it could not endure
> The common good of life,
> But lived as 'twere a king
> That packed his marriage day
> With banneret and pennon,
> Trumpet and kettledrum,

The Great Moment

> And the outrageous cannon,
> To bundle time away
> That the night come.

Here the soul would marry that which lies beyond time and mortality. Some fifteen years later he rendered the theme in prose: "Escape from time may be for individuals alone who know how to exhaust their possible lives, to set, as it were, the hands of the clock racing" (EX, 398). Such individuals know "that ecstasy . . . that extremity of life in which life seems to pass away like the phoenix in flame of its own lighting" (E, 57). In Yeats's eyes, Robert Gregory was such an individual:

> Some burn damp faggots, others may consume
> The entire combustible world in one small room
> As though dried straw, and if we turn about
> The bare chimney is gone black out
> Because the work had finished in that flare.
> Soldier, scholar, horseman, he
> As 'twere all life's epitome.
> What made us dream that he could comb grey hair?
>   (Y, 133)

As Keats wrote: "Verse, Fame, and Beauty are intense indeed, / But Death intenser—Death is Life's high meed" (K, 470).

Concomitant with passion or intensity is its seeming opposite, reverie or stillness. "I am certain," Yeats wrote, "that every high thing was invented in this way, between sleeping and waking (E, 277). "I am awake and asleep, at my moment of revelation, self-possessed in self-surrender" (E, 524). If passion is self-surrender, reverie is, paradoxically, a kind of self-possession; contrary emotional states are balanced, and the soul seems to hang "between sleeping and waking" (A, 227), "a state transcending sleep when forms, often of great beauty, appear minutely articulated in brilliant light" (E, 439). The imagination, thus liberated from the intellect and the will, receives images from the Great Memory. (Intellect and will return in sufficient degree, however, to prevent *hodos chameliontos*, Keats's "concatenation" discussed in chapter 3.) What Yeats is getting at by reverie seems paralleled by remarks in Keats: "Let us not therefore go hurrying about and collecting honey-bee like, buzzing here and there impatiently from a knowledge of what is to be arrived at: but let us open our leaves like a flower and be passive and receptive —budding patiently under the eye of Apollo and taking hints from every noble insect that favors us with a visit" (L1, 232). The passage may be compared to Yeats's remarks on rhythm, which possibly owe something to Wordsworth's discussion in the 1815 *Preface*: "The purpose of rhythm . . . is to prolong the moment of contemplation, the moment when we are both asleep and awake, which is the one moment of creation, by hushing us with alluring monotony, while it holds us waking by variety, to keep us in that state of perhaps real trance, in which the mind liberated from the pressure of the will is unfolded in symbols" (E, 159). "Is not sleep by the testimony of the poets our common mother?" he asks;[6] one thinks of the testimony of Keats's *Sleep and Poetry* and many references to creative sleep in his work. The wise passiveness that both poets describe is a kind of intense stillness within the self-possessed soul: "Nothing but stillness can remain when hearts are full / Of their own sweetness, bodies of their loveliness" (Y, 203). Yeats's most successful poem on this theme of stillness is *Long-Legged Fly*, familiar enough to require no commentary.

One of Keats's terms for this stillness or reverie was disinterestedness, which he rated the top of "spiritual honours" (L1, 205). Very few men, he felt, ever arrive at a complete disinterestedness: "Yet this feeling ought to be carried to its highest pitch, as there is no fear of its ever injuring society— which it would do I fear pushed to an extremity—For in wild nature the Hawk would lose his Breakfast of Robins and the Robin his of Worms. The Lion must starve as well as the swallow" (L2, 79). Disinterestedness should be pursued to the point where it reveals its own limits, its impossibility as an absolute standard for conduct if one is to survive. Just before that point, it will allow perception of process—the cycle of nature and the consolation that can be taken from process,

6. *Oxford Book of Modern Verse*, p. xxix.

the doctrine of reciprocity in the song of the Indian Maid. Hence it provides a vision by which one can accept the final necessity of doing without it for survival.

Disinterestedness is in one sense a name for the aesthetic distance by means of which one can see beauty in all things, even in a quarrel in the streets. It allows forgiveness, of others and of oneself. Such forgiveness was often necessary for Yeats before the Great Moment could come: "I enter upon it the moment I cease to hate" (M, 365); he does so in *Paudeen*, when he ceases to hate the shopkeeper, in *Demon and Beast*, and in *A Dialogue of Self and Soul*, when he ceases to hate himself.

The *Dialogue* begins with the Soul summoning the Self to climb the stair of spiritual transcendence, to "scorn the earth and intellect" and so be "delivered from the crime of death and birth" (the cyclical, determined process of nature; by implication, endless rebirth). The Soul would have the Self settle for nothing less than the Thirteenth Cone or sphere of Absolute Reality, where "intellect no longer knows / *Is* from *Ought*, or *Knower* from the *Known*." In this realm the world that we wish to have and that ought to be becomes the world that is, while subject and object, self and world coincide. It seems exactly what is desired. But the Self does not desire it, for the juncture with the One that the Soul proposes is not a union of two but the submergence of the Self and its world into the One. Darkness is indeed an emblem for the Soul, for darkness obliterates the separate identity of things. In the heaven of the Soul the world of Ought is; but in that heaven, the world of Self is not. If the Soul does not see this clearly, the Self does, and so pays no attention to the Soul's argument. Believing that it cannot exist in that heaven of the Soul, the Self accepts, in temporal images, mortal paradigms for a heaven in which its own nature and its own world would exist with the One. Works of art are such paradigms. Hence the Self holds as its emblems not the darkness and the tower of the Soul but Sato's "consecrated blade" and its embroidered sheath "from some court lady's dress"; male and female, war and love, interknit. (The sword, ironically, is shaped like the tower and is "still razor-keen" while the tower is "crumbling.") The sword, "unspotted by the centuries," is sufficient symbol for the timeless; the dress, "heart's purple," is poignant symbol for time and mortality. With these emblems the Self claims "as by a soldier's right / A charter to commit the crime once more . . . content to live it all again." What if it "be life to pitch / Into the frog-spawn" of mortality and endless process, "the blind man's ditch" of finite human knowledge? Man must accept "the fury and the mire of human veins" (Y, 243), accept process even when its cycle seems a tragic doom. To will acceptance of the mire and ditch is to transcend them and hence is to know joy and tragedy at once, an emotion more intense, more full of the mystery of being, more close to the Soul's heaven, than either emotion alone. Like a sacramental vision, this reconciliation in the Great Moment blesses:

> I am content to follow to its source
> Every event in action or in thought;
> Measure the lot; forgive myself the lot!
> When such as I cast out remorse
> So great a sweetness flows into the breast
> We must laugh and we must sing,
> We are blest by everything,
> Everything we look upon is blest.

Yeats shows toward himself a similar forgiveness in the course of *Vacillation*, a poem which, as its title indicates, moves through the contraries to be reconciled in the Great Moment. The first section presents the problem: "Between extremities / Man runs his course"; at the end of life "A brand, or flaming breath" destroys all the "antinomies," and "The body calls it death, / The heart remorse." To the body, its end is death, a finality. The heart would seem to concur; unable at death to make amends, it feels that remorse which will recur in section v. "But," the speaker asks, "if these be right / What is joy?" The rest of the poem, moving in vacillation from section to section, renders very nearly the same answer as *A Dialogue of Self and Soul*.

That answer is most clearly imaged in the second section.

The Great Moment

The tree described introduces the vegetation imagery which, with the image of fire, will recur in all sections but the last. The green foliage is physical life. The fire, as it was in section I, is the agent of death; later in the poem it also represents the soul or spirit. The double meaning of fire contributes to Yeats's rejection of the Soul's argument in section VII. The tree in section II is "half all glittering flame and half all green / Abounding foliage moistened with the dew. . . ." Water is associated with vegetation as a symbol of life. This fabulous tree is the very image of the mythic sense of life, death, and rebirth: "half and half consume what they renew," dying each other's life, living each other's death:

> And he that Attis's image hangs between
> That staring fury and the blind lush leaf
> May know not what he knows, but knows not grief.

Attis, an Asia Minor vegetation god, is himself a symbol of the cyclical process, life and death, represented by the tree. Hence to hang his image between the "glittering flame" and "green / Abounding foliage" is tantamount to proclaiming one's faith in process and the world of time, believing that the concept of process can reconcile "All those antinomies / Of day and night" (section I). He who so believes "May know not what he knows"—any paradoxical reconciliation to be found will not necessarily be amenable to the discursive intellect—"but knows not grief." However one is to define the emotion experienced in reconciliation, it is not grief, the "remorse" of section I that recurs in section V. This point is particularly important, in light of the Attis cult. In the yearly festival the god's followers castrate themselves. That they know, according to Yeats, no grief after such an event—an event separating them from the very fertility they celebrate—looks forward to the theme of acceptance found in section VI. They can, as it were, will the very sterility that old age will bring them and, like the aging poet, still affirm nature, time, and mortality. After the fabulous tree of section II, the "brand, or flaming breath" that causes death in section I is ambiguous and disturbing. A brand, of course, is a flaming stick—the miraculous tree in miniature. Process itself causes death; life dies of life. Yeats will accept and affirm this in section VI. Or is the event of death a "flaming breath"—the breath of the spirit longing for another home, the breath of God, or the mortal breath that consumes itself like the burning brand? The poem, I think, gives no answer.

Section III unweaves the flame and the green leaf, siding with each by turn. "Joy" is first thought to lie in intense, flame-like activity for material goods and worldly fame. "And yet . . . All women dote upon an idle man"; now it seems that joy is the quiet unpremeditated living of a green tree. But the vacillations run their course, for immediately Yeats adds that the children of women won in idleness "need a rich estate." The first stanza ends in contraries: "No man has ever lived that had enough / Of children's gratitude," which argues for the first mode of living, "or women's love," which argues for the second. In this quandary, Yeats advises one to throw off "Lethean foliage" and "begin the preparation for . . . death. . . ." Is he rejecting the foliage of time, this world and mortality altogether, or merely "Lethean" foliage? The second stanza suggests the latter. Foliage is "Lethean" when we let the love of life blind or drug us to mortality, when we seek to separate the two halves of the tree and take the foliage, leaving the flame. We must live always aware of death and perform work "suited for such men as come / Proud, open-eyed and laughing to the tomb." The section does not specify what such work would be, but it says clearly that any other work is "extravagance of breath," akin presumably to the labor for "gold and silver" and "ambition" in stanza 1, that work itself related to the "glittering flame" of section II, the "flaming breath" of section I. Such labor is a waste, a death-in-life that leads to death directly rather than through living life well. When life dies of life, as it does for Robert Gregory in earlier poems, a man goes "proud, open-eyed and laughing to the tomb." Here at the end of section III, the poem has discovered a kind of joy, an answer to the question posed in section I.

The next three sections form a unit, section IV presenting simple joy, section V remorse, and section VI tragic joy, a

union of the emotion in the two preceding sections. Section
IV is perhaps the most ambiguous section of the poem. Certainly it records a great joy, even a kind of Great Moment;
but there is almost nothing in it to suggest the reconciliation
of opposites, the awareness of process, or the fusion of joy
and pain in tragic joy that usually attend the Great Moment.

> My fiftieth year had come and gone,
> I sat, a solitary man,
> In a crowded London shop,
> An open book and empty cup
> On the marble table-top.

> While on the shop and street I gazed
> My body of a sudden blazed;
> And twenty minutes more or less
> It seemed, so great my happiness,
> That I was blessèd and could bless.

It is true that when Yeats's "body of a sudden blazed" he became himself like the tree in section II; and he had drained
his cup, taken the water of life into himself. But the experience is curiously unrelated to any cause, and when it is followed in the next section by a mood of remorse and near despair, the context suggests that it is a "Lethean" joy, no answer to the question at the heart of the poem. Just as he did in
section III, Yeats has again split his tree, as it were, separating
moods that must ultimately be, like the tree, one.

In section V the foliage imagery returns, but only glimpsed,
for the heart is so full of remorse that "I cannot look thereon." With section VI the poem finds the joy, now tragic joy,
imaged by the tree in section II. Observing "a rivery field"
(the water again mixed with foliage) and smelling "an odour
of the new-mown hay," the speaker—like Keats in the ode *To
Autumn*—cries acceptance: "Let all things pass away." The
last stanza of the section is the turning point of the poem:

> From man's blood-sodden heart are sprung
> Those branches of the night and day
> Where the gaudy moon is hung.
> What's the meaning of all song?
> "Let all things pass away."

The lines recapitulate the poem's central theme to this point:
the damp flaring tree of section ɪɪ is the human heart itself, in
which are rooted the "extremities" of section ɪ, the "antinomies / Of day and night." The human condition is one of
opposites, their only reconciliation the activity of the imagination (here, "the moon"), particularly in its mode of mythic
apprehension (the image of Attis in section ɪɪ). When the
mythic imagination understands process and the interconnection of life and death, it can accept death, which becomes its
theme: "Let all things pass away." As so often in Yeats, "joy"
is the moment of insight into process whereby "Chance" becomes one with "Choice." Only to the uninformed heart is
the end of life "remorse" (section ɪ). To a heart informed,
mutability can be accepted, even affirmed. This theme is announced first by "the great lord of Chou," next by "some conqueror," and last by Yeats himself, in the lines quoted above;
it is documented objectively and then, at the poem's climax,
subjectively declared. Section vɪ thus brings together the innocent joy of section ɪv and the remorse of section v, reconciling them in what Yeats calls elsewhere "tragic joy."

The last two sections of the poem, vɪɪ and vɪɪɪ, together
form an envoi. Section vɪɪ, a brief dialogue between the Soul
and the Heart, restates the dialectic of the poem and the affirmative position declared by the informed heart. The Soul,
misunderstanding the Heart's cry in the previous section
("Let all things pass away"), thinks it has found an opening
and importunes: "Seek our reality, leave things that seem."
But the heart knows that the soul's reality is an imageless
truth that would leave it without a theme, "struck dumb in
the simplicity of fire!" "Look on that fire," the Soul cries,
echoing the "staring fury" of the fire in section ɪɪ. But Yeats
sides with "the blind lush leaf": "What theme had Homer
but original sin?" The fire of the pure spirit, the spirit of the
saint, is no theme for the poet; to the spiritual fire he must
add the fire of human passion, of "original sin."

In section vɪɪɪ the mystic Catholic Von Hügel is cast in the
role of the Soul. But the dialogue is over and the section is a
monologue dismissing Christianity and, as in the previous

section, telling why. Yeats accepts the Christian miracles, and he knows that his heart, when troubled by remorse as in section 1, could find in the Christian heaven an answer to the question "what is joy?" But, he says, he plays "a predestined part." His destiny is to be a poet, loyal to Attis's image and the moon. This destiny means accepting the green of the tree as well as its flame, for the whole tree is the necessary symbol for the predestined human condition.

In *A Dialogue of Self and Soul* and *Vacillation*, Yeats finds the Great Moment in what he later called "tragic joy," an experience that arises from and partakes of both passionate intensity and stillness. He defines tragedy as a "passionate art" that sets us in "the intensity of trance" (E, 245); it is "a reverie of passion that mounts and mounts till grief itself has carried [the soul] beyond grief into pure contemplation" (E, 239). His concept of tragedy is, as B. L. Reid has noted, lyric rather than dramatic.[7]

Passion is, of course, *energy* itself, and "when its limit is reached it may become a pure aimless joy," as in section IV of *Vacillation*; at such moments "It has, as it were, thrust up its arms toward angels who have . . . returned into themselves in an eternal moment" (EX, 449). Since "the will, or energy, is greatest in tragedy" (EX, 449), tragedy must lead on to the same joy, the same moment. "No tragedy is legitimate unless it leads some character to his final joy" (EX, 448). The joy of tragedy, however, is "not joy as we understand that word, but ecstasy, which is from the contemplation of things vaster than the individual," a passion "rejecting character" (A, 286). Yeats's emphasis is on a passion so powerful that individual Character is subsumed in the representatively human, in Personality. Tragedy deals not with the man or even with men but with the ground of being—that "mould ethereal" as Keats called it—which all men share. The merely individual mind

7. *William Butler Yeats: The Lyric of Tragedy* (Norman, Okla., 1961), p. 56. Reid's work is an excellent study of Yeats's uses of the term and its variety of tones. Arra Gareb, *Beyond Byzantium: The Last Phase of Yeats's Career* (DeKalb, Ill., 1969), investigates the theme of acceptance in the mature work of Yeats, covering much of the ground in Reid's earlier work.

becomes a vehicle for the *anima mundi*, and through the Great Moment one is made ready to join himself with the Other or is at the threshold of such union.

II

"Fellowship Divine"

In the Great Moment the self joins or is made ready to join the Other. No clearer expression of this can be found in Keats and Yeats than the famous "fellowship with essence" passage in *Endymion* (1, 777–842). Reference to the passage was made in chapter 2, as part of my argument there that Keats meant by "essence" the immanent Power or universal Energy with which, in mythic apprehension, objects are invested. The "fellowship" that the passage describes may now be considered in some detail. The passage begins:

> Wherein lies happiness? In that which becks
> Our ready minds to fellowship divine,
> A fellowship with essence; till we shine,
> Full alchemiz'd and free of space. Behold
> The clear religion of heaven! Fold
> A rose leaf round thy finger's taperness,
> And soothe thy lips. . . .

And, Endymion continues, when music enters the winds, unbinding "with a sympathetic touch . . . Eolian magic from their lucid wombs," old songs will waken older stories and an older feeling of immanence that has since passed away. If we feel these things,

> —that moment we have stept
> Into a sort of oneness, and our state
> Is like a floating spirit's.

As the concrete and ideal come together in this apprehension of the object, so does the perceiving subject, its quest for transcendental evidence satisfied, come together with the object, becoming "full alchemiz'd" in an experience which, if

intense enough, can by extension reconcile other of life's opposites and allow a feeling of timelessness in time, of being
"free of space." Such an experience is the Great Moment.
"That which becks / Our ready minds" to the Great Moment of "fellowship divine" is any object manifesting the
numinous. Keats has listed material objects (the rose leaf)
and aesthetic objects (music, song, legend).

> But there are
> Richer entanglements, enthrallments far
> More self-destroying, leading, by degrees,
> To the chief intensity . . .

and that is fellowship with other persons, in friendship and
love. Because of the word "degrees" and Keats's description
of the passage as setting forth "gradations of Happiness even
like a kind of Pleasure Thermometer" (L1, 218), some critics
have been led to argue for a Neoplatonic hierarchy of objects.
But their argument must find its evidence in reading "essence" Neoplatonically, a reading I find oversimple. Furthermore, there is nothing in Keats's term "degrees" or in his
thermometer metaphor to demand a change in kind rather
than a change in degree. The change is not in the *quality* of
the objects, all of which are charged with essence; the change
is in the *quantity* of the response. There is evidence for this
in one of his lesser sonnets; it begins:

> Of late two dainties were before me plac'd
> Sweet, holy, pure, sacred and innocent,
> From the ninth sphere to me benignly sent
> That Gods might know my own particular taste.
> First the soft bag-pipe . . .
> The Stranger next . . .
> . . . .
> Alas! I could not choose.   (K, 537)

Clearly the aesthetic object is here as desirable as the person.
"Intensity" was for Keats a great value, but it was not a Neoplatonic moral value. The fellowship with persons is more intense than it is with natural or aesthetic objects because of its
potential for longer duration. In the reciprocal greeting of the

spirit, each person feeds the other and, as he says at the end of the passage, "Life's self is nourished by its proper pith, / And we are nurtured like a pelican brood" on the "unsating food" that is the essence of the other.

In the Neoplatonic reading of the passage, the self is seen as dissolving into the other, a mystical fusion of subject and object in which separate identities are obliterated. Building on the phrase "self-destroying," this reading ignores all the evidence which shows how that phrase is to be understood. There is, first, the word "entanglement": both subject and object retain some aspect of their own identity. Second, the passage clearly states that it is not the lover but love itself, the middle term between lover and beloved, into which "we *blend*, / *Mingle*, and so become *a part*" (italics added). Yeats, writing of his fellowship with Maud Gonne, described the same separateness-in-union: "it seemed that our two natures blent / . . . Into the yolk and white of the one shell" (y, 213). The egg is one, but the yolk and the white retain their own identity. In *A Vision* he wrote: "though there is still separation from the loved object, love accepts the separation as necessary to its own existence" (v, 136). Philip Wheelwright, in another context, has expressed this well: "If there is complete identification, the self becomes lost in its object and no longer confronts it; the poetic mode of consciousness becomes submerged in the mystical. . . ."[8] Fearing just this submergence, Keats wrote to Fanny Brawne: "It seems to me that a few more moments thought of you would uncrystallize and dissolve me—I must not give way to it" (L2, 142). The subject and the object, as he says in the passage a few lines later, "interknit" in what he earlier called "*a sort* of oneness" (italics added).

The passage describes a union which is a transformation of self, not its obliteration. The individual self-conscious ego is surrendered, its intentions are relaxed that the deeper self may come into play. The numinous quality of the Other enthralls the superficial self into a kind of quiescence (it is in

8. *The Burning Fountain* (Bloomington, Ind., 1954), p. 80.

this sense that love is "self-destroying"); and in the Great Moment of union, what Yeats called the Character is "full alchemiz'd," transformed through the released activity of the deeper self, the Personality. Through the elevation of the Moment, we stand "full alchemiz'd and free of space." The noun means here, I think, *time*, as it so often does in Keats (in fourteen of thirty occurrences). Certainly one of the chief characteristics of the unifying Great Moment is a sense of timelessness, or "the disengaging of a soul from place and history, its suspension in a beautiful or terrible light to await the Judgment" (E, 339), as Yeats wrote of art, a vehicle of the Great Moment. As in witnessing the greatest drama, one is "carried beyond time and persons [i.e., Character] to where passion . . . becomes wisdom" (E, 239).

In summarizing one of the Pantanjali commentaries, Yeats sets forth the stages of concentration that lead to this timeless state; the summary stirs echoes of Keats's "fellowship with essence" passage:

The first is the fixing of attention upon some place or object. . . . The second stage is this identity between idea and fact, between thought and sense. . . . The third stage is . . . complete disappearance of all but this identity . . . the man has disappeared as the sculptor in his statue, the musician in his music. One remembers the Japanese philosopher's saying "What the artist perceives through a medium, the saint perceives immediately."

(E, 461–62)

The fourth state comes when "all these states are as a single timeless act, and that act is pure or unimpeded personality, all existence brought into the words: 'I am.' " This state, he adds, is probably "an all but unattainable ideal . . . touched or it may be symbolized at some moment when some quality of life flowers" (E, 463). "All could be known or shown / If time were but gone" (Y, 253), if "time itself would be annihilate" (K, 465).

Keats wrote his brother Tom: "June 26—I merely put [the date] *pro forma*, for there is no such thing as time and space, which by the way came forcibly upon me on seeing for the first hour the Lake and Mountains of Winander—I cannot describe them—they surpass my expectation—beautiful water—shores and islands green to the marge" (L1, 298). Here the scene of still water and islands causes the experience of a timeless moment reconciling opposites: views of the lake, he adds, "make one forget the divisions of life. . . ." In *Sleep and Poetry*, the sonnet on Chapman's Homer, and elsewhere, he had used just such imagery of water and islands to symbolize the "vast idea" of the Great Moment and of process which reconciles the divisions of life. Both in the poetry and in the actual scene his sensual vision is refined, as he says in the letter, to the point where it perceives "the wonders of the great Power" (L1, 299). The Great Moment, revealing this immanent Power in things, has prepared him for union with the Other.

In his mature work Yeats came to use the sexual experience as an analogue for the Great Moment. Keats's fellowship with essence is carried to its logical conclusion. *Solomon and the Witch* is one of the earliest annunciations of the theme (1921). The poem renders through dialogue Yeats's speculation that the love-bed may offer the closest temporal equivalent this side of the grave, of the Great Moment. To the act of love

> each [lover] an imagined image brings
> And finds a real image there;
> Yet the world ends when these two things,
> Though several, are a single light,
> When oil and wick are burned in one.

Just as the two lovers join yet keep their identities, so the real and the ideal coalesce in balancing unity. If that perfect balance can be found, "Chance" or the real lover is "at one with Choice at last," with the ideal lover, and "All that the brigand apple brought / And this foul world were dead at last." The ground of this unity is again the universal Energy of which their deeper selves partake (the source, perhaps, of the "imagined image"). It is this that spoke through the Witch when, at the climax of their lovemaking, "I suddenly cried out in a strange tongue, not his, not mine."

The Great Moment

In 1926 Yeats wrote: "One feels at moments as if one could with a touch convey a vision—that the mystic way and sexual love use the same means—opposed yet parallel existences" (LY, 715). He wrote in *A Vision*: "The marriage bed is the symbol of the solved antinomy, and were more than symbol *could a man there lose and keep his identity*, but he falls asleep" (v, 52, the added italics recalling again my epigraph from Malraux). Sex as the Great Moment occupies many of the short lyrics that make up the sequences *A Man Young and Old, Words for Music Perhaps* and *A Woman Young and Old, Supernatural Songs, The Three Bushes*, and other separate lyrics in these mature volumes. By the time of *Words for Music Perhaps* (the Crazy Jane poems), the sexual act is decidedly a sacramental image.[9]

The first of the *Supernatural Songs, Ribh at the Tomb of Baile and Aillinn*, is one of Yeats's most remarkable uses of the sexual analogue. Here he would have us witness the perfect balanced union sought by Solomon and the Witch. It takes place, however, not between the earthly lovers but their "pure substance" transformed in the finer tone, after death. The heterodox Christian Ribh turns the pages of his holy book in the light cast by the lovers' consummation. Co-present with this Great Moment is the mythic sense of time. Ribh's monologue goes from the present to the historical past of Baile and Aillinn, to the timeless recreation of their spirits, and thence again to the present, making all time present time. Furthermore, the moment of the poem is "the anniversary of their death, / The anniversary of their first embrace"; time bends back to the renewing moment of creation, itself a fusion of death and rebirth. In this return to the renewing moment, two acts of generation exist simultaneously, the consummation of the spirit lovers and the creation of wisdom in the

---

9. William V. Spanos, "Sacramental Imagery in the Middle and Late Poetry of W. B. Yeats," *TSLL* 4 (1962): 224. Arguing from "Leda and the Swan," Spanos writes, p. 223: "Yeats came consciously to conceive of the sexual act as sacramental in the same sense that the eating of the god in primitive ritual was sacramental." The point is suggestive, but in basing it on *Leda and the Swan* Spanos begs the question of the poem's last lines, assuming an affirmative answer to the question there posed.

poet-priest Ribh.[10] The natural world itself has prefigured the lovers' union in the Great Moment: "all know what leaf and twig, / What juncture of the apple and the yew, / Surmount their bones." In the very choice of plants, sex (life) and death come together.

Chosen is another poem in which the speaker, through perception of process, moves to the Great Moment, figured again in sexual terms. The woman begins by saying: "The lot of love is chosen. I learnt that much / Struggling for an image on the track / Of the whirling Zodiac." She would find an image to embody the meaning of her love in time, where all is flux and change. The image she finds arises at the poem's end through the image of time itself, the Zodiac. It is fitting, then, that her concern in the first of the two stanzas be with the Zodiac, the cycle of seasons and time. As if she were thinking of the symbolic figures for each month of the Zodiac, she transforms herself and her lover into the protagonists of nature myth, into Zodiacal figures. Like the sun, her lover sinks to her bed at dark, finding "a subterranean rest / On the maternal midnight of my breast / Before I had marked him on his northern way." He departs like and with the sun but returns to her body, to an earth goddess, subterranean, maternal; she is also, by implied contrast, the moon.

The last line of the first stanza is ambiguous and must be seen in context:

> Scarce did he my body touch,
> Scarce sank he from the west
> Or found a subterranean rest
> On the maternal midnight of my breast
> Before I had marked him on his northern way,
> And seemed to stand although in bed I lay.

The departure in the penultimate line implies that with her love and yearning she was drawn after him, pulled figurative-

---

10. T. K. Dunseath, "Yeats and the Genesis of Supernatural Song," *ELH* 28 (1961): 399–416, analyzes the mode of time structuring the Songs, especially the first of them. Though he makes no special reference to mythic time, he shows clearly that that is the sense of time operative in the poems.

ly into standing position by her attachment to him. The parallel clauses beginning with "scarce" seem so obvious that the reader, supplying the absent comma after "breast" required by grammar, paraphrases the passage in this fashion: "Scarce did we touch, scarce did he come to my breast, before he left and I seemed to stand." But Yeats omits that comma—and supplies one after "way," making it impossible for the subject of "seemed" to be immediately clear. The ambiguity of Yeats's punctuation, then, suggests another reading: it is not merely in his departure but also in the Great Moment of sexual consummation ("Scarce did he my body touch") that the woman "seemed to stand although in bed I lay." It is into that present moment of their union that she projects his future departure.

In this reading the first stanza ends with a Great Moment, just as the second will:

> I take
> That stillness for a theme
> Where his heart my heart did seem
> And both adrift on the miraculous stream
> Where—wrote a learned astrologer—
> The Zodiac is changed into a sphere.

Here at the close of the poem the speaker finds her image for the Great Moment of love: the Zodiac—the cycles, wheels, and gyres of temporal existence—changes into the sphere, Yeats's favorite symbol for the transcendent Absolute, the *There* (Y, 284) beyond time. The Zodiac-sphere image, like the theme of completion in the Robert Gregory poems, recaptures that high Renaissance theme in Marvell's famous image: "Thus, though we cannot make our Sun / Stand still, yet we will make him run." Yeats caught the tone in his cry to "animate / The trivial days and ram them with the sun" (Y, 245). He wrote in *A Vision* that the Soul's object is "to pass rapidly around its circle and find freedom from that circle" (V, 236). Time may approach eternity through an intensity that makes of time a movement so swift that one seems to be on all points of the periphery at once.

Paradoxically, however, it is not swift energetic motion

that the speaker takes for her theme but "stillness"—that stillness "where his heart my heart did seem . . . both adrift . . ." She is not describing the moment of sexual union but the time after it, the hours before dawn when, their passion fulfilled, they lay embracing in a more profoundly emotional union. In these hours when they seem to drift, free of time, she is aware that he will leave her: "I struggled with the horror of daybreak . . ." So begins the second stanza. But she can accept that now; knowing their union soon must end makes this after time even more precious. Hence she adds, in the same sentence, "I chose it for my lot!" She has learned that "Chance" must become one with "Choice." When she can will her fate, in a moment of stillness added to intensity, she finds not only her image but, by implication, a Great Moment far exceeding the Great Moment of their sexual consummation. Here is the profound insight of the poem, somewhat unique in Yeats, who usually finds the Great Moment in sexual union itself, not in the different sort of union that follows it. Here, too. is probably the chief reason for the syntactic ambiguity of stanza one. Yeats punctuates there to imply the sexual union but does not want to bring it into climactic prominence, for his real theme and climax is the Great Moment after sexual union, a moment in which the speaker, her will having chosen the lot of love, comes to greater understanding.

Stanza 1. then. describes obliquely the moment of sexual union and the insight that comes with it: her lover will leave her shortly. Stanza 2 describes the union after sexual consummation and the insight that comes with it: she must accept her lover's departure. To the intensity of the union in stanza 1, now diminished, she brings the stillness after sex (already prefigured in the "rest" of stanza 1); in this paradoxical mood she finds her image. Her struggle with daybreak done, through her acceptance of the cycle of time, her struggle to find an image is likewise completed; that image merges from the very Zodiac with which she began. The stream of time is no longer "whirling," as in stanza 1, but is instead "miraculous."

The Great Moment

Yeats's finest poem using the sexual analogue is the magnificent sonnet *Leda and the Swan*, one of his greatest works. The poem recalls Eliade's remark that "myth describes the various and sometimes dramatic irruptions of the sacred into the world."[11] So brilliantly does the octave of the sonnet record an instance of this dramatic irruption that this may well seem to be the subject of the poem. This initial response, however, ignores the sestet, where the poem's real theme emerges. That theme is the mythic apprehension of time which leads to the Great Moment, and the rape is merely symbolic of that true subject: just as Zeus impregnates Leda in the octave, so in the first three lines of the sestet the future impregnates the present (or vice versa). The moment of sexual climax is seen simultaneously as the end of one event (the rape itself) and the beginning of new life (Helen and Clytemnestra) which, in turn, will be the end of a civilization (Troy). Helen's conception is the end of Troy, "the broken wall, the burning roof and tower," just as her sister's conception is "Agamemnon dead." Leda's womb becomes a microcosm of process, of the mythic interconnection of birth and death.

But the sestet presses on beyond the mythic concept of time to the question that defines the poem's theme: "Did she put on his knowledge with his power / Before the indifferent beak could let her drop?" Did *she*, in other words, recover the mythic consciousness of the gods, in particular the sense of time? Certainly she experienced the numinous, the union of the self with the Other. Did she, however, have the knowledge enormous that comes to Apollo in *Hyperion?* The poem's profundity lies, I think, in its refusal to assume that the experience of divine Power automatically entails divine knowledge. Was the moment for Leda anything more than an extravagant physical union? Was it experience as well as extraordinary sensation? This is the question, I think, that Yeats would ask the modern man who believes himself to have experienced the numinous or holy in Dionysian sensual frenzy. The very casual verb "put on," while it is meant to parallel the physical putting on of Zeus's body over hers, sug-

11. *The Sacred and the Profane* (New York, 1961), p. 97.

— 143 —

gests that she did not gain this knowledge. It is we who, through the poem, have the experience of knowledge that may have eluded Leda. Through mythic consciousness, as Eliade says, "one attains the beginning of Time [here, the moment of conception] and enters the Timeless—the eternal present" of the Great Moment.[12] Without that experience the poem will seem to be little more than the record of a rape.

Even in the drama of the octave, mythic apprehension is present. Each of its quatrains exhibits the double sense of awe felt before Power: attraction and withdrawal in fear. In the first quatrain the physical assault of Power is so sudden that Leda's reactions are hardly yet emotional. But the double sense of awe is there, the words "blow," "beating," "staggering" countered by "her thighs caressed." In the second quatrain an emotional response has come into play: her fingers are "terrified," lost (or "vague") in "that white rush," but the bird is now "the feathered glory," not a thing to fear totally. Both quatrains end with images of union that prefigure the climactic moment, the second expressing greater physical closeness than the first. In line 4 "He holds her helpless breast upon his breast." Critics have commented on the ambiguous position of "helpless," which describes not merely her breast but the fashion in which Zeus holds her; it has even been suggested that Zeus himself is helpless, caught in the throes of his passion. In line 8 it is her heart within her breast that feels "the strange heart beating where it lies."

The mythic theme is continued to the end. The "indifferent beak" is not only the god's spent sexual passion but, in the real theme, the passing or fading of the numinous moment. Leda is "dropped" from sacred time—from *ek-stasis*, a standing out, "being so caught up"—back into profane time and consciousness. The greatness of the poem is not merely in its execution but in its having employed a metaphoric vehicle rich enough to convey so many aspects of its theme, mythic apprehension.

Though he has no instances so dramatic, so fully realized, Keats also sees in sex the Great Moment and uses it for sym-

12. *Myth and Reality* (New York, 1963), p. 86.

The Great Moment

bol in his work. In *Endymion* the Indian Maid makes the same high claim for love as the chief intensity that Endymion himself made earlier in his speech on happiness. The love-dream in the poem is largely an extended metaphor for the kind of visionary experience first clearly articulated in *Sleep and Poetry* and serves to dramatize the emotional and psychological reality of that experience.[13] Elsewhere Keats imagines moments of eternal love. Cupid and Psyche are seen in the second stanza of the *Ode to Psyche* as having neither just completed nor just commenced loving; rather, they are enjoying love in a finer tone, without beginning or end, in a timeless moment, rather like the lovers on the Grecian urn. It is a passion Keats wished for himself when, in the *Bright Star* sonnet, he would be pillowed on Fanny's breast, "Awake for ever in a sweet unrest, / Still, still to hear her tender-taken breath, / And so live ever—or else swoon to death"(к, 475).

Yeats, by contrast, is more realistic about the sexual Great Moment possible in time, knowing that though boy and girl may cry "Forever," they will still awake "Ignorant what Dramatis Personae spake" (y, 286). The voice of the Other may speak through both at the Great Moment, joining boy and girl, but at best the union is temporary. Love may make "two things, / Though several . . . a single light" (y, 175), yet "Love no more than Discord [is] the changeless eternity" (v, 247). The physical union of man and woman is merely "a symbol of that eternal instant where the antinomy is resolved. It is not the resolution itself" (v, 214). Keats also knew this truth, which is among the lessons of *La Belle Dame Sans Merci*. One should remember that nowhere in the great odes is earthly love contemplated as genuine alleviation of human woe.

It is not only with friends and lovers that one joins in the Great Moment. One may also join with natural landscapes,

13. Stuart M. Sperry, Jr., "The Allegory of Endymion," *SIR* 2 (1962): 49. Sex seems, as well, to figure as an analogue for the act of artistic creation. Mario D'Avanzo, *Keats's Metaphors for the Poetic Imagination* (Durham, N. C., 1967), has noted how often it appears in conjunction with some story or tale.

natural objects, or aesthetic objects, finding "that union with
created things which assuredly must precede the soul's union
with the uncreated spirit" (E, 79). Yeats's poem *Stream and
Sun at Glendalough* describes such a union with the landscape:

> Through intricate motions ran
> Stream and gliding sun
> And all my heart seemed gay:
>
> . . . .
>
> What motion of the sun or stream
> Or eyelid shot the gleam
> That pierced my body through?
> What made me live like these that seem
> Self-born, born anew?

Through the "intricate motions" that suggest process, Yeats
experiences the mythic sense of renewal. Keats, remarking on
two views of Lake Winander, described a Great Moment of
reconciled opposites and awareness of divine power: "they
make one forget the divisions of life; age, youth, poverty and
riches; and refine one's sensual vision into a sort of north star
which can never cease to be open lidded and stedfast over the
wonders of the great Power" (L1, 299).

Through the landscape in *To Autumn* Keats experiences
the Great Moment and feels himself at one with the harmonious operations of Being in nature, which he sees as a paradoxical union of process and stasis. In stanza one Autumn is
perceived as universal Energy, a vital power filling, swelling,
plumping, o'er-brimming natural objects. In stanza two this
Energy is personified and seen in stasis, at a moment of fulfillment, "sitting careless on a granary floor . . . Or on a half-
reap'd furrow sound asleep." In the next image she "dos't
keep / Steady [her] laden head across a brook": motion and
stillness are part of one body. As the stanza ends she watches
"by a cyder-press, with a patient look . . . the last oozings
hours by hours." The oozings from the press parallel the o'er-
brimmed and clammy cells with which the first stanza's de-
piction of process ended; thus they bring the first stanza's
motion to the second stanza's stasis and prepare for the recon-

ciliation of motion and stasis which the third stanza explores. Images of process begin the stanza: "clouds bloom the soft-dying day, / And touch the stubble-plains with rosy hue." The clouds live while the day dies; the dead grass is touched by the living light—of the dying day. Reciprocity or an interchange of favors orders the landscape. In it Autumn now acts as music. Unlike the music on the Grecian urn, this music is played to the sensual ear, sounded by living creatures. Yet the idea of music as the abstract form, syntax, or structure within which Being, the living power, plays its changes, is not absent from the stanza, for it begins by saying that Autumn, like spring (like all the seasons, one assumes) has its own music or mode in which Being manifests itself. And that syntax or truth is again process: the wailful gnats move "borne *aloft* / Or *sinking* as the light wind *lives* or *dies*" (italics added); the lambs are "full-grown," filled with life, yet their "loud bleat" suggests a mournful dying fall. The swallows that conclude the poem suggest even wider operations of process. They are seen gathering in the skies, echoing the cluster of rising images dominant in stanza one; but their song is a "twitter," as if it were a slow ineffectual dying into silence. They fly away; and yet it is their nature to return with spring.

Keats's swallows lead one immediately to the bird imagery he shares with Yeats. For both poets birds are perhaps the chief natural objects through which the Great Moment is experienced, and their use of birds has often been compared, especially in the *Ode to a Nightingale* and *Sailing to Byzantium*. The Yeatsian parallels are in stanza seven of the ode: Keats's "hungry generations" anticipate Yeats's "dying generations"; the "emperor" is common to both poems; and the "perilous seas" of the ode are crossed by Yeats, whose Byzantium is among the "faery lands" generalized by Keats. But Keats's faery lands are forlorn of life, and herein lies a major difference between the two poems: Keats's living bird opens a vision of the beauty of nature (stanza 5), while Yeats's bird is a metal artifice opposed to nature. The heaven of *Sailing to Byzantium* is no realm where temporal existence is repeated in a finer tone; in this sense it is a faery land forlorn, rejected by Keats. And Keats's nightingale sings *to* past, present, and (presumably) future generations, while Yeats's sings *of* "what is past, or passing, or to come." The knowledge possessed by Yeats's golden bird is more closely paralleled by another of Keats's nightingales; in *Bards of Passion and of Mirth,*

> the nightingale doth sing
> Not a senseless, tranced thing,
> But divine melodious truth;
> Philosophic numbers smooth;
> Tales of golden histories
> Of heaven and its mysteries.

This nightingale, though in heaven, is very much an earthly bird repeated in a finer tone.

Because the golden bird expresses Yeats's momentary rejection of nature, his wild swans at Coole are better birds to compare to Keats's nightingale. The last two stanzas of Yeats's poem bear distinct Keatsian overtones. In the penultimate stanza are echoes again of the ode's stanza 7, wherein Keats introduces the paradox of permanence and change in the bird, "immortal" down the ages through its mythic eternal return in kind:

> Unwearied still, lover by lover,
> They paddle in the cold
> Companionable streams or climb the air;
> Their hearts have not grown old;
> Passion or conquest, wander where they will,
> Attend upon them still.

(The lines could, as well, describe Keats's lovers in their medium, the "cold pastoral" of the urn.) In the last stanza of the ode, the nightingale fades

> Past the near meadows, over the still stream,
> Up the hillside; and now 'tis buried deep
> In the next valley-glades:
> Was it a vision, or a waking dream?

Yeats closes his poem:

The Great Moment

Among what rushes will they build,
By what lake's edge or pool
Delight men's eyes when I awake some day
To find they have flown away?

Yeats's birds are often found in a poetic structure common
to him, one with similarities to Lévi-Strauss's definition of
mythic structure. Building a poem on opposites, Yeats will
employ a sudden single image or metaphor to resolve the conflict, a metaphor emerging from contraries and transcending
or transforming them at the moment of the poem's conclusion. Often the very cry of a bird is symbolic of this Great
Moment. As early as the *Responsibilities* volume of 1914
Yeats utilized birds in this fashion. in *Paudeen, Memory of
Youth, Friends.* and less obviously in *The Cold Heaven.* In
The Three Hermits he suggests the method by which such
images are achieved. The birds in his later poems are familiar
to those readers with even passing acquaintance with his
work. They usually seem touched by or possessed of universal
Energy, and they become symbols in Coleridge's sense, par-
taking of that which they reveal.

Aesthetic objects are likewise endowed with the numinous
and, through the reconciliation of opposites that each achieves,
become vehicles for the Great Moment. That numinous quality is the Keatsian "beauty" or "essence," the Yeatsian "energy" or "passion"; and, as I discussed at some length in chapter 2 (section 3), the *Ode on a Grecian Urn* is the paradigm
of art's reconciliation of that numinous quality with "truth,"
a reconciliation sought not only by aesthetic but also by
mythic apprehension.

In eliciting the Great Moment, works of art may also bring
into play the mythic sense of time. In the *Ode on a Grecian
Urn* Keats leaves the scene depicted on the urn to imagine the
town from which the procession came and to ask toward what
green altar it moves. In *Lapis Lazuli* Yeats moves from the
figures carved on the stone to an imagined "half way house"
toward which they climb and to "the tragic scene" on which
they will stare. Keats's vision moves horizontally, ahead of
and behind the present scene on the urn; Yeats's vision moves

vertically, up and down. In both cases the present moment is only a part of the whole.

In Yeats's poetry art objects often elicit what Keats called "the elevation of the Moment" (L1, 185). One finds the bust of Maud Gonne in *A Bronze Head*, other bronzes in *The Living Beauty*, and the images that nuns worship in *Among School Children*, keeping "a marble or a bronze repose." There are the portraits in *The Municipal Gallery Revisited* and the picture of a black centaur by Edmund Dulac. Sato's "consecrated blade" appears in *A Dialogue of Self and Soul, Meditations in Time of Civil War*, and several shorter lyrics. There are mosaics and gold-hammered birds in the two Byzantium poems. In *The Statues* Yeats praises Western art for its presentation of the transcendental in temporal form and material, somewhat as Keats did in his sonnet on the Elgin marbles. Some of these poems I have discussed elsewhere; all of them have been carefully read by other critics.

"The excellence of every Art," Keats wrote, "is its intensity." Like Yeats he would put passion, the expression of feeling, at the center of his aesthetics. Such intensity, he continued, is "capable of making all disagreeables evaporate, from their being in close relationship with Beauty and Truth" (L1, 192). If the intensity of a work is sufficient to reconcile Beauty and Truth—vital energy that presses for no restraint and the restraining form, motion and stasis—then pain is converted into a kind of joy; the disagreeables evaporate through transformation. The concept anticipates Yeats's tragic joy and a similar if more fully developed aesthetic.

"The subject of all art is passion," Yeats wrote, beginning in Keats's terms and insisting on the energy or being that the work must capture and communicate. But he is quick to add: "and a passion can only be contemplated when separated by itself, purified of all but itself" (EX, 155). He is more explicit in recognizing the contrary state. contemplation or disinterestedness, that must accompany passion in the Great Moment. He implies that the artistic form must be so structured that, through its effect of aesthetic distance, contemplation of passion is invited. As Edward Engelberg has noted, his poems are committed, like the souls in *Byzantium*, to both "trance" and "dance,"[14] just as the bounded figures on Keats's urn, though static, seem kinetically alive. This tension between passion and reverie is found in Yeats's description of the great poem as an art form "cold and passionate as the dawn" (Y, 146), like Keats's Grecian urn, and of the ideal family as one in which "passion and precision have been one" (Y, 93). This tension is likewise found in Keats's description of poetry as "might half slumb'ring on its own right arm" (K, 48).

When the state of disinterested contemplation—trance or revery, as Yeats called it—is coupled with passion or intensity—itself freed by disinterestedness from willed attachments or intellectually determined ends ("an aimless joy")—one is ready to experience the Great Moment, an experience of timelessness and reconciled contraries that reveals, often through apprehension of process, the solidarity of all life. In 1907, as he moved toward his mature work, Yeats wrote, "the nobleness of the arts is in the mingling of contraries, the extremity of sorrow, the extremity of joy, perfection of personality, the perfection of its surrender, overflowing turbulent energy, the marmorean stillness; and its red rose opens at the meeting of the two beams of the cross, and at the trysting-place of mortal and immortal, time and eternity" (E, 255). In terms of contemporary criticism, Yeats is describing a displaced or secularized sacramental vision. But it would be just as accurate to say that he is describing, through the terms of aesthetics and traditional symbolism, the very thrust of mythic apprehension, that mode of consciousness from which religions later arose. It has been my argument that Keats and Yeats move not away from religion but *behind* it, to its origin in mythic apprehension.

---

14. *The Vast Design* (Toronto, 1964), p. 89.

Chapter Five

Melancholy's Sovran Shrine

I

"The Shores of Memory"

"We begin to live," Yeats wrote, "when we have conceived life as a tragedy" (A, 116). To be properly understood, the sentence must be placed in the context of his mature definition of tragedy; then it may be paraphrased to read: We begin to live when we have affirmed tragic joy, the paradoxical vision and emotion offered by the reconciliation of opposites here in time.

Keats shared a similar belief. His concept of "melancholy" is all but synonymous with Yeats's term, a joy informed by pain or else a pain transformed by will into joy—a gestalt of joy and grief, of happiness and sadness. The idea dominates his work of 1819. What Yeats develops in his last work, Keats has already explored. In Keats, however, more often than in Yeats, "melancholy" is the result of the mythic sense of time defined by Cassirer. These two factors are so interwoven in Keats's sensibility that they require the special attention afforded them in this chapter. Several of his poems—in particular the *Ode to a Nightingale* and the *Epistle to Reynolds*—are not fully understood unless these factors are seen at the center of their concerns. The second section of the chapter deals exclusively with the two *Hyperions*. These poems explore fully not only the concepts of "melancholy" and mythic time but also the problem of consciousness, which becomes their theme. And for that theme they supply a narrative: mythic consciousness progresses to myth, whose subject is consciousness itself. In these poems mythic apprehension finds full realization.

Cassirer's definition of mythic time was introduced in

chapter 3 and other examples were discussed in chapter 4. Keats and Yeats often sees the past, the future, or both temporal extensions of an event simultaneously with its present —the time sense that brings grief to Yeats in, for example, *Fergus and the Druid* and stanza 3 of *A Bronze Head*. A month or so before composing the *Ode on Melancholy*, Keats set forth its thesis in a letter: "Circumstances are like Clouds continually gathering and bursting—While we are laughing the seed of some trouble is put into the wide arable land of events—while we are laughing it sprouts i[t] grows and suddenly bears a poison fruit which we must pluck" (L2, 79). Yeats paralleled the thought almost exactly: "Every movement, in feeling or in thought, prepares in the dark by its own increasing clarity and confidence its own executioner" (M, 340). Process was thus a two-edged sword. With the blade of compensation and eternal return, one could console himself for temporal loss. With the other blade, however, one's sense of temporal tragedy only increased; Yeats often found process to be tragic because the very fact of eternal return seems to doom man to repetition in time; Keats often found it tragic because the vision of the future end of the object or situation that it granted during experience of the present could only bring pain and sadness into the immediate joy. Thus if the apprehension of process in the first sense may lead to the Great Moment, apprehension of process in either of the second senses will force one to tragic joy or melancholy as components additional or prerequisite to the Great Moment.

The *Ode on Melancholy* is Keats's formal exploration of the theme. Robert Gittings is right to call it the poet's "most complete attempt to describe, explain and reconcile his own tendencies, harking back to many other attempts."[1] Well read as it has been by other critics, no more than summary is required here. The poem presents both aspects of Keats's concept: pain into joy and joy into pain. Stanzas 1 and 2 present the first, stanza 3 presents the second. The cancelled stanza

1. *John Keats* (Boston, 1968), p. 314. However, I do not agree with Gittings that the ode "repudiates" the Cave of Quietude passage.

(thought to be originally the first) says that death and sadness alone do not cause melancholy and, by concentration on them, "certes you would fail / To find the Melancholy" (к, 504). This stanza, sometimes considered morbid or "unhealthy," is probably meant as satire on the gothic trappings of the eighteenth-century Graveyard School of verse. Certainly the term "melancholy" is here established as standing for something more than it did for Blair and Young, a point indeed made by the whole poem.

The first stanza argues that neither suicide nor preoccupation with death as escape should be made "a partner in your sorrow's mysteries." The second stanza argues—through images of process ("weeping" cloud that "fosters" flowers, "April shroud," "morning rose," and the stationed moment of the rainbow on the wave)—that sorrow's partner should be joy in the beauty of what is, the *donné*; in this paradox is sorrow's "mystery" and in it true melancholy will be found. Life, as stanza 1 says, may be "the wakeful anguish of the soul." But willed acceptance of that anguish is preferred to drowsy numbness—a metaphorical death-in-life by which the soul, reduced to a shade, goes into the shade of death. Stanza 2 shows how that anguish, through acceptance, can be turned to joy. In particular, one accepts his mistress's "rich" anger and lets her rave, so compensated by and caught up in the rich energy and instress, the "glow of beauty in [her] eyes" (*Hyperion*, II, 237). The lines of the ode are identical with the letter discussed in chapter 2: "Though a quarrel in the streets is a thing to be hated, the energies displayed in it are fine; the commonest Man shows a grace in his quarrel" (L2, 80).

Stanza 3 reverses the proposition and shows that joy is truly joy only when, as Yeats would say, it is tragic: the beauty of the beloved (joy) is made intense only by knowledge of her mortality (tragedy); pleasure, consequently, is "aching," "turning to Poison while the bee-mouth sips."[2]

2. The germ of this image is found in *Isabella* (stanza xiii) a year before: "Even bees, the little almsmen of spring-bowers, / Know there is richest juice in poison-flowers."

Melancholy's Sovran Shrine

Ay, in the very temple of Delight
  Veil'd Melancholy has her sovran shrine,
    Though seen of none save him whose strenuous tongue
  Can burst Joy's grape against his palate fine. . . .

When Beauty, Joy, and Pleasure, while being experienced,
are seen as passing away (Beauty must die, Joy bids adieu,
Pleasure turns to poison), they will be experienced that much
more intensely (the "strenuous tongue" is metonomy for the
strenuous being, and looks back to "glut" and "feed deep,
deep" in the preceding stanza; the plea for intensity completes the first stanza's insistence on wakeful anguish). Under
these conditions they form the temple within which Melancholy has her shrine.

The theme is directly or indirectly present in each of the
other great odes. The intense joy taken in the landscape of
To Autumn is momentarily perplexed by the intrusion of the
past: "Where are the songs of Spring? Ay, where are they?"
But in the perception of process, "While barred clouds *bloom*
the soft-*dying* day" (italics added), the music that autumn
offers is accepted and affirmed. I suggest that the somewhat
awkward line "More happy love! more happy, happy love!"
in the *Ode on a Grecian Urn* appears less overstated if taken
with the pain introduced in the rest of the stanza. Keats experiences the ideal love of the figures on the urn at this high
pitch of intensity precisely because he now remembers the
painful imperfection attendant upon human love. The intense
sadness of the stanza's end is equal to and joined with the intense joy of its beginning. Just so is the wrenching picture of
the eternally-to-be-deserted village introduced in the next
stanza: the movement toward consummation (the altar)
leaves something desolate behind (the town); the procession
is another example of Keats's seeing in the present both the
future (the altar) and the past (the town). Hence if the urn
speaks of eternal joy, so does it, by implication to the poet,
argue for eternal grief; the two are parts of one experience.
The urn expresses not only a tale of beauty and truth, as explored in chapter 2, but a legend of tragic joy as well, its
Attic shape a cloudy trophy in veiled Melancholy's shrine.

Chapter Five

In the *Ode to Psyche* the theme is mentioned merely in passing; Keats says that within his mental temple dedicated to Psyche will be thoughts "new grown with pleasant pain." Here it is hardly more than that eighteenth-century oxymoron he showed such fondness for in his earliest work. But in the *Ode to a Nightingale* the theme returns to prominence. This ode, in fact, forms a companion piece to the *Ode on Melancholy* not only in its placement in the 1820 volume (the former ode begins the section of shorter lyrics, the latter one concludes it) but also in a more explicit parallel of theme than has yet been noted.[3]

The theme of the ode, put baldly, is this: Keats would "unperplex" joy and pain by transcending earth and its unhappiness but learns he cannot, except through death, which he rejects, or fancy which, he says, "cannot cheat so well / As she is fam'd to do"; when the nightingale departs, taking joy with her song, joy and pain are suddenly unperplexed and, that goal ironically achieved, he is left wondering if he wakes or sleeps. The poem thus struggles to undo, at the opening of the lyrical section of the 1820 volume, what the *Ode on Melancholy* closes the section by accepting: melancholy or the inextricable fusion of joy and pain. The former poem would reject tragic joy if it could and shows rejection to be impossible; the latter poem accepts it as a truth and affirms it as a goal.

The key to the emotional complexity of the *Ode to a Nightingale* is the opening stanza. With the very first phrase, "My heart aches," we are placed in the realm of "Melancholy's" "aching Pleasure"; the poet is, as he says a few lines later,

3. This remark is not meant to slight E. C. Pettet who, in *On the Poetry of Keats* (Cambridge, 1957), pp. 251–59 offers a brilliant reading of the opening stanza, relating it to the *Ode on Melancholy* and to other passages in Keats on the theme of mixed joy and pain. My own reading of that opening stanza, as well as of some other details in the poem, is largely Pettet's. We part company, however, over the general meaning of the ode. Pettet reads the fifth stanza (and by extension much of the poem) as "the expression of a luxurious death wish," p. 266, and concludes by disparaging the mixture of joy and pain—here and more especially in the *Ode on Melancholy*—as "superficial" and "unhealthy" Romanticism.

"too happy in thine happiness." His joy has been intensified to a point of pain, an ache.[4] Furthermore, "a drowsy numbness pains" his sense, as though he had drunk "some dull opiate . . . and Lethe-wards had sunk." Superficially the lines seem to say that he feels exactly as he might had he performed those ministrations in *Melancholy*'s opening stanza which are there rejected because they lead "shade to shade . . . too drowsily." But the apparent contradiction is resolved if one realizes that the *Ode on Melancholy* does not say melancholy cannot be drowsy; it merely says true melancholy cannot be "too" drowsy, so drowsy that it drowns "the wakeful anguish of the soul." In the reconciliation of opposites some drowsiness is to be expected. The term is synonymous with that stillness of Yeatsian "reverie" discussed in chapter 4. The key to it is Yeats's statement quoted there: "At my moment of revelation I am awake and asleep . . . self-possessed in self-surrender" (E, 524). Both drowsiness and reverie are states of consciousness suspended between the activity of wakefulness and the passivity of sleep, which is what the ode's last line affirms. Drowsiness is not, unless excessive, that nearly empty, self-reflecting consciousness described in the *Ode on Indolence*:

> my pulse grew less and less;
> Pain had no sting, and pleasure's wreath no flower . . .
> . . . .
> Unhaunted quite of all but—nothingness?
>
> (K, 448)

The drowsiness of the opening stanza is not of this kind, for it "pains." Strictly speaking, however, it is not drowsiness itself that pains; the pain is not a quality of the state of consciousness *per se* but a quality of feeling which the state allows: the ache of the heart and the pain of the senses enter the heart and senses with intensity only when the soul is in the state of suspended consciousness. Keats, then, is like Mad-

---

4. Pettet, p. 259, compares Peona's remark on seeing Endymion sad in the company of the Indian Maid: "Perhaps ye are too happy to be glad" (IV, 819).

elaine on first retiring: "In a sort of wakeful swoon, perplex'd she lay" (к, 248).

The poet says the ache and pain are "not through envy of thy happy lot. / But being too happy in thine happiness." The second of these assertions is clarified by the third stanza. There Keats describes the pain of human experience, which he would like to forget. The bird, in contrast to the poet, "hast never known / The weariness, the fever, and the fret" that the stanza details. Although the bird will certainly know hunger, discomfort, and death, Keats means that the bird—a simple, unself-conscious, unreflecting creature—lives only in the present, be that of comfort or woe; for the bird, joy and grief *are* unperplexed, and its present moment is one of pure joy. Man, by contrast, through self-consciousness and memory, finds it all but impossible not to interject the past and future into the present moment ("but to think is to be full of sorrow"), particularly the future dissolution of what he presently finds beautiful and loves. "The dull brain perplexes" joy with grief and so "retards" the experience of any unadulterated joy. It is knowledge of mortality, then, mixed with the ecstatic joy felt by Keats through the bird's song, which causes that aching pleasure in the heart declared by the poem's opening line. That ecstasy is the agency through which the wine of stanza 2 becomes an emblem of unperplexed joy. Yet the more intensely Keats feels that joy—developing his wine image for a full stanza—the more intensely does he recall the tragedy of mortality, likewise developing this half of his perplexed feeling for a full stanza. Stanzas 2 and 3, held together by the wine image, unperplex the aching pleasure of stanza one into its components of pleasure and of pain. The relationship between them parallels that which I have suggested exists in the *Ode on a Grecian Urn* between the beginnings and endings of stanzas 3 and 4 and between the imagined empty town and the actual scenes on the urn.

The implication of the first three stanzas seems to be that, were the drowsiness either more or less, the ache and pleasure might be disjoined, the joy and grief distinct. Less drowsiness would mean a more active, less self-conscious participation in the present, thus a restriction of that panoramic sense of time by which the future enters the present. More drowsiness would numb Keats to the pain—and to the pleasure, too, as in the lines already quoted from the *Ode on Indolence*. The paradox of the situation is that the bird's song can be intensely experienced only in a state of consciousness that invites the panoramic sense of time and so invites pain as well.

It is from this perplexed emotion that Keats would extricate himself; he would have joy alone. The poem, in a sense, renders experientially his remark: "I am a Coward, I cannot bear the pain of being happy" (L2, 160).[5] Thus it is that the first of his two assertions in stanza 1—"not through envy of thy happy lot"—is not altogether true; stanza 3 makes clear that it is precisely the unreflective lot of the bird which he envies. Unconsciously Keats has realized this envy himself before the second stanza begins, for his desire to reach the bird with wine or poetry—to fly away with it, not with its song—is most simply explained as envy. Keats would either slow down or, like the bird, have no consciousness of the temporal process leading to death that is the subject of the third stanza. He first envisions wine as the vehicle of escape, then in stanza 4 the wings of poetry; the conjunction is natural because the first was for Keats almost always a metaphor for the second.[6] In stanza 4 Keats's union with the bird is abruptly declared to have taken place; yet the result, as so many critics have observed, is only two lines of artificial verse describing the moon and "all her starry Fays." Unconsciously, with the word "Fays," Keats is already looking forward to his concluding judgment, where he will call the fancy, responsible for this abortive flight, a "deceiving elf."

At this point the poem makes its first major turn. The "two lines of futile ornament," as W. J. Bate has called them,[7] are

---

5. In the same letter to Fanny Brawne he writes: "I cannot resolve to mix any pleasure with my days . . . If I were to see you to day it would destroy the half comfortable sullenness I enjoy at present [turning it] into dow[n]right perplexities" (L2, 160).

6. Mario D'Avanzo, *Keats's Metaphors for the Poetic Imagination* (Durham, N. C., 1967), pp. 108–13.

7. Bate, *John Keats*, p. 505.

followed by "But here there is no light." Each stanza has a short tetrameter eighth line, and Keats felicitously uses it here to mark his turn. He does not continue with his fancy of the Queen-Moon and her Fays; rather, he returns to earth (earth is indicated by the light's coming "from" heaven and "through" trees and foliage). The turn is not an evident one, disguised as it is by what the short line introduces: the magnificent descriptive passage that completes stanza 4 and fills stanza 5. In darkness Keats imagines the beauty of budding life around him. And, in calling that darkness "embalmed," he indicates a belief that he has now escaped the fever and the fret; he is himself hardly conscious of any turn. Yet the remarkable and significant fact is that the list of trees and flowers culminates in images of process: "Fast fading violets . . . / And mid-May's eldest child, / The coming musk-rose. . . ." Fancy has led him back, unconsciously, to that very process he desired to escape in stanza 2—but with this difference: process is no longer merely a one-directional movement to the grave but an interchange of favors, a movement of compensation in which consolation may be found. Although he shows no conscious awareness of it, Keats has been led to accept process in the fashion discussed in chapter 2. Thus stanzas 4 and 5 lead one to conclude that the only image to be found for paradise is temporal; like Yeats's Thirteenth Cone, absolute transcendence is imageless. Keats obscurely senses this and turns from his artificial Queen-Moon to the myth of process on earth. He returns to time because he has only time, and fancy cheats if she pretends otherwise. This conclusion was foreshadowed in stanza 2 where, paradoxically, Keats employed the richest of earthly images to express what, by fading from the world with drink, he hoped to find.

Keats is not yet, however, aware of these truths; they are now before him but their meaning is yet to be grasped. Nor is he yet ready to grasp it: the beauties of stanza 5 are, it must be remembered, *imagined* beauties. Thus it is that in stanza 6 he continues his desire for joy unperplexed. Because his imagined union with the bird is so nearly complete he thinks it now "seems more than ever . . . rich to die, / To cease upon the midnight with no pain." Death would, he thinks, grant him the nightingale's ecstasy—and with "no pain." It is as if, wine and poetry having served him incompletely, death will now be his wings to a permanent union. But what was earlier called "the dull brain" now undermines this vehicle, too. For it once again brings the future into the present: at death "Still wouldst thou sing, and I have ears in vain—/ To thy high requiem become a sod." Death may indeed be the portal to the transcendent, "life's high meed" with which he is more than half in love. But he cannot carry empathy with the bird to the point of death; for death, though it might momentarily join him perfectly with the object, would also cause him to lose that object with which he desires total empathy, since the object would remain this side of death. It might be true that in losing the object in the moment after death, Keats would gain all else, other objects with which he might empathize perfectly, entering an absolute fellowship with essence. But that gain would be of little avail, since he was not led to want that other world in the first place except through active empathy with some particular object that seemed to promise it. Only when his passion, the feeling response, is intensely engaged does he really long for the other world; intellectual speculation or conception of that other world acquired in mundane, daily living is insufficiently felt to lead him to the point of daring death to gain that other world. So in neither mundane nor impassioned moments can he seriously entertain suicide. The *Ode on Melancholy* says one can—and does —entertain the idea when in despair. But the first stanza also says that genuine despair is so much a numbness that a person is too removed from the felt image or memory of happiness possible in another life (should there be one) to have the necessary incentive to end his life to reach it; he is so numbed that action of any sort is impossible.

This realization of the limits of empathy marks the second turning point of the *Ode to a Nightingale*. Keats has now exhausted all possible vehicles for a union with the unadulterated joy of the bird. Yet in this very exhaustion, step by step, he has unconsciously prepared the grounds for his final realization. Stanza 7 expresses that realization. Janet Spens has read this penultimate stanza as the climax of the poem. She is, it seems to me, both right and wrong. In it, she says, "the poet did feel himself to have 'stept' for a moment 'into a sort of oneness,' to have become like a 'floating spirit' independent of space and time."[8] Thus the stanza presents an "Eternal Moment" (her term echoes Yeats's), that experience discussed in the "fellowship with essence" passage in *Endymion*. This it does; but it does something else besides. The stanza is not so uniform in mood, for it recapitulates the movements and moods of stanzas 1 through 6. The climax offered is considerably complex.

Opening with a denial of the bird's mortality, the stanza would refute the mortality of stanza 3. Then, in the third line. Keats shifts terms as it were, from the bird to the bird's voice. This shift troubled several earlier critics; and those today who with no problem accept it as metonomy are still on occasion— some of them—troubled because the nightingale itself seems to shift in meaning as the poem progresses. Neither shift should be troublesome, I think; for the ode has shown itself, by the end of stanza 6, to be very much a poem that takes one step backward for every two steps forward.[9] Thus the stanza's opening reference to the "immortal Bird," rather than to the song, is a step backward to the creature whose lot the poet envied in stanzas 2–4. It is the bird that holds Keats's attention before the first turn in the poem; after stanza 1—an in-

8. Janet Spens, "A Study of Keats's 'Ode to a Nightingale,' " *RES* 3 (1952): 236. Maurice Bowra, *The Romantic Imagination* (Cambridge, Mass., 1949), p. 136, is of similar opinion.
9. With this metaphor I attempt to analyze a quality of the ode often noted. For example, D. G. James, *The Romantic Comedy* (London, 1948), believes the poem is "uncertain in its aim," and Kenneth Muir, "The Meaning of *Hyperion*," *EC* 2 (1952): 68, finds it "not the expression of a single mood but a succession of moods." Muir's judgment accords with my own reading and seems to me more nearly accurate than the statement of Earl Wasserman, *The Finer Tone* (Baltimore, 1953), p. 178, that "forces contend wildly within the poem," though Wasserman—like James and myself—finds these forces "without resolution."

troduction setting forth the complex problem of the poem—
the bird's song is not mentioned again until the end of stanza
6. When the first turn comes and is developed in stanza 5,
we find the only stanza in the poem that makes no reference
whatsoever to the bird or its song. At this moment when the
earth and process are being imaginatively rediscovered, the
bird is absent. I would suggest that in this interval—and because of it—Keats does shift his attention from the bird and
its previously envied lot to the bird's song. Here in stanza 5
where the groundwork for an acceptance of temporal mortality is laid. Keats begins to abandon the bird—the "thee" he
has been so ardently pursuing—for the song sent out "in such
an ecstasy" in the following stanza. From this line forward to
the end of the poem it is the song not the bird that is empha-
sized. At the end of stanza 6, in which this line occurs, Keats
realizes that an escape from mortality would mean loss of
the bird's song and, by implication, of the temporal beauty
imagined in stanza 5. Thus he is ready to abandon his earlier
quest for the bird and its lot, to settle for the bird's song. It
is the same retreat he makes in the *Ode on a Grecian Urn*
where he abandons the quest for the eternal passion of the
lovers and accepts a less self-destroying contemplation of the
urn as an artifice of eternity.

Stanza 7, then, like stanza 6, begins with a reference to the
bird, now called "immortal." After the painful realization by
Keats of the necessity of his own mortality, immediately preceding this line, he momentarily takes a step backward to the
whole mortality theme of stanza 3. In the complex turning of
his mood he wishes immortality for the bird if he himself is
to be denied it in the moment he desires it; in so wishing, he
obscures the real turn of his mood, which first emerges in
line 3 as he returns to the bird's song. Expressing there the
immortality of the song, he makes his most significant step
backward—to that sense of process first adumbrated in stanza
5: "The voice I hear this passing night was heard / In ancient days by emperor and clown . . ." As Wordsworth wrote
of the River Duddon, "The form remains, the function never
dies." The bird's song, a paradigmatic form like the fixed

number of swans at Coole Park, is eternal. At this point the
experience of the stanza is, as Janet Spens says, an "Eternal
Moment."

Yet when Keats proceeds by including Ruth, he not only
adds one more person to the circle of living and dying; he returns at last, as if ready for acceptance of it, to that perplexity
of joy and pain from which the poem began in stanza 1.
There Keats, like Ruth here, was "sick for home," the nightingale's imagined South. While the bird's song "found a path
/ Through the sad heart" of each of them, they stood amid
the knowledge of mortal process, which made the ripe corn
and the summer earth seem alien. But even now Keats is not
totally free from that desire to transcend limit, earth, and
pain. Almost as if the image of Ruth's perplexity of joy and
pain had recalled him to the heavy burden of his own, he
makes once more that movement toward transcendence which
he attempted in line 5 of stanza 4. Having moved two steps
forward, he moves backward again, seeing the song at the
stanza's conclusion to be

> The same that oft-times hath
> Charm'd magic casements, opening on the foam
> Of perilous seas, in faery lands forlorn.

The seas are indeed perilous, inviting that suicide mused
upon in stanza 6. The "vast idea" of process had been imaged
by "an ocean dim" spreading "awfully" before him; to turn
away from process is to sail, as Endymion said, into "the
monstrous swell / Of visionary seas!" (iv, 652–53) where the
lands are forlorn of all but "starry Fays." Such lands are as
imageless as that imagined union in stanza 4—an empty,
flowerless, personless unknown, an empty zero like Yeats's
Thirteenth Cone. The fancy, which would unperplex joy and
pain, and take one to the Queen-Moon or the magic seas,
"cannot cheat so well / As she is fam'd to do."[10] Carried by
the last line of the stanza into the land promised beyond the

10. Pettet would have these lines deny the entirety of stanza 7, thus
refuting Janet Spens's "Eternal Moment." But his reading oversimplifies
that stanza no less than does her own. Both make it the reflection of a
single mood where I read it as a rapid transition among several moods.

windows, Keats is once again projected into the future of a present moment; once more the dull brain perplexes and retards. Hence in the last stanza he withdraws to his "sole self," and the bird's song—now an echo of the tolling bell that was the word "forlorn"—is heard as a "plaintive anthem," the "high requiem" of stanza 6 now sung at a different, a metaphorical death. The terms are not inappropriate for the sound in Keats's aching heart, which, like the sad heart of Ruth, knows both pleasure and pain at the bird's song. Whether from this point Keats might have come to acceptance of that joy and pain, content with temporal process, it is impossible to say. For Keats, as if still unable to accept the logic of his own experience, has the nightingale withdraw at this very moment. He who would have faded with it has it fade away instead. With the bird's withdrawal, joy and pain are unperplexed; the initial conflict of the poem is neither accepted or resolved. The ending does no more for that conflict than reiterate the state of consciousness within which it was possible: "Do I wake or sleep?" It is for the *Ode on Melancholy* to accept the logic of the experience discovered here.

"Discovered" is not, however, an altogether accurate word. Strictly speaking neither of the odes may be said to have first discovered the logic of melancholy. Just as Yeats's use of the term "tragic joy" considerably predates its full embodiment in poetry, so the origin of Keats's melancholy goes back to his earliest verse, where it is prefigured in his fondness for eighteenth-century oxymoron. In the sonnet *To Lord Byron* (which he did not think enough of to include in the 1817 volume) he speaks of Byron's "sweetly sad" melody, his "tale of pleasing woe":

> O'ershading sorrow doth not make thee less
> Delightful: thou thy griefs dost dress
> With a bright halo, shining beamily. . . .
>
> (K, 477)

In *I Stood Tip-Toe* he speaks of "sweet desolation—balmy pain" (K, 9). More effective is the sonnet *Time's Sea*, in which the woman addressed, being vividly remembered after five years, "dost eclipse / Every delight . . . And grief unto my darling joys . . . bring" (к, 466).

The theme sounds throughout *Endymion*, with considerably more seriousness. E. C. Pettet, in fact, has suggested that Keats, in calling the "fellowship with essence" passage "my first step toward the chief Attempt in the Drama—the playing of Different Natures with Joy and Sorrow" (l1, 218–19), may have meant by "Drama" the action of *Endymion* itself; certainly the action of the poem reveals the various reactions of different natures toward joy and sorrow.[11] In book ii the sorrow and struggle of life are seen as

> bearing in themselves this good,
> That they are still the air, the subtle food,
> To make us feel existence. . . . (ii, 156–58)

They grant intensity, another familiar theme. Some lines further, when Endymion has plunged underground, Keats writes:

> Dark, nor light,
> The region; nor bright, nor sombre wholly,
> But mingled up; a gleaming melancholy. . . .
> (ii, 221–23)

In the *Ode on Melancholy* this mingled light and dark returns as the cloud that "hides the green hill in an April Shroud" and in the image of Melancholy's "cloudy trophies." It is absent from the *Ode to a Nightingale*. Just as Keats there wishes to unperplex joy and pain, so does he, at the moment of asserted union with the bird, unperplex light and dark; the natural beauties of stanza 5 are imagined in darkness. In *Endymion* Cynthia herself is aware of the Keatsian melancholy. "O bliss! O pain!" she cries (ii, 773) at the moment of her first union with the youth, asking: "Is grief contain'd / In the very deeps of pleasure . . . ?" (ii, 823–24). In an ear-

---

11. Pettet, p. 138. One might note, too, the program that Keats set for himself in *Sleep and Poetry*: to pass the realm of "Flora, and Old Pan" for "the strife / Of human hearts." When one remembers that this poem introduces the "vast idea," it seems that Keats is saying, not altogether conscious of it, that he will pass through the apprehension of process to tragic joy.

lier draft Keats had written "shrine" instead of "deeps"; the word returns to stay in the *Ode on Melancholy*, which answers her question affirmatively. Book 3 answers likewise. There Glaucus is informed by the scroll retrieved from the sea that the curse upon him will be lifted when, among other duties, he *"explores all forms and substances / Straight homeward to their symbol-essences"* (iii, 699–700), an empathy with inscape and instress discussed in chapter 1. The scroll further defines this as a "task of joy and grief" (iii, 702). Glaucus had opened his story with lines that all but paraphrase the first stanza of the *Ode to a Nightingale*:

> My soul stands
> Now past the midway from mortality,
> And so I can prepare without a sigh
> To tell thee briefly all my joy and pain.

Book iv continues the theme, with the song of the Indian Maid and the Cave of Quietude. One stanza of the song seems to paraphrase the very reading of the *Ode to a Nightingale* that I have offered:

> To Sorrow,
> I bade good-morrow,
> And thought to leave her far away behind;
> But cheerly, cheerly,
> She loves me dearly;
> She is so constant to me, and so kind:
> I would deceive her
> And so leave her,
> But, ah! she is so constant and so kind.
> (iv, 173–81)

In his famous letter to Bailey (l1, 182–86), Keats said that by the song one could know his favorite speculation. What that speculation is remains ambiguous, since its clausal antecedent is unclear. But the immediately preceding clause says that all our passions create "essential Beauty" (in effect they *are* beauty, as chapter 2 argued). By implication, then, sorrow must create or partake of beauty just as joy does. And since the song represents "the probable mode of operating in these

Matters," that mode, it is clear from the song's content, is process. Sorrow gives back to a second object what she takes from the first. What she takes is essence or instress: "the natural hue of health . . . lustrous passion . . . mellow ditties from a mourning tongue . . . heart's lightness." With this theory of an interchange of favors, Keats is already groping toward his concept of melancholy. Associating sorrow with beauty that must die, he looks forward to *Hyperion*, as later analysis of that poem will make evident.

The song, though it does not develop it well, hints at the question of perplexed and unperplexed joy. The Indian Maid says that, in her sorrow, Bacchus and revelers rode by, "To scare thee, Melancholy! / O then, O then, thou wast a simple name!" (IV, 203–204.) At the time of Bacchus's arrival, her sorrow had been "simple, uncomplicated by any attendant joy. In joining Bacchus, she leaves her sorrow ("I forgot thee, as the berried holly / By shepherds is forgotten, when . . . Tall chestnuts" bloom), tries to trade it for an unperplexed joy that does not remember the past. Unable to do this, however, she drops out of the train and reaffirms Sorrow: "of all the world I love thee best."

In the Cave of Quietude passage (IV, 513–48) Keats for the first time extends his theme imagistically. He characterizes the Cave as a place beyond our mundane speculations, a place of "glooms" where dark and light are mingled. One is led to it by "a grievous feud"; Endymion's present plight implies it to be a feud between grief and joy. "This native hell" is indigenous to man's mortal nature, and at one time or another all persons enter it, just as Keats does himself at the opening of the *Ode to a Nightingale*. Yet few men know how "calm and well" is "that deep den of all"; few penetrate beyond the strife of opposed emotions to that point where

> anguish does not sting; nor pleasure pall:
> Woe-hurricanes beat ever at the gate,
> Yet all is still within and desolate.

"Happy Gloom! / Dark Paradise!" Keats cries, bringing together light and dark, joy and sorrow. This moment comes, as Middleton Murry says. "when misery has reached its extreme point; then the misery marvelously changes into a profound content."[12] The soul comes to acceptance of misery, ceases to fight against it and, instead, takes refuge in the center of misery itself. At that moment one finds that "never since thy griefs and woes [MS: *joys*] began, / Hast thou felt so content." Tragic joy is won. Near the end of the passage Keats says that in the Cave "those eyes are the brightest far that keep / Their lids shut longest in a dreamless sleep." Had he written "open" instead of "shut" he would have prefigured almost perfectly the eyes of Moneta which, "with a benignant light," seem "visionless entire . . . Of all external things" and "in blank splendor [beam] like the mild moon" (K, 516). Middleton Murry is right in believing the whole passage describes a complexity of mood most fully presented in the silent face of Moneta.[13]

Sometime during 1818, possibly while he was revising *Endymion*, Keats wrote the little song of opposites *Welcome Joy and Welcome Sorrow*. The poem is sometimes called the germ of the *Ode on Melancholy*, but its light, carefree, rather artificial handling of the ode's theme differs little from that theme's expression in the earliest verse. A more likely candidate is the verse *Epistle to Reynolds*. It is here, I think, that Keats first intensely experiences and genuinely understands the mixture of joy and pain that in the Cave of Quietude passage remained more nearly literary metaphor than experienced truth. Here he prefigures fully the problem of consciousness as it appears in the great odes and in *The Fall of Hyperion*. Like Walter Evert, though for somewhat different reasons, I think the poem marks a turning point in Keats's thought and concerns.[14]

12. *Keats* (New York, 1962), p. 175.
13. Ibid., p. 170.
14. Walter Evert, *Aesthetic and Myth in the Poetry of Keats* (Princeton, 1965), pp. 194–211, offers the most careful reading of the poem to date; yet, as my own reading will show, he seems to me wrong in his interpretation of lines 26–68 and 75–85. He thinks that Keats's response to the painting described in the first passage is, "beyond any question, perverse," that Keats makes of the painting "a collective metaphor for

Chapter Five

Keats begins the *Epistle* by listing "Things all disjointed," the "wonted thread / Of Shapes, and Shadows and Remembrances" coming to one before sleep:

> Two witch's eyes above a Cherub's mouth,
> Voltaire with casque and shield and Habergeon,
> And Alexander with his night-cap on—
> Old Socrates a tying his cravat;
> And Hazlitt playing with Miss Edgeworth's cat;
> And Junius Brutus pretty well so, so,
> Making the best of's way towards Soho.
> (K, 484–85)

Critics usually read the passage as the disordered play of fancy.[15] Certainly there is a sense in which Keats is being led on by what he called "the Loadstone Concatenation" into Yeats's *Hodos Chameliontos*, the customary phantasmagoria of the imagination loosed from all bounds. But what should be noted is the progression among these images. The first represents total incongruity between two elements in an imaginary realm. The remainder speak of actual human beings and the incongruity in human character. The great men are seen not in positions impossible to them but positions which, altogether possible and human, "vex" the pure or simple notion of their greatness. With each passing instance, man's mortality and human frailty increases, a frailty disharmonious with the image one would like to hold of unperplexed greatness. The intellectual Voltaire is seen fighting not with his mind but his body. The great conqueror Alexander is seen as an ordinary mortal in bedclothes. Socrates, so disdainful of his personal appearance, is caught in a moment of vanity. Hazlitt, Keats's philosophic mentor, is trivially playing with

---

the internal disharmony of the perceiving mind's own impulses," p. 200. Believing the "it" of line 84 to refer to the imagination, he reads the second passage—and hence the poem—as a critique of the imagination.

15. See, for example, the most recent reading, Stuart M. Sperry, Jr., "Keats's *Epistle to John Hamilton Reynolds*," *ELH* 36 (1969): 562–74. Sperry says the images "neither suggest nor lead on to anything more," p. 564, and he follows directions similar to Evert's in reading lines 26–68 and 78–85. He finds the poem's chief preoccupation to be "the degree of idealization—both in a good and bad sense—that art can achieve in its transcendence of actuality," p. 566.

a cat. Junius Brutus, actor of so many noble roles, is now ignobly drunk. The only impossible incongruity here lies in historically anachronistic items chosen to make the point in the first three instances; yet Keats, as he progresses to contemporary persons, progresses to historically consistent items in the last two instances. What begins in imagination and aesthetics—the witch's eyes and cherub's mouth—moves quickly to human character and contemporary reality. Underlying this progression in the list of men is perception of human frailty in the midst of human greatness. It is always "remembrances" of the former that "vex" and "shadow" the "shapes" of the latter. In this vexation the first stanza looks forward to the last, where Keats projects future death into present life.

Just as there are few men who are not led to the Cave of Quietude, so "few there are who escape these visitings." Those few so doing, the second stanza says, see "young Aeolian harps personified . . . Titian colours touch'd into real life." They have what Yeats would call Unity of Being and their world is like that in the painting Keats now describes for the greater part of the poem. The first description of this world shows its inhabitants in ritual acts of devotion, thus implying that some religious, universal harmony is perceived by those within it. Nothing is said of process as that principle of harmony, yet the sacrifice of the heifer and the image of the pontiff knife suggest an acceptance of death as part of a universal plan.

Keats next invokes Apollo's "sacred word" to describe the castle and the landscape composing the scene. The castle stands upon the edge of a lake dotted with isles, suggesting the "ocean dim, sprinkled with many an isle" that was image for the "vast idea" of process in *Sleep and Poetry.* The trees "seem to shake / From some old magic-like Urganda's Sword," and the elements of the landscape, which in other paintings "are but half animate,"

> Here do they look alive to love and hate;
> To smiles and frowns; they seem a lifted mound
> Above some giant, pulsing underground. (38–40)

Chapter Five

Natural things are so touched by, filled with, some divine force that they radiate that instress discussed in chapter 2; even the earth seems organic, a living thing. In a world with immanent deity, objects seems almost subjects; epistemological opposites are one. The castle is described (lines 41–48) as having been built over the course of several thousand years, by persons of many religious beliefs. Keats here reiterates his belief in a "parent of all the more palpable and personal Schemes of Redemption" (L2, 103), that "older religion than Christianity" (E, 149) which Yeats rightly felt Keats shared. The lines are best glossed by Keats's letter of the following spring: "As one part of the human species must have their carved Jupiter; so another part must have the palpable and named Mediator and savior, their Christ their Oromanes and their Vishnu" (L2, 103). The castle indicates that all religions arise from, partake of, and attempt to order the same fundamental religious impulse; and the sense of universal harmony they reflect is symbolized by the mythic noumenon in the landscape, which is the ground from which the castle arises. Thus the castle and its landscape bear some resemblance to the shrine and fane Keats will build for Psyche in the following year.

With the next stanza Keats anticipates several of the major poems:

> The doors all look as if they oped themselves,
> The windows as if latch'd by fays & elves—
> And from them comes a silver flash of light
> As from the Westward of a Summer's night;
> Or like a beauteous woman's large blue eyes
> Gone mad through olden songs and Poesies—
> (49–54)

The "magic casements" of the *Ode to a Nightingale* are prefigured here, and the eyes of the beautiful woman are seen again in the *Ode on Melancholy*:

> Or if thy mistress some rich anger shows,
> Emprison her soft hand, and let her rave,
> And feed deep, deep upon her peerless eyes.

Melancholy's Sovran Shrine

They reoccur too in *Lamia* (1, 84), where Hermes addresses the heroine, happy-sad (sometime mortal woman—now "immortal" serpent), as "thou beauteous wreath, with melancholy eyes." In the *Ode on a Grecian Urn* they bear the *Ode on Melancholy*'s weight of transience and are coupled with yet another of Keats's favorite terms: "Where Beauty cannot keep her lustrous eyes." In *Hyperion* (II, 237) this association carries pronounced implication of instress or essence: "With such a glow of beauty in his eyes." De Selincourt long ago noted the anticipation of the *Ode on a Grecian Urn* in the scene of sacrifice and in line 77. I would suggest a further anticipation in line 55. Introducing elements not in the painting, "See what is coming from the distance dim!" echoes "Who are these coming to the sacrifice?" which in the ode introduces scenes not depicted on the urn. The rest of this stanza looks backward to *Calidore*.

His description of the painting complete, Keats turns to a commentary on it. He wishes that, sleeping or waking, dreams "Would all their colours from the sunset take; /From something of material sublime"—just as the castle windows take their light from the sun, surrounded by those trees and earth that seem of material sublime. But, as in stanza 1, our dreams usually "shadow our own soul's day-time / In the dark void of night." Remembrance of mortal frailty shadows our waking dreams with intimations of failure, even of death; indeed, "in the world / We jostle." Remembering his own lack of philosophical study, Keats now breaks off: "philosophize / I dare not yet!" Then in rapid shift anticipating the shifts in stanza 7 of the *Ode to a Nightingale*, he moves from "yet" to "never":

> Oh never will the prize,
> High reason, and the lore of good and ill
> Be my award. Things cannot to the will
> Be settled, but they tease us out of thought.
> Or is it that Imagination brought
> Beyond its proper bound, yet still confined,—
> Lost in a sort of Purgatory blind,
> Cannot refer to any standard law
> Of either earth or heaven?—It is a flaw

Chapter Five

In happiness to see beyond our bourn—
It forces us in Summer skies to mourn:
It spoils the singing of the Nightingale.
(74–85)

Here is the heart of Keats's poem. He sees that what he quests for is "the lore of good and ill," some "high reason" by which he might understand and accept the fusion of joy and grief, of good and ill, of pleasure and pain that his experience brings him. He has entered what he will call, five weeks hence in a letter to Reynolds, "dark passages" of consciousness leading out of "the Chamber of Maiden-Thought": "We see not the ballance of good and evil. We are in a Mist" (L1, 280–81). Yet in his quest Keats doubts—as he has always doubted—if the intellect can solve a paradox that teases one out of thought. Then in a marvelous moment of self-knowledge, Keats wonders if it is not the imagination itself that causes the paradox. The imagination transcends its proper bound—the present moment of the object of its attention—by investing that present with glimpses of the past or future. And, if the imagination cannot reconcile these images of present and future into some larger harmony which the soul can accept, then it is "still confined,— / Lost in a sort of Purgatory blind." The standard law of earth has been transcended but the standard law of heaven has not yet been perceived. When the future enters the present, we "see beyond our bourn" and indeed mar happiness. With the last two lines of the stanza Keats anticipates both of his great odes on the subject of this perplexed joy and pain. The "summer skies" vexed by mourning are to return in stanza 2 of the *Ode on Melancholy*; and the paradox of joy and pain brought on by the imagination's investment of the present with the future is precisely what informs the *Ode to a Nightingale*.

It is in contrast to this vexation that the painting plays its role in the *Epistle*; within its world these perplexities are resolved. The persons depicted there make devotion to some principle of universal harmony that grants acceptance of death. The landscape depicted there is, without contradiction, "alive to love and hate, / To smiles and frowns"—the very contradiction Keats would solve with "lore of good and ill." Because of these harmonized contraries, the castle is called "enchanted" and two mythical enchanters are mentioned, Urganda and Merlin. If they are agents of sinister enchantment, the painting is able to harmonize their ominous implications as well.

In his own life Keats is unable to effect the reconciliations. And, having come to guess in the abstract the imagination's role in perplexing joy and pain, he concludes the *Epistle* with an example of its operation in his own life. He was, he says, upon the shore one calm evening and "should have been most happy":

> but I saw
> Too far into the sea; where every maw
> The greater on the less feeds evermore;—
> But I saw too distinct into the core
> Of an eternal fierce destruction,
> And so from Happiness I far was gone. . . .
>
> (93–98)

Into the present moment he projected the future, just as in stanza 1 he projected a past or future of frailty into images of human greatness. And, he continues, though he has gathered flowers the very day of writing Reynolds, "Still do I that most fierce destruction see." In the *Ode to a Nightingale* he is likewise to remember mortality the more intensely he experiences the joy of the bird's song. In his new understanding he calls the awareness "moods of one's mind" and wishes it away. The poem ends with his saying he would rather be a devout unthinking believer in some orthodox religious creed ("a clapping bell / To some Kamschatkan missionary church") "Than with these horrid moods he left in lurch." He had implied as much before, when he called this state a "Purgatory blind."

Seven weeks before writing the *Epistle*, Keats tentatively considered its subject in the sonnet *To the Nile* (K, 484). Thinking of the river, Keats finds its accepted significance coming automatically to mind: "We call thee fruitful." Yet "that very while" the imagination projects another, equally true, aspect of the river: "A desert fills our seeing's inward span." This simultaneous perception of two aspects of a thing foreshadows the opening section of the *Epistle to Reynolds*. Keats continues by saying that he hopes such "dark fancies"—"moods of the mind" he calls them in the *Epistle*— may err. It is, he says, "ignorance that makes a barren waste / Of all beyond itself," just as, in the *Epistle*, it is ignorance of a final principle or mode of reconciliation that leaves imagination stranded in a Purgatory blind. Unlike the *Epistle*, however, the sonnet proposes some reconciliation. Keats says the river

> dost bedew
> Green rushes like our rivers, and dost taste
> The pleasant sun-rise. Green isles hast thou too,
> And to the sea as happily dost haste.

Keats does not deny the desert; rather he turns his attention to what fruitfulness the river surely has, green rushes by its banks and small green isles. In that bit of green and in the river's free motion toward fulfillment of its process in the sea he finds consolation. His acceptance of what is, this calm joy in what is given, is found again in the concluding stanza of the ode *To Autumn*.

The summer after writing the *Epistle to Reynolds*, Keats made the Scottish walking tour. One of the sonnets composed then exhibits the *Epistle*'s awareness of the double-vision in mythic time. *On Visiting the Tomb of Burns* was written, Keats said, "in a strange mood, half asleep" (L1, 309), that mood discussed earlier in the reading of the *Ode to a Nightingale* as perquisite to the experience of joy and pain perplexed. Keats says that the landscape round the tomb is beautiful—but "cold—strange," like the ripe corn which is strange and "alien" in the Nightingale Ode. It seems "as in a dream, / I dreamed long ago, now new begun." Already the sense of the past penetrates the present moment and alters it to strangeness. Keats is experiencing what the psychologist would probably calle *déjà vu*, a psychic phenomenon paralleled in the mythic sense of temporal interconnection. In the next two lines the imagination now brings the future into the present moment: "The short-liv'd paly Summer is but won / From Winter's ague, for one hour's gleam." At the very moment of experiencing the beauty of summer, Keats is simultaneously aware of the brevity of summer, of winter's coming on. The title of the poem, too, should not be overlooked: the landscape may be beautiful in the summer of living fulfillment, but it surrounds a tomb, a reminder of death. So Keats is forced to say: "All is cold beauty; pain is never done." Joy and pain have become perplexed precisely as they will at the opening of the *Ode to a Nightingale*. Keats then wonders if anyone

> has a mind to relish, Minos-wise,
> The real of Beauty, free from that dead hue
> Sickly imagination and sick pride
> [Cast?] wan upon it?

He seems to say that all men at some time so perplex their responses, just as he said all men come to the Cave of Quietude, very few persons being able to escape the "visitings" of the first section of the *Epistle*. Though H. W. Garrod substitutes "sickly" for "fickly," the word found in Keats's letter-copy of the poem, I suspect J. C. Maxwell is right in arguing that Keats meant the word he wrote, perhaps having found it in *King Lear*.[16] The imagination is fickle, in that it cannot remain fixed upon the present moment alone but must continually vex that moment with some other dimension of time. Keats concludes the sonnet by calling this imaginative investment of the moment a "sin" against the present, just as in the sonnet on the Nile and in the *Epistle* he wished away "dark fancies" and "moods of one's mind."

Thus in the *Epistle to Reynolds* the mythic sense of time brings Keats to his first full recognition of the nature of his imagination and the double-edge of process. In announcing his vast idea of process in *Sleep and Poetry*, he admitted that he had not enough "spanning wisdom" to speak it clearly. In concluding the *Epistle* he says, "I have a mysterious tale, /

---

16. "Keats' Sonnet on the Tomb of Burns," *KSJ* 9 (1955): 77–80.

And cannot speak it." To express himself he uses in both instances the image of the sea. In *Sleep and Poetry*, as in the
sonnet on the Nile and in the painting in the *Epistle*, the body
of water is seen with islands; process offers pattern and consolation. But as Keats's imagination matures, he sees "too far
into the sea"; perception of process spoils the present moment.
Yet if the *Epistle* says he sees too far, it implies just as strongly that he does not see far enough. Having left the Chamber
of Maiden-Thought, he is wandering in "dark passages" of
consciousness. But he understands that the problem of consciousness cannot be resolved by disavowing consciousness;
he knows that he must press on to a wider perspective, a
mode of conciousness that will allow him to reconcile "good
and ill."

Many of the poems written after the *Epistle* explore its
dark passages, particularly those written on the Scottish walking tour. The odes of May, 1819, again take up the problem
of consciousness. Like poems by Yeats, they vacillate between
solutions (the *Ode to Psyche* and the *Ode on Melancholy*)
and struggle (*Ode to a Nightingale*). When Keats came in the
following summer to write *Lamia*, he took as his theme the
attempt of man to disavow the complex awareness of his consciousness, to separate good from ill, joy from pain. What
chiefly characterizes his heroine as a supernatural being is
her power

> To unperplex bliss from its neighbor pain;
> Define their pettish limits, and estrange
> Their points of contact, and swift counterchange;
> Intrigue with the specious choas, and dispart
> Its most ambiguous atoms with sure art. . . .

"Every word" she wrote to Lycius "entic'd him on / To unperplex'd delight and pleasure known" (1, 326–27). Because
he would have the joy and pain distinct, Lycius, by his own
folly, is led to destruction. The poem dramatizes the failure
that comes to one who will not press on beyond the contradictions of consciousness to a state of mind in which those contradictions are accepted and consequently transformed into a

vision of the harmonious operation of the cosmos. Somewhere Hegel has said that the hand that inflicts the wound must also be the hand that heals it. Keats would have affirmed the maxim, and his culminating statement on the nature and transformation of consciousness is his last long poem and its revision. There the post-mythic poet, in an act of mythic apprehension, reaches a threshold beyond dark passages.

II

The Two *Hyperions*

Keats's last major assault on the problem of mythic time and its ensuing melancholy is *Hyperion* and its revision. In both versions of the poem Keats attempts to reconcile his apprehension of process with the perplexity of joy and grief resulting from it. Unable to disavow his vast idea or his particular apprehension of time, he has no recourse but to accept the paradoxical emotion they bring him. He comes to see in *Hyperion* that the increased consciousness implied by the imagination's investment of the present with the future is not a sickness, a "sin" against nature as he had thought in the sonnet *On Visiting the Tomb of Burns*. Rather, this mode of apprehension places man above the other creatures in nature and in this sense deifies him. Only more consciousness can solve the problem of consciousness. The poems show, to borrow Kleist's phrase, that the gates of Paradise can only be unlocked when man eats of the fruit of the tree again.

Hyperion is an epic on the theme of consciousness, more particularly on the origin of two kinds of consciousness: the Titans' fall into self-consciousness, into the human condition, the separation of the self from the world, attended by awareness of time, sorrow, and mortality; and, in Apollo's deification, the birth of a new and more expansive mode of consciousness that transcends but does not cancel that separation, the mode of melancholy or tragic joy. The poem's theme is closely related to one of Yeats's favorite thoughts: "two states of consciousness, being or persons, which die each other's life, live each other's death" (LY, 918). Through its theme and plot the poem transcends its mythological apparatus to become not merely an expression of mythic apprehension but, in Eliade's terms, a mythic narrative or myth proper. According to Eliade, "the myth proclaims the appearance of a new cosmic situation or of a primordial event. Hence it is always the recital of a creation; it tells how something was accomplished, began to *be*."[17] Every myth shows how a reality came into being, "whether it be the total reality, the cosmos, or only a fragment—an island, a species of plant, a human institution."[18] Clearly, *Hyperion* and its revision fit Eliade's definition. Both poems narrate the coming of something into being: human consciousness and a higher god-like consciousness that man can attain. Both poems record "primordial events in consequence of which man becomes what he is today"[19] (self-conscious) and, one should add, what it is possible for him to become tomorrow.

Had Keats realized more clearly that his real subject was both of these events, he might have reshaped his existing materials to bring the two themes into better balance—or he might have delayed Apollo's deification until Hyperion's fall. But committed as he was to *Paradise Lost* as his epic model, he let the structure of Milton's work blind him to the fact that his own epic was about not only Paradise Lost but also Paradise Regained. In plot and handling of scene he committed himself to the former theme; but in sympathy and dramatic thrust he committed himself to the latter. Hence there were indeed too many Miltonisms in the poem, at a level more damaging than style alone.

Quite possibly Keats did not become aware that his theme was double and that Paradise Regained was the true thrust of his intention until he had written the scene of Apollo's deification. In a thematic sense the action of *Hyperion* is complete with that scene; but in a dramatic sense the action has barely

17. *The Sacred and the Profane* (New York, 1961), p. 95.
18. Ibid., p. 97.
19. *Myth and Reality* (New York, 1963), p. 11.

begun. Realizing this flaw Keats did two things. First, under the influence of Dante, he recast the poem as a dream; by means of Dante he could perhaps keep his plot free enough from Milton's epic for his real theme of Paradise Regained to be dramatically balanced with his original theme of Hyperion's fall. Second, in order to make his real theme clear he wrote an Induction in which he himself experiences Apollo's deification. This Induction, perhaps the height of Keats's poetic career, is a summary of the theme of consciousness that the epic proper is meant to dramatize. In repeating in his own person what is to be the subject of his myth—and doing so under the tutelage of a priestess—Keats brings his poem close to ritual. In ritual, Eliade writes, "the imitation of an archetypal model is a reactualization of the mythical moment when the archetype was revealed for the first time."[20] Keats means his Induction to be evidence that his epic is a paradigm for human experience. Eliade is to the point: "myths provide [man] with an explanation of the World and his own mode of being in the World . . . by recollecting the myths, by reenacting them, he is able to repeat what the Gods, the Heroes, or the Ancestors did *ab origine*."[21] In the Great Moment of mythic apprehension the Golden Age can briefly return.

In Apollo-Keats's deification, however, it is not the first Golden Age that returns but a new Golden Age. Keats's concept of time in *Hyperion* is spiral rather than circular; it is a compromise between purely mythic time and historical time. Within the poem Oceanus's view of events is couched in historical terms; some critics have therefore believed a theme of evolution or progress to be at the center of the poem. But this is to oversimplify Keats's apprehension of time and to overlook the more central theme of consciousness. Although Oceanus says that profane or historical time may yet see a higher consciousness or greater beauty than Apollo's come to reign, his remark is made within the context of the theme of process. Furthermore, *The Fall of Hyperion* implies that, should

20. *Cosmos and History* (New York, 1959), p. 76.
21. *Myth and Reality*, p. 13.

Chapter Five

Apollo be dethroned by a higher consciousness, Keats would again, as he does in *The Fall* itself, celebrate that higher consciousness by returning, *in illo tempore*, to the time of its creation or birth, its coming to be.

Keats's apprehension of mythic time is central to his theme. The Titans and the Olympians belong to differing levels of consciousness because they have differing perceptions of time. The Titans live in the present alone, unperplexed by the past or the future. Theirs is an unself-conscious identity with the world through which they rule natural processes while remaining unaware of process or time itself, except in so far as they know the eternal return of seasonal and stellar events. Linear time is unknown to them and so, consequently, is death. Though gods, they are like the men of Latmos in *Endymion*, of whom Keats wrote: "High genitors, unconscious did they cull / Time's sweet first-fruits" (I, 320–21). Thea, for example, is called "a Goddess of the infant world" (I, 26), and it is clear that Keats meant the Titans to represent "the infant or thoughtless Chamber, in which we remain as long as we do not think" (LI, 280). With their fall, however, they enter "dark passages," as Keats phrased it in his letter (LI, 280), the world of time, mortality, and self-consciousness. In book III of *Hyperion* Enceladus bemoans the Titans' new condition. His grief, he says, is not merely for his lost realm; more grievous is the loss of "days of peace and slumberous calms," days "innocent of scathing war." It had been the Titans' nature to take simple pleasure in the moment, unreflecting and unperplexed by thought of past or future. Their pleasure—and their rule—was "before we knew the winged thing, / Victory, might be lost, or might be won." The Olympians, in rebelling, have introduced the Titans to a new consciousness of time, mortality, and self division for which their natures are unsuited. Unable to accommodate this new knowledge, they are unable to hold their realms.

In contrast, the Olympians, represented by Apollo, are evidently at the poem's beginning in something like the state to which the Titans fall. That is, they bear the knowledge of time and mortality, the perplexity of joy and grief. Their revolt lies in their ability to move to a level of consciousness in which these elements, while preserved, are transformed by their placement in a wider view of the cosmos; and this wider view restores, again transformed, the virtues of the Titans' unfallen state. Apollo's deification is the expansion of his consciousness to a breadth which synthesizes the Titans' fallen and unfallen states. He moves out of the Chamber of Maiden Thought, through dark passages, to the next chamber, for which Keats had no term. He moves, as Blake would say, from "experience" to "organized innocence," and the poem implies that this movement is possible for fallen man through the employment of mythic apprehension.

Characteristic of the Titans' fallen state is a general sense of division; they are sundered from their harmonious union with the world and are separated from their former natures, left indeed without a sense of self. Saturn has obviously been separated from the elements (1, 55–63), from his power (1, 106–12), from his previous self (1, 112–16). This crescendo of loss climaxes with a Lear-like cry of pathos: " 'Thea! Thea! where is Saturn?' " (1, 134.) No modern could express with greater anguish the crisis of self-identity. Saturn does not know who he is because he has never had to ask the question and so has never been conscious enough of the self as an entity separate from the world to formulate an answer. His "soul-making" is just begun. He says, "I am smother'd up, / And buried from all godlike exercise / Of influence" (1, 106–108); both verbs bespeak a self isolated from the world, a self turned inward. A few lines later he says:

> I am gone
> Away from my own bosom: I have left
> My strong identity, my real self,
> Somewhere between the throne, and where I sit
> Here on this spot of earth.
> (1, 112–16)

Caught in the Sartrean *en soi*, his perceiving ego or now fallen self is unaware of separation from the world—and therefore from that unself-conscious pre-fallen self he would like to think of as still real. The pre-fallen unself-conscious harmony

of the ego and the world has now not only divided; it has
fallen into three. No wonder he cries "Where is Saturn?" He
asks if he cannot create another world (1, 141–45). In light of
the more urgent task before him, the creation of a self, the
question is as naive as the fancies in Keats's early verse.

Hyperion has not yet fallen, so his situation is more subtle.
In him we see develop a characteristic of the fall, the consciousness of future time and its anxious uncertainty. He is
visited by omens that "fright and perplex" him. Though these
are not intimations of mortality (in *The Fall* Saturn cries
"there shall be death—Moan. moan"), they nevertheless alter
his relationship to the world:

> Why do I know ye? why have I seen ye? why
> Is my eternal essence thus distraught
> To see and to behold these horrors new?
> (1, 231–33)

Will they, he wonders. dispossess him of his home—which he
describes in Edenic terms (1, 235–39). climaxed by "the
blaze, the splendor, and the symmetry."

> Even here, into my centre of repose,
> The shady visions come to domineer,
> Insult, and blind, and stifle up my pomp.—
> (1, 243–45)

"Blind and stifle up"—again the verbs bespeak a self shut off
from the world. To counter these forebodings and to test his
power, he rushes to the sun before his usual time:

> Fain would he have commanded, fain took throne
> And bid the day begin, if but for change.
> He might not:—No, though a primeval God:
> The sacred seasons might not be disturb'd.
> (1, 290–93)

"If but for change"; the phrase is richly suggestive. By his
very action to counter his growing consciousness of the future, Hyperion shows himself changed, out of harmony and
out of timing with the element and function in the world
that hitherto has been his unselfconscious identity. The curve
of his fall has begun. His father says:

> Now I behold in you fear, hope, and wrath;
> Actions of rage and passion; even as
> I see them, on the mortal world beneath,
> In men who die.   (i, 332–35)

Human, all too human. For this is, in terms of consciousness, what the Titans become when they fall. Thea sees Saturn fallen to this same mortality:

> There saw she direst strife; the supreme God
> At war with all the frailty of grief,
> Of rage, of fear, anxiety, revenge,
> Remorse, spleen, hope, but most of all despair.
> Against these plagues he strove in vain; for Fate
> Had pour'd a mortal oil upon his head . . .
>   (ii, 92–97)

Consciousness of the self and world are born. The Titans fall.

In the complaint of Clymene (ii, 252–99), we learn of the inability of the fallen Titans to bear the perplexity of pleasure and pain that will characterize Apollo's apprehension. The beginning of her story echoes the sonnet *On Visiting the Tomb of Burns*, with the difference that she, unlike Keats in the sonnet, would chastise the landscape for its simple mode of moment to moment existence:

> I stood upon the shore, a pleasant shore,
> Where a sweet clime was breathed from a land
> Of fragrance, quietness, and trees, and flowers.
> Full of calm joy it was, as I of grief;
> Too full of joy and soft delicious warmth;
> So that I felt a movement in my heart
> To chide, and to reproach that solitude
> With songs of misery, music of our woes . . .
>   (ii, 262–69)

As she sang there came, from "an island of the sea" just opposite the shore, "enchantment," "a golden melody" so blissful that "a living death was in each gush of sound." The "living death" of this music made Clymene "sick / Of joy and grief at once." In book iii Mnemosyne follows suit:

> all the vast
> Unwearied ear of the whole universe

Chapter Five

> Listen'd in pain and pleasure at the birth
> Of such new tuneful wonder.
>
> (III, 64–67)

Clymene is experiencing melancholy, which she is unsuited by nature to bear.

We learn in the third book that the melody Clymene heard was made by the young Apollo, evidently while gaining intuitive knowledge of process from the sea surrounding his isle:

> Throughout all the isle
> There was no covert, no retired cave
> Unhaunted by the murmurous noise of waves,
> Though scarcely heard in many a green recess.
> He listen'd, and he wept, and his bright tears
> Went trickling down the golden bow he held.
>
> (III, 38–43)

By placing Apollo on "an island of the sea"—a sea into which Clymene sees too far, as Keats had done in the *Epistle to Reynolds*—the poet returns to his principal metaphor for the "vast idea" passage and the sonnet on Chapman's Homer. Thus it is not surprising that, of all the Titans, it is Oceanus who argues at the council for acceptance of process, recognition that "We fall by course of Nature's law, not force / Of thunder, or of Jove" (II, 181–82). "Nor are we," he adds, "thereby more conquer'd, than by us the rule / Of shapeless Chaos" (II, 215–17); in cosmic process nothing is totally lost. His lengthy speech on the interconnection of all elements of creation has already been discussed in chapter 3.

This speech lies between his insistence that the Olympians are "A power more strong in beauty, born of us / And fated to excel us, as we pass / In glory that old Darkness" (II, 213–15) and his repetition of the idea: " 'tis the eternal law / That first in beauty should be first in might" (II, 228–29). It thus implies that it is their knowledge of process which makes the Olympians "first in beauty." But a closer look at the speech is very revealing.

Oceanus's example of the interchange of favors moves from darkness and "shapeless Chaos" through earth (Saturn's mother, line 20) and forest-trees (the Titans) to eagles (the

Olympians) "who do tower above us in their beauty." The vehicles in the extended metaphor move from sheer matter through unconscious life to a sentience with spiritual overtones. The parent-child relationship among them, in an example of mythic interconnectedness, more importantly establishes a continuous spectrum of consciousness, from its absence through its presence to a higher consciousness not understood by Oceanus, since he lacks it.

If Keats's metaphor is taken seriously, what else can "beauty" mean but a kind of energy, or a kind of consciousness? Chapter 2 argued that Keats generally meant the former; the present chapter has given evidence that the second could apply. I think, in fact, that Keats is trying to bring together in the poem two of his favorite speculations, beauty and melancholy. When beauty is energy, it follows that those possessing the greatest amounts of it will be "first in might"; Oceanus's successor has "such a glow of beauty in his eyes" that the Titan bids farewell to his empire. When beauty is Apollo's kind of consciousness, its possessor also has power, the power that comes with greater knowledge and makes a god of him—or, in Apollo's case, a greater god. Experiencing that greater knowledge entails a great intensity of feeling. So through the factor of intensity both aspects of beauty meet.

The Olympians' beauty is primarily determined by their new consciousness. The Titans' beauty, now surpassed, resided in their unself-conscious identity with the natural world, their very having sentience and energy—an Adamic innocence unaware of the radical subject-object duality known to mortals. The ambiguous description of Thea's face is related to Keats's theme: "How beautiful, if sorrow had not made / Sorrow more beautiful than Beauty's self" (1, 35–36). Either Thea's face has been made more beautiful by its sudden plunge into melancholy, or her face would be more beautiful if she were capable of bearing melancholy, whose beauty far exceeds the unperplexed beauty of simple joy. In either case the description foreshadows the face of Moneta in *The Fall*.

It is Mnemosyne—Memory—who brings Apollo to the

new mode of apprehension. He has, in looking at nature, at the sea, intuited her presence (III, 51–59). Mnemosyne asks him why he weeps and he replies: "Why should I tell thee what thou so well seest?" Keats here implies that theme taken up in so much of his work since the *Epistle to Reynolds*: the power of memory and its agent, the imagination, to invest the present moment with other temporal dimensions. Apollo continues: "I strive to search wherefore I am so sad, / Until a melancholy numbs my limbs." By his intuited vision he is numbed as Keats was numbed in the opening stanza of the Nightingale Ode. He longs for greater knowledge.[22] "Are there not other regions than this isle?" What divinity causes the thunder "While I here idle listen on the shores / In fearless yet in aching ignorance?" He quests for greater consciousness, just as Keats had done in the sonnet *To Homer*, "Standing aloof in giant ignorance . . . As one who sits ashore and longs perchance / To visit dolphin-coral in deep seas" (K, 463).

When he looks into Mnemnosyne's silent face he finds the "wondrous lesson" and "knowledge enormous" he has sought. He wins that state Keats had hoped, a year before, he might in time attain: "high-rife / With old Philosophy, / And mad with glimpses of futurity!" (K, 480) Memory makes him conscious of process:

> Names, deeds, gray legends, dire events, rebellions,
> Majesties, sovran voices, agonies,
> Creations and destroyings, all at once
> Pour into the wide hollows of my brain,
> And deify me. . . .
>
> (III, 114–18)

Here indeed is the Great Moment in which the mythic apprehension of process is reconciled with joy and pain. Apollo accepts the vision of temporal suffering and so transcends it; he

---

22. In this longing he wants to explore straight homeward the essence of the stars and dart empathically into them (lines 99–102). Compare *Endymion*, I, 97–99: the altar fire has made the clouds a pyre of such brightness that "therein / A melancholy spirit well might win / Oblivion and melt out his essence fine. . . ."

"dies into life" as Yeats does in *A Dialogue of Self and Soul.*
Tragic joy is won.

"In dreams begin responsibilities." This is the epigraph to
the volume of verse with which Yeats entered his maturity as
a poet. It might well stand in like position in *The Fall of Hyperion*, where the experience of *Hyperion* is now seen in the
mode of dream or vision; Apollo's deification is transferred to
Keats himself and placed as an Induction to the epic proper.[23]
In this Induction Keats first imagines himself by a screen of
forest trees and arbor of teeming vines. Finding the remnants
of a meal, he is overcome with hunger and thirst; he eats, and

> pledging all the Mortals of the world,
> And all the dead whose names are in our lips,
> Drank. That full draught is parent of my theme.
> (I, 44–47)

The draught leads him to the sanctuary wherein he finds Moneta, and in this obvious sense is parent to his theme. But the
actual pledge he takes has as its theme human mortality and
process and hence is parent to the theme of the entire poem.

The sanctuary is vast and represents the whole history of
man and nature's building and destruction, just as the Enchanted Castle in the *Epistle to Reynolds* represented the
whole history of man's religious endeavors:

> So old the place was, I remembered none
> The like upon the earth: what I had seen
> Of grey Cathedrals, buttress'd walls, rent towers,
> The superannuations of sunk realms,
> Or Nature's Rocks toil'd hard in waves and winds,
> Seem'd but the faulture of decrepit things
> To that eternal domed monument.
> (I, 65–71)

As has often been noted, the "strange vessels and large draperies" that lie about invoke religious connotations. The col-
umns supporting the temple run "north and south, ending in

23. The most generally satisfying interpretation of the poem's Induction is, I think, offered by Brian Wicker, "The Disputed Lines in *The
Fall of Hyperion*," *EIC* 7 (1957): 28–41. I am not convinced, however,
that the Christian parallels are so strong as Wicker believes them to be,
and I offer a different reading of the disputed lines.

in mist / Of nothing." The images that open the *Epistle* likewise "come from north and south," directions in opposition to
Keats's favorite compass point, the west, so often his source of
harmonious vision. The west of this sanctuary presents a huge
image, later defined as Saturn's, and the raised altar tended by
Moneta.

Westward Keats moves, to the base of the altar. The con-
frontation between the poet and Moneta bears some similarity
to that between Yeats and Rocky Voice in *The Man and the
Echo*. Yeats descends, doubts his life work, and is told to "Lie
down and die," before he finds the strength to affirm his life.
Moneta commands Keats to ascend or die. Before he can begin
the climb, a "palsied chill / Struck from the paved level up
my limbs . . . I strove hard to escape / The numbness." With
this word we are returned once more to that paradoxical emotion at the opening of the Nightingale *Ode*. "One minute before death" his "iced foot" touches "the lowest stair" and mi-
raculously he is elevated to Moneta's height. The passage was
prefigured in the Cave of Quietude:

> Enter none
> Who strive therefore: on the sudden it is won.
> Just when the sufferer begins to burn,
> Then it is free to him. . . .
>
> (IV, 531–34)

Keats asks Moneta why he was spared. She begins her reply by positing two general categories of men: (1) All those
"who find a haven in the world, / Where they may thoughtless sleep away their days." These, one assumes, form the
bulk of mankind—the insensitive, the unimaginative, the un-
sympathetic. (2) "Those to whom the miseries of the world /
Are misery and will not let them rest," who "love their fel-
lows even to the death" and "Labour for mortal good." Only
these, Moneta says, "can usurp this height." Keats, telling her
that there must be "thousands" in the world belonging in this
second category, asks why he is there alone. (Compare the
ode's "Veil'd Melancholy has her sovran shrine, / Though

seen of none save him . . .") With her reply—that these others are "no visionaries . . . no dreamers weak"—Keats introduces two terms whose ambiguous use is to trouble the rest of his argument.

At Moneta's reply, the second category (2) is further divided, into (*a*) others—those who don't come to the temple, who "seek no wonder but the human face"—and (*b*) Keats, who is there because he is "less than they . . . a dreaming thing" and by implication a visionary and a dreamer, unlike the others. The others do not come because they *accept* the miseries and do not try to escape them as visionaries like Keats do. Visionaries know the miseries as well as the "others" do but can't accept and so attempt to escape them as Keats did in his early "visionary" poetry. Moneta would have Keats accept: "think of the Earth," she admonishes. Visions are finally no escape ("What bliss even in hope is there for thee?") and earth is Keats's home ("every creature hath its home"), the lesson Endymion learned.

On earth "Every sole man hath days of joy and pain / . . . The pain alone; the joy alone; distinct." The dreamer (the argument does not speak about the "others" in category 2) "venoms all his days" by mixing the two, as Keats did in the *Epistle to Reynolds*, imagining there future woes beyond the present joy and thus "bearing more woe than all his sins deserve." At the same time, if one is so constituted that this mixed mode of perception is inevitable, inherent as it were (a "sickness not ignoble"), then he must learn to respond to it not by complaint or escape but by acceptance. For such instruction or initiation ("that cause") Keats and others are admitted to the mystery of Process ("are suffer'd in these temples") and so "standest safe beneath this statute's knees." So ends the first passage of the argument.

In one transcript of the poem, the remaining part of the argument (lines 186–210) bears a note that Keats "seems to have intended to erase this." Certainly the passage is problematic; but ambiguous as the word "dreamer" now becomes, I do not find this second passage inconsistent with the preceding argument (lines 147–85). What Keats does is introduce a new term or category, "poet," which, like the term "dreamer," is handled with ambiguity and not clearly fitted into the two categories with which his argument began. My own suspicion is that he intended not to cancel but to rewrite this second passage (lines 186–210), to bring its terms "poet" and "dreamer" more clearly into line with his opening argument.

To this point no mention has been made of poets, as such. In the ambiguous second passage (lines 186–220), Keats introduces the "tribe" of poets. "Sure a poet," he says, "is a sage," and by implication poets are placed in the second category (2). But he says he feels that he is no poet himself and asks "What am I then?" Moneta replies that he is "of the dreamer tribe" and says the two tribes are "distinct, / Diverse, sheer opposites, antipodes." The ambiguity in the argument results from this: neither Keats nor Moneta makes clear that a poet is, first, a man who writes poetry, and that what the man knows, as man, may or may not be realized in his verse. If he is a man with wisdom and that wisdom is realized in his verse, he is a true poet. If he is a man without wisdom —or if he has wisdom but cannot embody it in his verse— then he is a dreaming poet. The true poet "pours out a balm upon the world, / The other vexes it." The true poet, that is, gives the world example of acceptance. But dreaming poets, like the dreamers and visionaries in the previous argument, "vex" the world with their complaints ("mock lyrists . . . careless Hectorers in proud bad verse") or with their escapes (specifically, exhibitions of ego, "large self worshippers"). Keats is a poet in the first sense; he is a man writing poetry. But he is not a true poet because his verse has not yet fully realized the wisdom of the man; moreover, that wisdom is not yet fully formulated, he but stands at the threshold of it, as he stands before Moneta. Keats's poetry has been that "of the dreamer tribe." But as a man, however, he is not a dreamer; as a man he intuits the myth of process and the act of acceptance, tragic joy, and his task is henceforth to get his knowledge into verse and so write true poetry. Because he is capable of coming into further knowledge that will allow him to realize his wisdom in poetry, he is able to mount the steps.

So read, the ambiguous second passage is not discontinuous with the lines preceding it. Its argument merely divides the second category of men (2) into three types rather than the two types found in the first argument. There are: (*a*) dreamers and visionaries, who *may* also write "poetry" ("mock lyrists"), but who as men or as poets either complain of or escape from the miseries and never come to full knowledge of tragic joy; (*b*) other men, non-artists, who accept, with or without special knowledge, the miseries. Neither of these groups comes to Moneta's temple; the first lacks the capacity for her instruction, the second has no need for it. The third group (*c*) contains the true poets, those writing, with acceptance and tragic joy, of Moneta's vision. If, like Keats, they have capacity for her wisdom and need of it before succeeding as true poets rather than as dreaming "poets," then they are allowed to ascend the steps of her temple. They are still "dreamers," in the sense that they can dream of worlds where miseries are not. But if they do not remain in those worlds they do not remain mere dreamers. They are certainly equal to the "others" in (*b*), the non-artists, and are "less than they" only in their consequent need of reinstruction.

That the argument of these two passages is not sufficiently worked out says what has so often been said about Keats: his wisdom, the wisdom of the letters, is often ahead of the realized content of the poetry. Together, however, the two versions of the argument indicate by the opposition of "poet" and "dreamer" that Keats meant the Induction to parallel the opposition in the epic proper between the Olympians and the Titans.

These definitions established. Keats next wishes to know whose temple he is at and who it is that ministers there. Moneta gives him her name. defining the image as Saturn's. It it fitting that the temple she tends be Saturn's: the Titan's mode of consciousness before his fall—an Edenic innocence,

the self in harmony with nature—is what man strives to gain
for himself, as an image of eternity, through means that do
not deny his mortal nature; Moneta will teach these means.
Her name, however, creates new ambiguities. Mnemosyne in
Hyperion was "an ancient Power" who had "forsaken old
and sacred thrones / For prophecies" of Apollo's coming (III,
76–78). Here her counterpart is "Sole Priestess" of the fallen
Saturn, "the pale Omega of a wither'd race" (I, 288) and, at
the same time, foster mother of Apollo (I, 286). Evidently
Keats intends her to be, as Kenneth Muir suggests, "the
priestess of Truth, who had outlived the various manifestations of truth in different ages of the world."[24]

That she is this the sanctuary surrounding Saturn's temple
has established. But the poem defines this truth in more specific terms. Moneta is the "Shade of Memory" (I, 282)—and
the foster mother of Apollo because the poetic imagination re-
lies on memory. The poem suggests, like the *Ode to Psyche*,
that the imagination itself, operating mythically, comes to
replace that older set of myths no longer operative in the
modern world.

Being the shade of Memory, Moneta will also be, like her
counterpart in *Hyperion*, instructress in process, the mythic
sense of time, serving Keats as Yeats's instructors served him.
Keats intimates this even before she lifts her veils:

> There was a silence while the altar's blaze
> Was fainting for sweet food: I look'd thereon,
> And on the paved floor, where nigh were pil'd
> Faggots of cinnamon, and many heaps
> Of other crisped spicewood—then again
> I look'd upon the altar and its horns
> Whiten'd with ashes, and its lang'rous flame,
> And then upon the offerings again;
> And so by turns. . . .   (I, 232–40)

Keats looks from the present of the woods to their future as
ash, and so back again, in cycle. Presently Moneta lifts her
veils.

24. "The Meaning of *Hyperion*," *EIC* 2 (1952): 65.

Melancholy's Sovran Shrine

> Then saw I a wan face,
> Not pin'd by human sorrows, but bright blanch'd
> By an immortal sickness which kills not;
> It works a constant change, which happy death
> Can put no end to; deathwards progressing
> To no death was that visage; it had pass'd
> The lily and the snow; and beyond these
> I must not think now, though I saw that face. . . .
>
> (I, 256-63)

"All changed, changed utterly: / A terrible beauty is born" (Y, 178). Her face is the very image of process. In describing it Keats uses the same word, "sickness," that hovered about his own similar vision in earlier work, there to criticize it. Now, however, the vision of process and the imagination's investment of the present with memory of man's pain and foreknowledge of his mortality become the supreme statement of his faith. He has realized his insight of a year before: "Until we are sick, we understand not;—in fine, as Byron says, 'Knowledge is Sorrow'; and I go on to say that 'Sorrow is Wisdom'" (L1, 279). When, some moments later, he "sees" what she sees, it is a visual melancholy, a "shrouded vale" (I, 311) reminiscent of the ode's "green hill in an April shroud," and he writes:

> Without stay or prop
> But my own weak mortality, I bore
> The load of this eternal quietude,
> The unchanging gloom, and the three fixed shapes . . .
> A whole moon.
> For by my burning brain I measured sure
> Her silver seasons shedded on the night
> And ever day by day methought I grew
> More gaunt and ghostly—Oftentimes I pray'd
> Intense, that Death would take me from the vale
> And all its burthens—Gasping with despair
> Of change. . . .
>
> (I, 388-99)

Keats, like Oceanus, is learning to accept process, "to bear all naked truths, / And to envisage circumstance" (*Hyperion*, II, 203-204).

Chapter Five

Moneta herself suffers her vision:

> My power, which to me is still a curse,
> Shall be to thee a wonder; for the scenes
> Still swooning vivid through my globed brain
> With an electral changing misery
> Thou shalt . . . behold,
> Free from all pain, if wonder pain thee not.
>
> (I, 243–48)

It is a curse to her because, as an immortal goddess, she must bear it eternally; there is no escape from it just as there is no apparent escape from the round of rebirth in Yeats. As a mortal Keats will, presumably, fall back into "unperplexed" vision (compare lines 172–75 and my comment on them above) and so be, ironically, similar to the Titans before their fall. Nor should one forget that Moneta is herself a Titan. What suffers in her is not that Olympian part of her nature she shares with the fallen Titans. As their natures left them unable to deal with melancholy—with consciousness of time and process and thus with consciousness of the self's separation from the world—so the Titan aspect of her nature is pained by that same knowledge. Mortals—and Olympians— are by nature forced to live with the self's separation from nature. Though mortals may desire to live as Titans, just as Keats had done, their nature forbids that option, allowing them only the affirmation of self-consciousness and its attendant sorrows by which Olympian consciousness is superior to that in both men and Titans. If Keats were to view Moneta's knowledge without experiencing it, it would be merely "wonder" to him and he would be one of the "visionaries . . . dreamers weak." But he is not of that kind, which Moneta momentarily forgets (after the ambiguities of their long argument, this is not surprising). Thus she is wrong to think that he will see "free from all pain"; when Keats does see, it is with much pain, as the passage quoted above (I, 388–99) makes clear.

Keats's description of Moneta's face shows her to be similar to "Veil'd Melancholy," both figures foreshadowed by the

eyes described in the Cave of Quietude passage.[25] It makes of
her face what Yeats saw in his "rough beast": "a vast image
out of *Spiritus Mundi*" (y, 185). To his image each poet responds with some incomprehension: Yeats ends his poem in
question and Keats concludes his description saying "beyond
these / I must not think now." And, like the song of Yeats's
golden bird, which is fixed in or near a dome as Moneta is
placed in a huge sanctuary "with roof august" (1, 62), the
face of Keats's priestess contains what is past, present, and to
come.

When Keats is allowed to see within "the dark secret chamber of her skull," the epic proper begins. At this moment, as
Yeats wrote in another context, "All thought becomes an
image and the soul / Becomes a body . . . cast away / Beyond
the visible world" (y, 162). Keats is transported from the
present moment to that event *in illo tempore* whereby the
Olympians took ascendency over the Titans. In Moneta's
brain this past event is *the* event, forever relived, in the eternal return of mythic consciousness. Keats is initiated into
Moneta's knowledge by reliving the event, at least as specta-
tor. As Eliade says of mythic ritual, "the participants . . . become contemporaries of the mythical event."[26] Keats writes:
"there grew / A power within me of enormous ken, / To see
as a God sees" (1, 302–304). Eliade, writing of the initiate,
defines Keats's situation: "He who ascends by mounting the
steps of a sanctuary . . . ceases to be a man; in one way or
another, he shares in the divine condition."[27] Such initiation
is the Great Moment: "One attains the beginning of Time
and enters the Timeless—the eternal present. . . ."[28]

The god-like power of enormous ken that envelops Keats
is a power to "take the depth / Of things as nimbly as the

25. One remembers, too, the face of poetry described in *Sleep and
Poetry* (lines 394–95): "From off her throne / She overlook'd things that
I scarce could tell."
26. *The Sacred and the Profane*, p. 88.
27. Ibid., p. 119.
28. *Myth and Reality*, p. 86.

outward eye / Can size and shape pervade." He stresses here once more that empathy with essence, energy, or instress through which, in mythic apprehension, the solidarity of all life is affirmed, the theme that was the subject of chapter 2. The passage lends support to Middleton Murry's suggestion that Moneta's vision—now Keats's—represents "Being itself, made conscious."[29]

Yeats, I think, would have agreed with Murry. He said of Keats in 1921, quoting Ben Jonson, that he was "so crammed with life he can but grow in life with being."[30] Certainly he understood Moneta in some fashion similar to that set forth above, for twice he wrote as if he had both *Hyperions* in mind:

> He can only create the greatest imaginable beauty who has en- dured all imaginable pangs, for only when we have seen and fore- seen what we dread shall we be rewarded by that dazzling un- foreseen wing-footed wanderer. (M, 332)

> Again and again, [Lady Gregory] and I felt that we had got down, as it were, into some fibrous darkness, into some matrix out of which everything has come, some condition that brought together as though into a single scheme "exultations, agonies'. . . . (E, 429)

Writing of Balzac at the end of his life, he used terms more nearly fitting for himself and for the Keats who created Moneta: "Something . . . constrained him to think of the human mind as capable, during some emotional crisis . . . of containing within itself all that is significant in human history and of relating that history to timeless reality" (E, 440). The words describe not only the conviction but the presentational task of two of our greatest poets as, through mythic appre- hension, they win from acceptance of process a Great Moment

---

29. *Keats and Shakespeare* (London, 1964), p. 92. Though our inter- pretations differ considerably in detail, Murry's general response to Moneta is essentially my own: "She was 'the vast idea.' . . . She had become 'the mighty abstract idea of beauty in all things'; and Keats had struggled through 'purgatory blind' for a vision of her, face to face." Murry's book, in spite of its biographical excesses and the sometimes embarrassingly personal tone, still remains centrally accurate, I think, about the inner nature of Keats's imagination.

30. Letter in *The John Keats Memorial Volume*, ed. G. C. Williamson (London, 1921), p. 216. ·

transforming joy and pain into that tragic joy Keats found in melancholy. "We artists," Yeats wrote, "are the servants not of any cause but of mere naked life, and above all of that life in its nobler forms, where joy and sorrow are one, Artificers of the Great Moment" (E, 260).

Conclusion
Adam's Dream

Throughout his work Eliade insists that myths are the endeavor of man to maintain contact with being: "through the reactualization of his myths, religious man attempts to approach the gods and to participate in being."[1] To the man of mythic apprehension, being first reveals itself as Power, the Numinous. All myths, in subject, are probably about the relationship of man to Power, generally manifested as the gods. Creation myths exhibit that relationship in showing the gods to have made us. These myths are of primal importance because they establish the primal relationship. They validate the belief that such a relationship *is* real because it *was* real, *in illo tempore*. Myths that do not involve men validate the relationship of the gods to the material world, which they made. Hence, myths are narratives because action—especially creation—is the nature of Power and the nature of the relationship: the cosmos exists because the gods, with their power, acted, and act to sustain or destroy it. In this action, matter is transformed. Metamorphosis is a manifestation of the gods' power, and that power is the point of mediation between two things, events or states. It is only through the gods, for example, that man retains his junction with nature. As the mediating agent between man and nature, the gods share in and partake of both and so hold both in harmony. Hence the further man removes himself from nature, the further he removes himself from the gods or Power. History, in Eliade's sense, is nothing more than a temporal sequence in which all three participants—man, nature, and the gods—recede from one another. History is, indeed, the nightmare man wakens into, and it becomes the intent of mythic consciousness to deny linear time, the drift of things away from being into separation and ultimately death, physical or spiritual.

1. *The Sacred and the Profane* (New York, 1961), p. 106.

Cassirer does not, like Eliade, couch his analysis of mythic consciousness in ontological terms; epistemology is the center of his attention. Yet his contention that myth, religion, and art share some basic structure of consciousness allows one to say that they share, as well, the same ontological assumptions or intentions. One of Yeats's beliefs points in this direction: "All our thought seems to lead by antithesis to some new affirmation of the supernatural" (EX, 214).

Yeats's statement suggests, I think, a possible definition not merely of Romantic aesthetics but of the ground of aesthetics in general. Art—and literature is our particular concern—strives to express the mystery of being. Through this intention it distinguishes itself from decoration or entertainment, and in this intention is its relationship to myth and religion. I have in mind Gabriel Marcel's definition of mystery: "A mystery is a problem which encroaches upon its own data, invading them, as it were, and thereby transcending itself as a simple problem. . . . [It is] a reality rooted in what is beyond the domain of the problematical . . . a thing of which I cannot doubt without falling into contradiction."[2] Being is a concept that escapes definition, but I think Marcel will again suffice: "Being is what withstands—or what would withstand—an exhaustive analysis bearing on the data of experience and aiming to reduce them step by step to elements increasingly devoid of intrinsic or significant value."[3] When art seeks to organize its materials into a form identical to its content, an organic form, it moves toward its intention through means that particularize it as art. When I have experienced art, as Yeats wrote, "I have added to my being, not my knowledge" (E, 340).

If myth, religion, and art share the same ontological intention, it is almost impossible to say conclusively at what point religion is to be distinguished from myth or art is to be distinguished from both. I noted in my Introduction that Cassirer believes religion diverges from the matrix of mythic

2. Gabriel Marcel, *The Philosophy of Existence* (London, 1948), pp. 8, 11.
3. Ibid., p. 5.

apprehension through increased self-consciousness and the particularization of Power as localized, generally anthropomorphic deities, a distinction he pursues in *Language and Myth*. He offers, however, no analysis of the distinction between mythic and aesthetic apprehension, beyond saying that the artist is indifferent to the existence or non-existence of his object, art being conscious of its images, of their discrepancy from logos. I will suggest that myth wishes to *describe* what is, the cosmos; poetry, homologously, wishes to *create* a model of what is, the heterocosm. Poetry will be most like myth when, as in much Romantic poetry, it affirms the virtual identity of the model and the reality.

Through the act of creation the artist joins the priest in becoming, more than other men, like unto the gods. While the priest is in the presence of divine power, while he may be filled with it as a potency, a potential, the artist seems to exercise it. The audience, in turn, shares in this power of creation by the act of recreating the art work in experiencing it. Through the creation and experience of art, being is revealed. By means of rite and myth the religious man with creed can pass from ordinary temporal duration to the elevated Moment of sacred or mythic time. The religious man without creed—Keats or Yeats—can do so by means of art. Keats wrote: "Imagination and its empyreal reflection is the same as human life and its spiritual repetition" (L1, 185). Because art and myth offer parallel experiences, the elevation of the aesthetic moment promises us that "Adam's dream will do" (L1, 185). This is what Arnold dimly perceived when he predicted that poetry would come to fill many of the functions previously performed by religion.

When still a young man Yeats came to Arnold's conclusion: "whatever the great poets had affirmed in their finest moments was the nearest we could come to an authoritative religion, and . . . their mythology, their spirits of water and wind were but literal truth" (A, 55). In his early twenties, deprived of his childhood religion by Huxley and Tyndall, he "made a new religion, almost an infallible church of poetic tradition," believing that whatever the poets spoke "may be the nearest I can go to truth" because they spoke "out of the deepest instinct of man" (A, 71).

Yeats describes here a religious situation he shared with many post-Enlightenment writers, a situation by virtue of which Romantic literature has perhaps its central characteristic: the *quest* for being. The chief agents in creating this situation were two. The rise of science threatened to empty the physical universe of the numinous; being, like God, became an *ens absconditus*. British empiricism and its continental followers left the status of the self and of consciousness highly problematic. Because of these two interweaving reasons, being was not as available to immediate experience as it had been in the past. Romantic literature, then, can be seen as an attempt to confirm being's continued presence in the world and its availability to experience, in spite of scientific and epistemological doubt. This confirmation, however, can be made only after struggling with the very questions that epistemology raises, especially the questions of the self and of consciousness. This exploration, this search, is the paradigmatic *praxis* of Romantic literature: quest. Its object, as I say, is being. Romantic literature, like literature in general, has as its ultimate concern ontology. But the path to that concern, forced on it by history, is epistemology.

Faced with an epistemological crisis and the consequent necessity to quest for being, many Romantic poets fell back on what Yeats called "the deepest instinct of man" or, in the terms that I have borrowed from Cassirer, mythic apprehension. To defend, believe in, or even keep alive what had been the experience within organized religion, Christianity in particular, it became necessary not so much to secularize that experience as to reach behind it to the matrix in human nature from which it came. An endeavor that began with Blake, Wordsworth, Coleridge, and Keats became highly conscious in Yeats and in Eliot's *The Waste Land*; it continues in recent poets of lesser stature, Edwin Muir, Kathleen Raine, Dylan Thomas, and Theodore Roethke.

What the Romantic poet wishes to overcome is the sense of separation of himself from the world and hence from the divine or holy which actualizes both. He wishes, in short, to heal the wounds of radical self-consciousness. Probably the chief factor in the origin of self-consciousness is memory. Man can remember past events; and from their discrepancy with the present arises a sense of difference, of separation. We have only the word "forethought" for that faculty by means of which we project a future. But our ability to project a future different from the present likewise contributes to a sense of separation of events and things. Hence man is self-conscious to the extent that he lives in time and is aware of time. Through time man is separated from the world. His fall into self-consciousness is actually a fall into time; and the first thing time makes him aware of is death. Through his sense of time man learns the fact that he will die: others *have*, he *will*. What mythic consciousness and Romantic imagination must do, then, is harness memory to its own ends and deny the fact of death, affirm the solidarity of all life, of being.

The progression of time is negated, however, not by denying the existence of past and future but through subsuming them into an expanded present. Cassirer implies as much when he speaks of mythic time as the fusion of past, present, and future. Eliade, then, is surely correct in believing that the central intent of mythic narrative is to deny history or linear time. In his analysis myth accomplishes this by its eternal return to the beginning, to *illud tempus*.

If time past, present, and future are apprehended simultaneously, all events are seen as parts of a process. Process becomes the syntax of mythic apprehension, manifested in the insistence on metamorphosis; everything is connected to everything else and may change into everything else: life, death, the elements, the seasons. Here mythic apprehension coincides with the shift in concept by which being has been understood since 1800. Before the crisis to which Romanticism was the response, being had been generally understood as stasis, as a stable, static entity like Newton's absolute space and time or the pre-Humean self. With the Romantic movement, being came to be seen not as stasis but as process. The Romantic poets and philosophers, like Aristotle and Heraclitus before them, discovered that being manifests itself in a particular kind of change. Modern physics has carried this concept to the point where reality is thought of not as entity at all but merely as relationship, structure. Substance—physical or otherwise—has curiously disappeared, and patterns of motion are reality, along of course with forces, such as gravity, electricity, and magnetism. Being is now energy and force, known in its relationships, its structures or syntax. Whitehead was not wrong to speak of the aesthetics of science.

Through mythic apprehension one discovers, as Yeats said of two visions he experienced, "proof of the supremacy of imagination, of the power of many minds to become one, overpowering one another . . . till they have become a single, intense, unhesitating energy" (E, 36) that Keats called essence or beauty. Through a feeling response, in Keats's phrase "a greeting of the spirit," one comes into union with the Other: lovers, friends, the landscape, natural objects, or art objects. One may go out to their being in empathy, as Keats did, or like Yeats, draw them into himself, there to discover that *being* he shares with them. In either case the self comes to experience its own real being, being in the other, and the mode of existence that being takes in time, the mode of process, reciprocity, and metamorphosis. These revelations may occur simultaneously or one may lead to the others. This elevation of the Moment, in which being is revealed, the solidarity of all life affirmed, and death denied, validates the significance of the cosmos. Keats wrote: "An extensive knowledge is needful to thinking people—it takes away the heat and fever; and helps, by widening speculation, to ease the Burden of the Mystery" (LI, 277). For post-mythic man a "widening speculation" or consciousness is possible through mythic apprehension, leading him beyond dark passages of self-consciousness and separation to the mystery of being. Mythic apprehension becomes, as Keats wrote of the god Pan, "Dread opener of the mysterious doors / Leading to universal knowledge" (K, 73).

The Great Moment, however, is impossible to sustain. Mortal beauty, being energy, is tenuous and limited, it "drifts

away / Like the waters" (Y, 80). "Man is in love and loves
what vanishes, / What more is there to say?" (Y, 205) We
dwell with Beauty—"Beauty that must die"—and our lives
are spent in quest of Great Moments promising some world
more perfect than our own. In Keats the quest to sustain the
Great Moment becomes through repetition almost a myth itself. The pattern of action in *La Belle Dame Sans Merci* is a
paradigm for the action of *Endymion* (before its ending),
Lamia, Ode on a Grecian Urn and the *Ode to a Nightingale.*
At the failure of the quest, "A sense of real things comes
doubly strong, / and, like a muddy stream, would bear along /
My soul to nothingness" (K, 55). The very sense of self, of
one's own continuous being, is threatened when the self is
removed from that for which it yearns, that source of self toward which its energies are directed. Endymion cries, when
his vision is fled, "how crude and sore / The journey homeward to habitual self!" (II, 275–76)

When we are returned to the world of ordinary experience,
we are left questioning the truth of the idea we carry away
from the moment of insight. "All that I have said and done . . .
Turns into a question till I . . . never get the answers right"
(Y, 337). It seems that the consoling acts and constructs of
the imagination may be no more than imaginary—that one's
favorite speculations, institutions, his system of belief, may
at worst be fiction or at best have little objective authority.
This disjunction between the experience of value in the Great
Moment and the questioning of value after the moment has
passed ("Do I wake or sleep?") is a distinguishing characteristic of modern literature.[4] It is this questioning that makes
the believing lyre of mythic apprehension also, in Keats's
word, "fond." The adjective undercuts a total commitment—
impossible to post-mythic man—just as does Yeats's reiterated
verb "seem" in the poetic expression of his beliefs. Keats
wrote: "I am sometimes so very sceptical as to think Poetry
itself a mere Jack a lanthern to amuse whoever may chance
to be struck with its brilliance" (L1, 242). When the values

4. See Robert Langbaum, *The Poetry of Experience* (New York,
1957).

experienced in the Great Moment are no longer felt to be real in the publicly accepted idea of nature held by a culture as the given, one is forced, on the one hand, to question the validity of his experience, and, on the other, to quest for the experience again and again, that it may validate his everyday experience which, without it, increasingly lacks significance.

Just before the turn of the century Yeats wrote, "in the beginning of important things—in the beginning of love, in the beginning of the day, in the beginning of any work— there is a moment when we understand more perfectly than we understand again until all is finished" (E, 111). That moment of understanding at the beginning might well have been *The Wanderings of Oisin* which, as others have pointed out, curiously contains so many of Yeats's mature themes, just as so much of the mature Keats is held in suspension in his 1817 volume. Yeats "often had the fancy that there is some one myth for every man, which if we but knew it, would make us understand all that he did and thought" (E, 107). Like others before me, I have tried to explore the myth that I see in the work of Keats and Yeats. That myth is their quest for the mystery of being through mythic apprehension.

When all was finished, at the end of his life, Yeats felt that he understood again the meaning of his myth. In the last of his published letters, dated three weeks before his death, he wrote: "It seems to me that I have found what I wanted. When I try to put it all into a phrase I say, 'Man can embody truth but he cannot know it' " (LY, 922). His phrase means that truth is vital, essentially non-discursive, and all but synonymous with being. It can be lived—suffered, even— but it cannot have some finally objective status abstracted from the knowing subject. He said the same thing in verse:

> The signs and shapes;
> All those abstractions that you fancied were
> From the great Treatise of Parmenides;
> All, all those gyres and cubes and midnight things
> Are but new expression of her body
> Drunk with the bitter sweetness of her youth.
>
> (Y, 444)

Conclusion

"Her body" reconciles opposites and embodies being just as surely as the magnificent images that close *Among School Children*, the dancer and the chestnut tree. In these images, as in the flaming tree of *Vacillation*, beauty is truth and truth beauty. The idea was expressed some years earlier in *A Vision*. His instructors, he said, repeatedly held out to him the sun-dried skeletons of birds, and it seemed to him that they meant by these bones that he should turn his own thought away from abstractions to the living bird: "That bird signifies truth when it eats, evacuates, builds its nest, engenders, feeds its young; do not all intelligible truths lie in its passage from egg to dust?" (v, 214). In that bird is the energy of being, and its syntax or truth is the vast idea of process, perceived mythically as metamorphosis; past and future are part of the present, and in the birth of the young birds there is an eternal return to the beginning. Yeats was surely right to make this passage the climax of his chapter on "The Completed Symbol."

Bibliography

Abrams, M. H. *Natural Supernaturalism: Tradition and Revolution in Romantic Literature.* New York: W. W. Norton & Co., 1971.

Adams, Hazard. *William Blake: A Reading of the Short Poems.* Seattle: University of Washington Press, 1963.

——. "Yeats, Dialectic and Criticism." *Criticism* 10 (1968): 185–99.

Allen, Glen O. "The Fall of Endymion: A Study in Keats's Intellectual Growth." *KSJ* 6 (1957): 37–57.

Allot, Kenneth. "Keats's 'Ode to Psyche.'" *EIC* 6 (1956): 278–301.

Allot, Miriam. "'Isabella,' 'The Eve of St. Agnes' and 'Lamia.'" In *John Keats: A Reassessment,* edited by Kenneth Muir. Liverpool: Liverpool University Press, 1958.

Ball, Patricia M. *The Central Self: A Study in Romantic and Victorian Imagination.* London: University of London, Athlone Press, 1968.

Bate, Walter Jackson. *From Classic to Romantic: Premises of Taste in Eighteenth-Century England.* 1946. Reprinted. New York: Harper & Row, 1961.

——. *John Keats.* Cambridge: Harvard University Press, 1963.

——. *Negative Capability: The Intuitive Approach to Keats.* Cambridge: Harvard University Press, 1939.

Baumgartner, Paul R. "Keats: Theme and Image in a Sonnet." *KSJ* 8 (1959): 11–14.

Bayley, John. *The Romantic Survival: A Study in Poetic Evolution.* London: Constable, 1957.

Beja, Morris. *Epiphany in the Modern Novel.* Seattle: University of Washington Press, 1972.

Benziger, James. *Images of Eternity: Studies in the Poetry of Religious Vision from Wordsworth to T. S. Eliot.* Carbondale: University of Southern Illinois Press, 1962.

Bibliography

Beyer, W. W. *Keats and the Daemon King*. 1947. Reprinted. New York: Octagon Books, 1969.

————. "Some Notes to Keats's Letters." *JEGP* 51 (1952): 336–44.

Bidney, David. "On the Philosophical Anthropology of Ernst Cassirer and its Relation to the History of Anthropological Thought." In *The Philosophy of Ernst Cassirer*, edited by Paul Arthur Schilpp. New York: Tudor Publishing Co., 1958.

Blackstone, Bernard. *The Consecrated Urn: An Interpretation of Keats in Terms of Growth and Form*. London: Longmans, Green, 1959.

Bloom, Harold. *The Ringers in the Tower: Studies in Romantic Tradition*. Chicago: University of Chicago Press, 1971.

————. *The Visionary Company: A Reading of English Romantic Poetry*. New York: Doubleday & Co., 1963.

————. *Yeats*. New York: Oxford University Press, 1970.

Bolle, Kees. *The Freedom of Man in Myth*. Nashville: Vanderbilt University Press, 1968.

Bornstein, George. *Yeats and Shelley*. Chicago: University of Chicago Press, 1970.

Bowra, C. M. *The Romantic Imagination*. Cambridge: Harvard University Press, 1949.

Bradley, A. C. *Oxford Lectures on Poetry*. 1909. Reprinted. London: Macmillan and Co., 1950.

————. "Keats and 'Philosophy.'" In *The John Keats Memorial Volume*, edited by G. C. Williamson. London: John Lane, Bodley Head, 1921.

Bush, Douglas. *Mythology and the Romantic Tradition in English Poetry*. Cambridge: Harvard University Press, 1937.

Cassirer, Ernst. *An Essay on Man*. 1944. Reprinted. New Haven: Yale University Press, 1962.

————. *Language and Myth*. New York: Dover Publishers, 1946.

————. *The Myth of the State*. 1946. Reprinted. New Haven: Yale University Press, 1971.

Bibliography

————. *Mythical Thought*, vol. 2 in *The Philosophy of Symbolic Forms*. New Haven: Yale University Press, 1955.

Coleridge, Samuel Taylor. *Biographia Literaria*. 2 vols. Edited by John Shawcross. London: Oxford University Press, 1907.

Cook, Thomas. "Keats's Sonnet 'To Homer.' " *KSJ* 11 (1962): 8–12.

Cornwell, Ethel F. *The "Still Point."* New Brunswick, N. J.: Rutgers University Press, 1962.

D'Avanzo, Mario L. *Keats's Metaphors for the Poetic Imagination*. Durham, N. C.: Duke University Press, 1967.

Donoghue, Denis, and J. R. Mulryne, eds. *An Honored Guest: New Essays on W. B. Yeats*. London: Edward Arnold, 1965.

Dunseath, T. K. "Yeats and the Genesis of Supernatural Song." *ELH* 28 (1961): 399–416.

Eddins, Dwight. *Yeats: The Nineteenth Century Matrix*. University, Alabama: University of Alabama Press, 1971.

Eliade, Mircea. *Cosmos and History: The Myth of the Eternal Return*. New York: Harper & Row, 1959.

————. *Myth and Reality*. New York: Harper & Row, 1963.

————. *The Sacred and the Profane: The Nature of Religion*. New York: Harper & Row, 1961.

Ellmann, Richard. *The Identity of Yeats*, 2nd ed. New York: Oxford University Press, 1964.

————. *Yeats: The Man and the Masks*. New York: E. P. Dutton & Co., 1948.

Engelberg, Edward. " 'He Too Was in Arcadia': Yeats and the Paradox of the Fortunate Fall." In *In Excited Reverie*, edited by A. Norman Jeffares and K. W. G. Cross. London: Macmillan, 1965.

————. *The Vast Design: Patterns in W. B. Yeats's Aesthetic*. Toronto: University of Toronto Press, 1964.

Evert, Walter. *Aesthetic and Myth in the Poetry of Keats*. Princeton: Princeton University Press, 1965.

Fogle, Richard Harter. *The Imagery of Keats and Shelley: A Comparative Study*. 1949. Reprinted. Hamden, Conn.: Archon Books, 1962.

Bibliography

————. "Keats's 'Ode to a Nightingale.'" *PMLA* 67 (1953): 211–22.

————. "A Note on Keats's Ode to a Nightingale." *MLQ* 8 (1947): 81–84.

Ford, George H. *Keats and the Victorians.* 1944. Reprinted. Hamden, Conn.: Archon Books, 1962.

Ford, Newell F. "Endymion—A Neo-Platonic Allegory?" *ELH* 14 (1947): 64–76.

————. "The Meaning of 'Fellowship with Essence' in Endymion." *PMLA* 62 (1947): 1061–76.

————. *The Prefigurative Imagination of John Keats: A Study of the Beauty-Truth Identification.* 1951. Reprinted. Hamden, Conn.: Archon Books, 1966.

Forsyth, R. A. "The Myth of Nature and the Victorian Compromise of the Imagination." *ELH* 31 (1964): 213–40.

Fraser, G. S. *Vision and Rhetoric.* New York: Barnes & Noble, 1960.

Frye, Northrop. *Anatomy of Criticism: Four Essays.* Princeton: Princeton University Press, 1957.

————. "The Rising of the Moon: A Study of *A Vision*." In *An Honored Guest: New Essays on W. B. Yeats,* edited by Denis Donoghue and J. R. Mulryne. London: Edward Arnold, 1965.

————. *A Study of English Romanticism.* New York: Random House, 1968.

Gareb, Arra. *Beyond Byzantium: The Last Phase of Yeats's Career.* DeKalb: University of Northern Illinois Press, 1969.

Gérard, Albert S. *English Romantic Poetry: Structure and Symbol in Coleridge, Wordsworth, Shelley, and Keats.* Berkeley: University of California Press, 1968.

Godfrey, Clarisse. "Endymion." In *John Keats: A Reassessment,* edited by Kenneth Muir. Liverpool: Liverpool University Press, 1958.

Halpern, Martin. "Keats and the 'Spirit that Laughest.'" *KSJ* 15 (1966): 69–86.

Hamilton, K. M. "Time and the 'Grecian Urn.'" *DR* 34 (1954): 246–54.

Bibliography

Harrison, Robert. "Symbolism of the Cyclical Myth in *Endymion*." TSLL 1 (1960): 538–54.

Hartman, Geoffrey H. "Romanticism and 'Anti-Self-Consciousness.' " *CentR* 6 (1962): 553–65.

———. *The Unmediated Vision*. New Haven: Yale University Press, 1954.

Haven, Richard. *Patterns of Consciousness: An Essay on Coleridge*. Storrs: University of Connecticut Press, 1969.

Heinan, Hubert. "Interwoven Time in Keats's Poetry." *TSLL* 3 (1961): 382–88.

Henn, Thomas Rice. *The Lonely Tower: Studies in the Poetry of W. B. Yeats*. London: Methuen, 1965.

Hirsch, E. D. *Wordsworth and Shelling: A Typological Study of Romanticism*. New Haven: Yale University Press, 1960.

Hobsbaum, Philip. "The 'Philosophy' of the Grecian Urn: A Consensus of Readings." *KSMB* 15 (1965): 1–7.

Hoffman, Daniel. *Barbarous Knowledge: Myth in the Poetry of Yeats, Graves, and Muir*. New York: Oxford University Press, 1967.

Hopkins, Gerard Manley. *Further Letters of Gerard Manley Hopkins*. Edited by Claude Colleer Abbott. 2nd ed. London: Oxford University Press, 1956.

———. *The Journals and Papers of Gerard Manley Hopkins*. Edited by Humphrey House and Graham Storey. London: Oxford University Press, 1959.

———. *Poems of Gerard Manley Hopkins*. Edited by W. H. Gardner and N. H. Mackenzie. 4th ed. London: Oxford University Press, 1967.

———. *The Sermons and Devotional Writings of Gerard Manley Hopkins*. Edited by Christopher Delvin, S.J. London: Oxford University Press, 1959.

Hough, Graham. *The Last Romantics*. New York: W. W. Norton & Co., 1964.

Jacobs, Edward C. "Yeats and the Artistic Epiphany" *Discourse* 12 (1969): 292–305.

James, D. G. *The Romantic Comedy: An Essay on English Romanticism*. London: Oxford University Press, 1948.

Bibliography

Jaspers, Karl. *Truth and Symbol*. New York: Twayne Publishers, 1959.

Jeffares, A. Norman. *W. B. Yeats, Man and Poet*. New Haven: Yale University Press, 1949.

Jeffares, A. Norman and K. G. W. Cross, eds. *In Excited Reverie: A Centenary Tribute to William Butler Yeats, 1865–1939*. London: Macmillan, 1965.

Jones, James Land. "Keats and Yeats: 'Artificers of the Great Moment.' " *XUS* 4 (1965): 125–50.

Jones, Leonidas M. "The Ode to Psyche: An Allegorical Introduction to Keats's Great Odes." *KSMB* 9 (1958): 22–26.

Keats, John. *The Letters of John Keats, 1814–1821*. Edited by Hyder Rollins. 2 vols. Cambridge: Harvard University Press, 1958.

————. *The Poetical Works of John Keats*. Edited by H. W. Garrod. 2nd ed. London: Oxford University Press, 1958.

Kermode, Frank. *Romantic Image*. New York: Macmillan Co., 1957.

Kirk, G. S. *Myth: Its Meaning and Function in Ancient and Other Cultures*. Berkeley: University of California Press, 1970.

Knight, G. Wilson. *The Starlit Dome: Studies in the Poetry of Vision*. 1941. Reprinted. London: Methuen & Co., 1959.

Koch, Vivienne. *W. B. Yeats: The Tragic Phase: A Study of the Last Poems*. Baltimore: Johns Hopkins Press, 1952.

Kuhn, Albert J. "English Deism and the Development of Mythological Syncretism." *PMLA* 71 (1956): 1094–1116.

Langbaum, Robert. *The Modern Spirit: Essays on the Continuity of Nineteenth and Twentieth Century Literature*. New York: Oxford University Press, 1970.

————. *The Poetry of Experience: The Dramatic Monologue in Modern Literary Tradition*. New York: W. W. Norton & Co., 1957.

Lentricchia, Frank. *The Gaiety of Language: An Essay on the Radical Poetics of W. B. Yeats and Wallace Stevens*. Berkeley: University of California Press, 1968.

Levine, Bernard. *The Dissolving Image: The Spiritual-Es-*

Bibliography

thetic Development of W. B. Yeats. Detroit: Wayne State University Press, 1970.

Lévi-Strauss, Claude. "The Structural Study of Myth." *Myth: A Symposium,* edited by Thomas A. Sebeok. Bloomington: University of Indiana Press, 1965.

Magaw, Malcolm. "Yeats and Keats: The Poets of Romanticism." *Bucknell Review* 13 (1965): 87–96.

Marcel, Gabriel. *The Philosophy of Existence.* London: Harvill Press, 1948.

Maxwell, J. C. "Keats's Sonnet on the Tomb of Burns." *KSJ* 4 (1955): 77–80.

Miles, Josephine. *Pathetic Fallacy in the Nineteenth Century: A Study of a Changing Relation Between Object and Emotion.* Berkeley: University of California Press, 1942.

———. "The Romantic Mode in Poetry." *ELH* 20 (1953): 29–38.

Miller, Bruce E. "On the Meaning of Keats's *Endymion.*" KSJ 14 (1965): 34–54.

Miller, J. Hillis. *The Disappearance of God.* Cambridge: Harvard University Press, 1963.

———. *Poets of Reality: Six Twentieth-Century Writers.* Cambridge: Harvard University Press, 1965.

Muir, Kenneth, ed. *John Keats: A Reassessment.* Liverpool: Liverpool University Press, 1958.

Muir, Kenneth. "The Meaning of *Hyperion.*" EIC 2 (1952): 54–75.

Murry, John Middleton. *Keats.* New York: Noonday Press, 1962.

———. *Keats and Shakespeare.* 1925. Reprinted. London: Oxford University Press, 1964.

Parkinson, Thomas. *W. B. Yeats, The Later Poetry.* Berkeley: University of California Press, 1964.

———. *W. B. Yeats, Self-Critic: A Study of His Early Verse.* Berkeley: University of California Press, 1951.

Patterson, Charles I., Jr. *The Daemonic in the Poetry of John Keats.* Urbana: University of Illinois Press, 1970.

———. "Passion and Permanence in Keats's 'Ode on a Grecian Urn.'" *ELH* 21 (1954): 208–20.

Bibliography

Pearce, Donald. "Yeats and the Romantics." *Shenandoah* 8 (1957): 40–57.

Peckham, Morse. *The Triumph of Romanticism.* Columbia: University of South Carolina Press, 1971.

Perkins, David. *The Quest for Permanence: The Symbolism of Wordsworth, Shelley, and Keats.* Cambridge: Harvard University Press, 1959.

Pettet, E. C. *On the Poetry of Keats.* Cambridge: Cambridge University Press, 1957.

Piaget, Jean. *Structuralism.* New York: Basic Books, 1970.

Poulet, Georges. "Timelessness and Romanticism." *JHI* 15 (1954): 3–22.

Quinn, Sister M. Bernetta. *The Metamorphic Tradition in Modern Poetry.* 1955. Reprinted. New York: Gordian Press, 1966.

Reid, B. L. *William Butler Yeats: The Lyric of Tragedy.* Norman: University of Oklahoma Press, 1961.

Schanzer, Ernest. " 'Sailing to Byzantium,' Keats and Anderson." *ES* 41 (1960): 376–80.

Schulz, Max F. "Keats's Timeless Order of Things: A Modern Reading of 'Ode to Psyche.' " *Criticism* 2 (1960): 55–65.

Seiden, Morton Irving. *William Butler Yeats: The Poet as Mythmaker, 1865–1939.* East Lansing: Michigan State University Press, 1962.

Shackford, Martha Hale. "The 'Ode on a Grecian Urn.' " *KSJ* 4 (1955): 7–13.

Shaw, Priscilla Washburn. *Rilke, Valéry and Yeats: The Domain of the Self.* New Brunswick, N.J.: Rutgers University Press, 1964.

Sherwood, Margaret. *Undercurrents of Influence in English Romantic Poetry.* Cambridge: Harvard University Press, 1934.

Smith, Barbara Herrnstein. " 'Sorrow's Mysteries': Keats's 'Ode on Melancholy.' " *SEL* 6 (1966): 679–91.

Southam, B. C. "The Ode 'To Autumn.' " *KSJ* 9 (1960): 91–98.

Bibliography

Spanos, William V. "Sacramental Imagery in the Middle and Late Poetry of W. B. Yeats." *TSLL* 4 (1962): 214–27.

Spears, Monroe K. *Dionysus and the City: Modernism in Twentieth-Century Poetry.* New York: Oxford University Press, 1970.

Spender, Stephen. *The Struggle of the Modern.* London: Hamish Hamilton, 1963.

Spens, Janet. "A Study of Keats's 'Ode to a Nightingale.' " *RES* 3 (1952): 234–43.

Sperry, Stuart M., Jr. "The Allegory of *Endymion.*" *SIR* 2 (1962): 38–53.

————. "Keats's *Epistle to John Hamilton Reynolds.*" *ELH* 36 (1969): 562–74.

Spitzer, Leo. "The 'Ode on a Grecian Urn,' or Content *vs.* Metagrammar." *CL* 7 (1955): 203–25.

————. "On Yeats's Poem 'Leda and the Swan.' " *MP* 51 (1964): 271–76.

Stallman, Robert Wooster. "Keats the Apollonian: The Time and Space Logic of His Poems as Paintings." *UTQ* 16 (1947): 143–56.

Stauffer, Donald. *The Golden Nightingale: Essays on Some Principles of Poetry in the Lyrics of William Butler Yeats.* New York: Macmillan Co., 1949.

Stillinger, Jack. "Keats's Grecian Urn and the Evidence of the Transcripts." *PMLA* 63 (1958): 447–48.

Tate, Alan. "Yeats's Romanticism: Notes and Suggestions." *Southern Review* 7 (1942): 591–600.

Teich, Nathaniel. "Criticism and Keats's Grecian Urn." *PQ* 44 (1965): 496–502.

Thorpe, Clarence D. *The Mind of John Keats.* 1926. Reprinted. New York: Russell & Russell, 1964.

Unger, Leonard. "Keats and the Music of Autumn." *The Man in the Name.* Minneapolis: University of Minnesota Press, 1957.

Unterecker, John. *A Reader's Guide to William Butler Yeats.* New York: Noonday Press, 1959.

Ure, Peter. *Towards a Mythology: Studies in the Poetry of*

Bibliography

W. B. Yeats. 1946. Reprinted. New York: Russell & Russell, 1967.

———. "Yeats's 'Demon and Beast.'" *Irish Writing* 31 (1955): 43–50.

Van der Leeuw, Gerardus. *Religion in Essence and Manifestation.* 2 vols. 1938. Reprinted. New York: Harper & Row, 1963.

Van Ghent, Dorothy. "Keats's Myth of the Hero." *KSJ* 3 (1954): 7–12.

Vendler, Helen Hennessy. *Yeats's Vision and the Later Plays.* Cambridge: Harvard University Press, 1963.

Wagner, Robert D. "Keats's 'Ode to Psyche' and the Second 'Hyperion.'" *KSJ* 11 (1964): 29–41.

Wasserman, Earl R. *The Finer Tone: Keats's Major Poems.* Baltimore: Johns Hopkins Press, 1953.

Watts, Harold H. "Yeats and Lapsed Mythology." *Renascence* 3 (1951): 107–12.

Weisinger, Herbert. "The Proper Study of Myth." *CentR* 12 (1968): 237–67.

Wellek, René. *Concepts of Criticism.* New Haven: Yale University Press, 1963.

———. *A History of Modern Criticism.* Vol. 2. New Haven: Yale University Press, 1955

Wheelwright, Philip. *The Burning Fountain: A Study in the Language of Symbolism.* Bloomington: University of Indiana Press, 1954.

———. *Metaphor and Reality.* 1962. Reprinted. Bloomington: University of Indiana Press, 1968.

Whitaker, Thomas R. *Swan and Shadow: Yeats's Dialogue with History.* Chapel Hill: University of North Carolina Press, 1964.

Whitley, Alvin. "The Message of the Grecian Urn." *KSMB* 5 (1953): 1–3.

Wicker, Brian. "The Disputed Lines in *The Fall of Hyperion.*" *EIC* 7 (1957): 28–41.

Wigod, Jacob D. "Keats's Ideal in 'Ode on a Grecian Urn.'" *PMLA* 72 (1957): 113–21.

Bibliography

————. "The Meaning of *Endymion*," *PMLA* 68 (1953): 779–90.

Wilcox, S. C. "Seasonal Motif of Keats's Ode 'To Autumn.'" *PQ* 35 (1956): 194–95.

Wilkie, Brian. *Romantic Poets and Epic Tradition.* Madison: University of Wisconsin Press, 1965.

Yeats, W. B. *The Autobiography of William Butler Yeats.* New York: Macmillan Co., 1953.

————. *The Celtic Twilight and a Selection of the Early Poems.* Edited by Walter Starkie. New York: New American Library, 1962.

————. *Collected Poems of W. B. Yeats.* New York: Macmillan Co., 1956.

————. *Essays and Introductions.* New York: Macmillan Co., 1951.

————. *Explorations.* New York: Macmillan Co., 1962.

————. "Introduction" to *The Oxford Book of Modern Verse.* New York: Oxford University Press, 1936.

————. *The Letters of W. B. Yeats.* Edited by Allan Wade. London: Rupert Hart-Davis, 1954.

————. *Letters on Poetry from W. B. Yeats to Dorothy Wellesley.* 1940. Reprinted. London: Oxford University Press, 1964.

————. *Letters to the New Island.* Edited by Horace Reynolds. Cambridge: Harvard University Press, 1934.

————. *Mythologies.* New York: Collier Books, 1959.

————. *A Vision.* New York: Macmillan Co., 1961.

————. *W. B. Yeats and T. Sturge Moore: Their Correspondence 1901–1937.* Edited by Ursula Bridge. London: Oxford University Press, 1953.

————. *Wheels and Butterflies.* London: Macmillan Co., 1934.

Zwerdling, Alex. "The Mythographers and the Romantic Revival of Greek Myth." *PMLA* 79 (1964): 447–56.

————. "W. B. Yeats: Variations on the Visionary Quest." *UTQ*, 30 (1960): 72–85.

Index

Abrams, M. H., 15n
Alan, Glen O., 68n
Anima mundi. See Self
Arnold, Matthew, 14, 17, 26, 29, 91, 202
Art: relation to myth and religion, 8, 201–2

Ball, Patricia M., 18–19n
Balzac, Honoré de, 198
Bate, W. J., 69n, 159
Beauty: as energy, 65, 71, 72, 76, 78, 80, 205–6; and melancholy, 167–68, 186–87; and eye image, 173. *See also* Beauty and truth; Truth
Beauty and truth: Keats on, 65–73, 77–81; as being, 68–69, 72, 78–81; defined, 71, 207–8; Yeats on, 73–78; intensity for their fusion, 150, 151. *See also* Beauty; Truth
Beckett, Samuel: his character Murphy, 17, 21, 30
Being: as ground of the self, 11, 12, 17–18, 20, 32, 39, 46, 49, 205; ontological content of mythic thought, 12, 200–201; as the holy, 51–53; as mana, power, 53–54, 147; and Hopkins's instress, 55, 82; as energy, 57–61; as Keats's "essence," 62–64; as passion, 65, 123, 133; and beauty, 68–69, 72, 115; and form, 79; symbolized by water, 97–99, 98n; revealed by intensity and stillness, 123; Gabriel Marcel's definition of, 201; mystery of the subject of art, 201; relation to Romantic literature, 203; process as post-1800 concept of, 204–5; mentioned, 15, 33. *See also* Beauty and truth
Benziger, James, 121n
Berkeley, George, 25, 57, 58
Beyer, W. W., 68n
Bidney, David, 8n

Bird image, 147–48, 149
Blackstone, Bernard, 68n, 92n
Blake, William, 20, 22, 41, 42, 44–45, 74n, 100, 120, 183, 203
Bloom, Harold, 14, 22n, 41n
Bornstein, George, 41n
Bradley, A. C., 14, 71n
Browning, Robert, 4, 120
Bush, Douglas, 1
Byron, George Gordon, Lord, 18, 26n, 38n, 41, 195

Cassirer, Ernst: general position, 5–7; criticized, 5–6, 8; characteristics of mythic thought, 6–7, 82; on myth and religion, 6, 8, 51; on feeling response, 16, 36, 50; self in mythic thought, 32; solidarity of life, 50–51; on mana, the numinous, 53, 80n; on metamorphosis, 83; on mythic space, 90; on reciprocity in process, 102–3; on mythic time, 106; denial of death in myth, 113–14; mentioned, 10–11, 201
Chase, Richard, 1
Coleridge, Samuel Taylor: on Hamlet, 14; on the self, 19–20; on godhead, 22; on Shakespeare and Milton, 39; on creative process, 83; on symbol, 149; mentioned, 35, 36, 46, 54, 71, 120, 121n, 203
Comte, Auguste, 49
Conrad, Joseph, 14, 26
Consciousness: and Romanticism, 6, 15, 21, 203–4; stages of, 16–17, 19–21; and Keats's "Chamber of Maiden Thought," 20, 174, 178, 182, 183; theme of *Hyperion*, 179–81, 188; and Keats's term "beauty," 186–87; in *The Fall of Hyperion*, 193–94, 198; and birth of sense of time, 204; and Great Moment, 205. *See also* Mythic consciousness

Index

Cook, A. B., 2
Cornford, Francis, 2
Cornwell, Ethel, 121n

Darwin, Charles, 49
D'Avanzo, Mario, 145n
Death: denial of in myth, 113–18; fulfillment in ("life's high meed"), 114–15, 124–25; mentioned, 7, 12
Descartes, René, 3, 14, 19, 42, 46
Dunseath, T. K., 140n

Ecstasy: fulfillment of soul, 65, 100, 125; as timeless moment, 100, 144; and tragic joy, 133; mentioned, 47, 163
Eliade, Mircea: on mythic time, 7–8, 107, 144; position on myth, 8–9; criticized, 8, 9n; ontology in myth, 12, 200; on self in mythic thought, 32; on being or the numinous, 53, 200; fullness as being, 56; energy as being, 61, 62; on mythic space, 90, 91; natural elements in myth, 95, 97, 98; denial of death in myth, 114; on mythic narrative, 180; on ritual and initiation, 181, 197; mentioned, 5, 10, 11
Eliot, T. S., 1, 120, 121n, 203
Energy: universal power perceived in mythic consciousness, 53–54, 146; in Yeats, 56–60; and instress, 57; in Keats, 57–59, 61; synonymous with beauty, 65, 68, 71, 72, 75, 76, 77, 78, 80, 181, 205; and as passion, 65, 123, 133, 150–51; as love, 67; manifest in metamorphosis, 83; ground of the self and the Other, 134, 138, 205; as intensity, 148; mentioned, 12
Engelberg, Edward, 123n, 150–51
Epiphany. See Great Moment
Essence: synonymous with beauty and being, 12, 65, 68–69; term in Keats, 62–64; and energy, 77, 198
Evert, Walter, 2, 40, 92n, 169

Faulkner, William, 14
Fergusson, Francis, 2

Feuerbach, Ludwig, 21
Fogle, Richard Harter, 123
Fontenrose, Joseph, 2
Ford, Newell F., 62–63, 71–72
Frazer, James, 2
Frye, Northrop, 1, 6, 14, 121n

Gareb, Arra, 133n
Garrod, H. W., 177
Gérard, Albert, 79–80n
Gide, André, 4
Gittings, Robert, 153
Great Memory. See Self
Great Moment: defined, 12, 119–21, 151, 199, 205; intensity perquisite to, 123–25, 141, 150–51; death a mode of, 124–25; stillness or reverie perquisite to, 125–27, 142, 150–51, 157; and process, 127–28, 130, 140–42, 188–89; 197; and tragic joy, 133; as fellowship with essence, 134–51, 205; Keats's "elevation of the Moment," 137, 150, 205; timelessness in, 137–38, 141, 142, 197; sexual union analogue for, 138–45; reveals power, 138, 197–98; and mythic time, 143–44, 197; union with natural and aesthetic objects, 145–50; union of passion and reverie, 150–51; as expanded consciousness, 205; brevity of, 205–7

Harrison, Jane, 2
Hartman, Geoffrey, 14
Heraclitus, 109, 204
Hierophany: defined, 95
Hoffman, Daniel, 2
Hopkins, Gerard Manley, 4, 42, 54–55, 56, 57, 58, 70
Hume, David, 17, 18, 46
Husserl, Edmund, 9, 10
Hyman, Stanley Edgar, 2

Imagery: natural elements as, stationing of, 88–90; 94–101. See also Bird image; Water image
Imagination: as Keats's "greeting of the Spirit," 11, 16, 36–38, 46, 67–68, 72, 135–36; heart as met-

Index

onymy for, 24, 33–34, 68, 132; in mythic consciousness, 35–36; Romantic concept of, 35; contrasting modes of, 39–41, 45–47; related to divinity, 61; and Keats's term "passion," 66–67; and Great Memory, 125; and mythic time, 174–75, 177, 188; and memory, 187–88, 194, 205

Inscape, 70

Instress: relation to mythic consciousness, 54; Hopkins's definition, 54–55, 57; synonymous with being, 55; defined as energy, 57; synonymous with Keats's "beauty," 68, 71; mentioned, 167, 172, 173

James, D. G., 162n
Jones, Leonidas M., 68n, 79n
Joyce, James, 1, 121
Jung, Carl G., 31

Kant, Immanuel, 3, 9, 41
Keats, John: development in 1818, 12–13, 21, 169, 176, 178; "Chamber of Maiden Thought," 20, 174, 178, 182, 183; "soul making," letter on, 23–24; "mould ethereal," 31–32; "sensations," 36; "ethereal things," letter on, 36–38; and empathy, 39–40; on religion, 51–52, 172; and energy, 56, 58–59, 61–62, 64; "essence," 62–64; on beauty and truth, 65–73, 77–81; "passion," 66–68; imagination, letter to Bailey on, 66–68, 72, 167–68, 202; "abstract," 69–70; and metamorphosis, 84–85, 92; "stationing," 88–89; his "vast idea," 93–94; on origin of myth, 98; and death, 114, 116, 117, 161; and opposites, 121–22; "fellowship with essence" passage, 134–37; and intensity, 135, 150. See also Imagination; Melancholy; Mythic time; Process
—Works by: After Dark Vapours, 104, 114; Bards of Passion and of Mirth, 117, 148; Bright Star, 98,

105, 145; Calidore, 103, 173; Endymion, 38, 39–40, 67, 73, 84, 94–103 passim, 108, 112–13, 118, 121–22, 157, 134–37, 145, 166–67, 188, 190, 206; Epistle to Reynolds, 16, 64, 87, 101, 169–75, 176, 177–78, 186, 188, 189, 190, 191; The Fall of Hyperion, 33, 38, 40, 52, 66, 181, 190–99; Four Seasons, 104, 110, 114; The Grasshopper and the Cricket, 103; Hyperion, 40, 77, 84, 96, 103–4, 143, 173, 179–88; Isabella, 39, 108, 154n; I Stood Tip-toe, 96, 101, 103, 165; Lamia, 84, 108, 122, 123, 173, 178–79; Ode on a Grecian Urn, 78–80, 116, 149, 150, 155, 158, 163, 173; One on Indolence, 157; Ode on Melancholy, 59, 66, 153–55, 156n, 157, 161, 165, 166, 169, 172, 173, 174, 178; Ode to a Nightingale, 13, 156–65, 167–78 passim, 188, 190; Ode to Psyche, 48–49, 84, 145, 156, 172, 178, 194; On Fame ("How fever'd"), 105; On First Looking into Chapman's Homer, 97, 98, 99; On the Sea, 99; On Visiting Staffa, 99; On Visiting the Tomb of Burns, 176–77, 179, 185; Sleep and Poetry, 61, 88, 93–94, 96, 113, 126, 145, 166n, 177–78, 197n; Time's Sea, 165; To Autumn, 103, 104, 146–47, 155, 176; To Homer, 34, 95–96, 97, 188; To Lord Byron, 165; To My Brothers, 96; To the Nile, 175–76; To Sleep, 15; Welcome Joy and Welcome Sorrow, 169; What the Thrush Said, 34; Why Did I Laugh?, 114

Kermode, Frank, 43–44
Kleist, Heinrich von, 20, 179
Knight, G. Wilson, 84

Langbaum, Robert, 14
Lawrence, D. H., 26
Leach, Edmund, 9
Lentricchia, Frank, 22n
Levine, Bernard, 22n
Lévi-Strauss, Claude: general posi-

— 223 —

Index

tion and its problem, 9–10; relation to Cassirer on myth, 9, 82; myth as reconciliation of opposites, 10, 120, 149; defines structure of myth, 93, 120; mentioned, 5, 10, 11, 84
Lewis, Wyndham, 74
Locke, John, 42, 46
Lovejoy, A. O., 3

Maeterlinck, Maurice, 44
Mallarmé, Stéphane, 42, 43, 44
Malraux, André, 6, 10, 84, 139
Marcel, Gabriel, 201
Marvell, Andrew, 141
Marx, Karl, 49
Maxwell, J. C., 177
Melancholy: defined, 119, 152; in Keats, 153–79 passim, 185–86, 188, 195, 196; and beauty, 167–68, 173, 186–87; mentioned, 12, 108
Metamorphosis: Cassirer on, 83; in Keats, 84–85, 92; in Yeats, 85–87, 92, 115; manifests power of gods, 200; and process, 204; mentioned, 7, 12
Miller, Bruce, 64
Milton, John, 21, 39, 88, 180, 181
Moore, T. Sturge, 73
Muir, Edwin, 203
Muir, Kenneth, 162n, 194
Murray, Gilbert, 2
Murry, John Middleton, 169, 198
Myth: ritual theory of, 1–2; and religion, 6, 8, 9, 51, 201–2; ontology as content, 12, 200–201; Keats on origin of, 98; mediation of opposites in, 120, 149
Mythic consciousness: characteristics of, 6–7, 82–83; feeling response in, 35–41, 46, 50
Mythic space: and stationing of images, 88–90, 91; defined, 90, 91; as bowers, 90, 117; in Yeats, 90–91
Mythic time: defined, 7–8, 106–7; in Keats, 107–8, 112–13, 149, 153, 155, 158–59, 161, 165, 171, 173, 174–78, 181–83, 188, 194, 197; in

Yeats, 108–12, 124, 139, 143–44, 149; and history, 200
Mythoids: defined, 101

Neoplatonism, 62, 63–64
Newton, Issac, 42, 204

Otto, Rudolph, 53

Pater, Walter, 21, 120
Patterson, Charles I., Jr., 40n
Peckham, Morse, 3, 19
Perkins, David, 70n, 92, 104
Personality. See Self
Pettet, E. C., 156n, 157n, 164n, 166
Piaget, Jean, 9
Pierce, Charles, 84
Plotinus, 63, 71
Power: synonymous with being, the holy, 53–54; Keats's diction for, 56; manifest in metamorphosis, 83, 200; perceived in natural elements, 94–95; and ecstasy, 100; and process, 113; content of mythic narrative, 200
Process: defined, 92–93; as Keats's "vast idea," 93–94, 171, 177–78, 186; in Yeats, 93, 109–12, 127–33, 140–42; and natural elements, 94–101; as reconciliation of opposites, 101–3; reciprocity and compensation in, 102–3, 160, 168, 176, 186; in Keats, 103–6; 146–47, 154, 155, 160, 163–64, 168, 186–87, 188, 194–95; and Great Moment, 119, 140, 153; tragic aspect of, 153
Pythagoras, 63, 71, 74

Raine, Kathleen, 203
Reid, B. L., 133
Rimbaud, Arthur, 18, 20, 26
Roethke, Theodore, 203
Romanticism: Wellek's definition, 3–4; related to structuralism, 9n; and consciousness, 14–15, 19–21, 203–4; concept of the self, 18–23, 32; concept of godhead, 21–23; concept of imagination, 35; subject-object problem in, 40–41; concept of symbol, 43–44; con-

Index

Index